PROTECTING RELIANCE:
THE EMERGENT DOCTRINE OF EQUITABLE ESTOPPEL

For Beth

Protecting Reliance: The Emergent Doctrine of Equitable Estoppel

MICHAEL SPENCE

BA LL.B (Sydney), D. PHIL (Oxon)

Solicitor (NSW)

·HART·
PUBLISHING

OXFORD – PORTLAND OREGON

1999

Hart Publishing
Oxford and Portland, Oregon

Published in North America (US and Canada) by
Hart Publishing c/o
International Specialized Book Services
5804 NE Hassalo Street
Portland, Oregon
97213-3644
USA

Distributed in the Netherlands, Belgium and Luxembourg by
Intersentia, Churchillaan 108
B2900 Schoten
Antwerpen
Belgium

Distributed in Australia and New Zealand by
Federation Press
John St
Leichhardt
NSW 2000

Hart Publishing Ltd is a specialist legal publisher based in Oxford, England.
To order further copies of this book or to request a list of other
publications please write to:

Hart Publishing Ltd, 19 Whitehouse Road, Oxford, OX1 4PA
Telephone: +44 (0)1865 434459 or Fax: +44 (0)1865 794882
e-mail: hartpub@janep.demon.co.uk

British Library Cataloguing in Publication Data
Data Available
ISBN 1 901362–62–0 (cloth)

Typeset by Hope Services (Abingdon) Ltd.
Printed and bound in Great Britain
by Biddles Ltd, Guildford and Kings Lynn

Contents

Table of Cases

Table of Statutes

Uniform Commercial Code (1978)

I

The Duty to Ensure the Reliability of Induced Assumptions

1. INTRODUCTION

One party induces an assumption in the mind of another. Three overlapping moral duties might rest upon the inducing party, each of which has found expression in English and Australian law. First, there is the duty to keep promises. Although the point has been a contentious one for twenty years, the duty to keep promises is probably the moral basis of contract law.[1] Second, there is the duty not to lie. This duty underpins the tort of deceit. Third, there may also be a more general duty to ensure the reliability of induced assumptions. This third duty may have influenced the development of several common law and equitable doctrines. These include the various types of estoppel, the tort of negligent misstatement and, perhaps, the duty that a fiduciary owes in the giving of advice under *Nocton* v *Lord Ashburton*.[2]

In this book I argue that the third of these moral duties – the duty to ensure the reliability of induced assumptions – can be used to shape a new and developing doctrine of estoppel in Australia. The book describes the duty to ensure the reliability of induced assumptions, distinguishing it from the duty to keep promises and the duty not to lie, and making some suggestions about the rôle that these three may have to play in the private law of obligations.[3] The book then uses the duty to shape the estoppel doctrine that emerged in *Waltons Stores (Interstate) Ltd* v *Maher*[4] and *Commonwealth of Australia* v *Verwayen*,[5] two decisions of the High Court of Australia. Finally, it demonstrates the utility of the doctrine in a series of problematic cases at the edge of contract law. The book is a comprehensive treatment of neither the duty to ensure the reliability of induced assumptions, nor the current English or Australian law of estoppel. It is an attempt to show that the estoppel doctrine described in *Waltons* and

---

[1] See below at n. 19.

[2] [1914] AC 398.

[3] This book is concerned only with private law. Questions such as the extent to which public law concepts of "legitimate expectation" and "estoppel" have, can or ought to give expression to the duty to ensure the reliability of induced assumptions are specifically excluded. Such questions raise complex issues regarding the philosophy and pragmatics of government which could only deflect attention from the central issues in this discussion.

[4] (1988) 164 CLR 387 (hereafter "*Waltons*").

[5] (1990) 170 CLR 394 (hereafter "*Verwayen*").

Verwayen, a doctrine often criticised as indeterminate, can be given a satisfactory basis in principle.

To identify the doctrine that emerged in *Waltons* and *Verwayen*, I will use the widely accepted term "equitable estoppel". It would surprise many of the Australian judges to hear that doctrine described as "new".[6] They have called it "equitable estoppel" because they have seen it as a development of traditional estoppel doctrines such as "promissory" and "proprietary" estoppel. In fact, "equitable estoppel" is a problematic term, both because of the historical claim that it implies[7] and because estoppel is emerging as a single doctrine operative in equity and at common law.[8] But it would be a Herculean task to trace the roots of the estoppel doctrine described in this book in the confusion of the traditional doctrines – Leopold has identified twelve of them and his list is not exhaustive[9] – and to settle the validity of the term "equitable estoppel". I adopt the term because of its wide currency without in any way endorsing it.

2. THE DUTY TO ENSURE THE RELIABILITY OF INDUCED ASSUMPTIONS

The duty to ensure the reliability of induced assumptions places primary and secondary obligations on a party who (i) induces an assumption in the mind of another party and (ii) induces the other party to rely upon that assumption. The primary obligation is that the inducing party must, in so far as he is reasonably able, prevent harm to the relying party. "Harm" consists in the extent to which the relying party is worse off because the assumption has proved unjustified than he would have been had it never been induced. The secondary obligation is that, if the relying party does suffer harm of the relevant type, and the inducing party might reasonably have prevented it, then the inducing party must compensate the relying party for the harm he has suffered.

It is inducing reliance, rather than merely inducing an assumption, that attracts the duty to ensure the reliability of induced assumptions. The question

---

[6] Although it would not surprise all the judges. Sir Anthony Mason has claimed that the Australian developments in estoppel "have no precise counterpart in other jurisdictions" (Sir Anthony Mason, "The Place of Equity and Equitable Remedies in the Contemporary Common Law World", (1994) 110 *LQR* 238 at 256).

[7] Spencer Bower and Turner object to the term "equitable estoppel" and claim that ". . . no satisfactory high authority is discoverable offering any firm foundation for the view that estoppel in equity is different in any essential respect from estoppel at common law, whatever may have been the case in the 19th century when the doctrine was in its embryonic stages." (A K Turner (ed.), *Spencer Bower and Turner: The Law Relating to Estoppel by Representation* 3rd edn (London, Butterworths, 1977) at 12) But cf. R P Meagher, W M C Gummow, and J R F Lehane, *Equity: Doctrines and Remedies* 3rd edn (Sydney, Butterworths, 1992) at 406.

[8] See below at pp. 26–30.

[9] A Leopold, "Estoppel: A Practical Appraisal of Recent Developments", (1991) 7 *Aust Bar Rev* 47 at 71–73. The list does not include, for example, estoppel by negligence, estoppel by silence or the so-called estoppel "by homologation". A possible categorisation of the estoppel cases before *Waltons* is offered in Chapter Two.

of whether reliance has been induced, and if so how strongly, determines whether, and if so how strongly, the duty to ensure the reliability of induced assumptions applies. Seven aspects of the parties' dealings and relationship must be considered in determining whether, and if so how strongly, reliance was induced. Four of these seven considerations concern the parties' dealings. They are: (i) the way in which the assumption and reliance upon it were induced (a claim that reliance has been induced and that the duty is owed is more plausible when there has been an express representation, than it is when there has merely been conduct or silence), (ii) the content of the assumption (a claim that reliance has been induced and that the duty is owed is more plausible when the relevant assumption relates to present fact, than it is when it relates to evidently less reliable matters such as another party's intentions), (iii) the relative knowledge of the parties (a claim that reliance has been induced and that the duty is owed is more plausible when the inducing party knew that the relying party would rely upon the relevant assumption) and (iv) the parties' relative interest in the activities undertaken in reliance on the assumption (a claim that reliance has been induced and that the duty is owed is more plausible when the relying party is providing the inducing party with some service in the relevant activities in reliance). Three of the seven considerations concern the parties' relationship. They are: (i) the nature and context of the parties' relationship (the claim that reliance was induced and that the duty is owed is less plausible in contexts in which a high degree of self-reliance might be expected, such as highly competitive contexts), (ii) the parties' relative strength of position (the claim that reliance was induced and that the duty is owed is more plausible in situations in which there is a disparity in the parties' strength of position in favour of the inducing party), and (iii) the history of the parties' relationship (the claim that reliance was induced and that the duty is owed is more plausible as between parties with long-standing relationships of trust). I do not claim that this list of seven considerations is necessarily exhaustive. Nor do I claim that there is no overlap between them. For example, if parties enjoy a longstanding relationship in a context of close co-operation, it might be assumed that one party knew that the other would rely upon an assumption he induced. However, any consideration of the claim that one party induced another to rely upon a particular assumption must involve assessment of at least these seven aspects of the parties dealings and relationship.

Two aspects of the duty to ensure the reliability of induced assumptions merit particular consideration. These are (i) the justification of the duty, and (ii) the distinction between this duty and the duties to keep promises and not to lie. In distinguishing this duty from the duty to keep promises, particular attention will be paid to the notion that the duty to ensure the reliability of induced assumptions can apply even to assumptions about the inducing party's intentions.

(a) Justification of the duty

Justification of the duty to ensure the reliability of induced assumptions might be found in the general duty not to cause preventible harm. From this general duty, MacCormick derives a more specific duty regarding reliance upon induced assumptions. He argues that:[10]

". . . if one person acts in a potentially detrimental way in reliance upon beliefs about another's . . . conduct, and if the latter person has by some act of his intentionally or knowingly induced the former to rely upon him [in the sense that he 'intended', 'knew', 'thought it likely' or 'ought to have realized' that the other party would rely],[11] then the latter has an obligation not to act in a manner which will disappoint the other's reliance."

MacCormick illustrates the operation of this duty by painting the following scene:

"Suppose that Jones has been swimming from a beach at the foot of a cliff on a stormy day. He has failed to notice the speed with which the tide is rising, and is now in such a position that a desperate dash along the beach will perhaps enable him to reach the path up to safety before he is cut off by the tide. MacDonald happens just then to be strolling along the cliff top carrying a few hundred feet of stout climbing rope. He spots Jones's predicament and lowers the rope down the cliff-face to him. Jones sees what he is doing and waits for the rope to reach himself, thus losing time so that he can no longer conceivably reach the path before the tide comes in."[12]

MacCormick argues that, from the moment at which it ceases to be possible for Jones to save himself, MacDonald is under an obligation not to abandon the enterprise and that it would be wrong for him to do so even if he could then save another person.[13] Otherwise, by inducing reliance, MacDonald would have caused preventible harm.

MacCormick's specific duty obviously bears a close resemblance to the duty to ensure the reliability of induced assumptions and his work can be used to justify that duty. However four refinements of MacCormick's work are necessary to equip it for this task.

First, MacCormick actually uses his specific duty to justify promissory obligation. Raz points out that induced reliance cannot be the basis of promissory obligation because it would then be possible neither to distinguish "promising" from other types of inducing reliance such as "advising" or "informing", nor to explain why "promises once made and understood are binding even if not relied upon."[14] Responsibility for induced reliance is better seen, not as the basis of

---

[10] N MacCormick, "Voluntary Obligations and Normative Powers I", (1972) 46 *PASS* 59 at 68.
[11] Ibid. at 67.
[12] Ibid. at 67.
[13] Ibid. at 68.
[14] J Raz, "Voluntary Obligations and Normative Powers II", (1972) 46 *PASS* 79 at 101.

promissory obligation, but as the basis of the different obligation to ensure the reliability of induced assumptions.

Second, MacCormick's example involves the situation of an induced assumption concerning intention, presumably because he means to explain promissory obligation. However, as he himself suggests, his argument applies with equal force to induced assumptions concerning fact.[15] Imagine, for example that the rope MacDonald lowered was unsound for climbing and that he was in a position to know this. By inducing reliance upon an assumption about its fitness for climbing, he would be just as responsible for causing preventible harm as he would be if he abandoned the enterprise.

Third, MacCormick too readily conflates inducing reliance with knowing, either actually or imputedly, that reliance will eventuate. On the one hand, there are circumstances in which one party might know, in the sense that he foresees, that another party will rely upon an induced assumption and yet it cannot be said that he has induced the reliance. On the other hand, a party may induce reliance quite unwittingly. The distinction between inducing reliance and foreseeing it, is an important one. Whether, and how strongly, a party has induced reliance is a difficult question the determination of which will be dependent upon the many different considerations outlined above. The relative knowledge of the parties is just one of those considerations. Thus in the situation of Jones and MacDonald, it is not simply because MacDonald knows that reliance is likely that he may be said to have induced it. It is because of the combined effect of (i) his knowledge of the likelihood of reliance, (ii) the context of the parties' relationship and (iii) their relative strength of position. Jones must make a split second decision. By lowering the rope, MacDonald has assumed the rôle of a rescuer. All these factors together support the claim that MacDonald induced reliance.

Fourth, a party may induce reliance and thereby cause harm which is not, in any practical sense, preventible. This is a possibility that MacCormick does not explicitly discuss, but it is why the duty to ensure the reliability of induced assumptions places a primary obligation on the inducing party to prevent the relevant harm from arising only *in so far as he is reasonably able*. This is a significant limitation on the duty. In particular, when the relevant assumption relates to the future, it will create a distinction between situations in which whether the assumption proves unjustified is within the control of the inducing party and those in which whether the assumption proves unjustified is outside the control of the inducing party. Someone who induces an assumption about the state of tomorrow's weather based on the best meteorological practice has done all that he can to ensure that a party who relies upon that assumption does not thereby suffer harm. Someone who induces an assumption about his own future intentions, even if those intentions are accurately stated at the time of the inducing, has not necessarily done all that he can to ensure that a party who

---

[15] N MacCormick, "Voluntary Obligations and Normative Powers I", (1972) 46 *PASS* 59 at 65.

relies upon those assumptions does not suffer harm if he simply changes his mind. Thus, in MacCormick's illustration, MacDonald would not be responsible for the harm caused by the inducement of the assumption if an entirely unexpected wave, which Jones might have avoided by his dash along the beach, were to sweep Jones off the cliff face. However, MacDonald may not simply change his mind and give up the attempt to rescue Jones.

With these four modifications, MacCormick's work offers a helpful justification of the duty to ensure the reliability of induced assumptions based in the general duty not to cause preventible harm.

(b) Distinguishing the duty from the duty to keep promises and the duty not to lie

Having briefly outlined and justified the duty to ensure the reliability of induced assumptions, I should distinguish it from the duty to keep promises and the duty not to lie. Consider first the distinction between the duty to ensure the reliability of induced assumptions and the duty to keep promises. There are two reasons why these duties might sometimes be confused.

First, the duties might be confused because, although it is less likely that the duty to ensure the reliability of induced assumptions will attach to an assumption regarding the future than it will to an assumption regarding fact, it is possible that the duty will attach to such an assumption, and even to an assumption regarding another party's intentions. The proposed formulation of the duty means that a party who has induced a perfectly accurate assumption regarding the state of his intentions involving no false claims of fact, and who has not made any promise regarding those intentions, may not be free simply to change his mind. This is because the inducement of reliance upon an assumption regarding intentions, may be just as much a source of preventible harm as the inducement of reliance upon an assumption regarding present fact. MacCormick's paradigm concerning Jones and MacDonald is a situation of precisely this type.

However, although both duties may attach to an induced assumption regarding intention, there is a distinction between the two duties in the obligations that they place upon a party who has induced such an assumption. A promise is a commitment to perform, or to refrain from performing, a particular act. The duty to keep promises gives rise to a primary obligation to perform or to refrain from performing the particular act, and a secondary obligation, if the promise is not kept, to put the party to whom the promise has been made in the position in which he would have been if it had been kept. Either as a matter of primary or secondary obligation, a party who, by a promise, induces an assumption in the mind of another must ensure that the other party is in the position that he would be in if the assumption were justified. The duty to ensure the reliability of induced assumptions places quite different obligations upon the party upon whom it lies. This duty imposes a primary obligation upon the party inducing the assumption, in as much as he is able, to prevent harm to the relying party. The harm he must prevent is that the relying party is worse off because the assumption has proved unjustified than he would have been had it never been induced. If the relying party suffers harm and the inducing party might have done more to have prevented it, the duty imposes a secondary obligation upon the inducing party to put the relying party, not in the position in which he would be if the assumption were justified, but in the position in which he would have been had the assumption never been induced.

Second, the duty to ensure the reliability of induced assumptions and the duty to keep promises might sometimes be confused because they may, either as a matter of primary or secondary obligation, require the same practical response of the party who has induced the assumption. This will be in the situation in which the *only*, or *only satisfactory* means of avoiding harm to the relying party is the same as the *only* or *only satisfactory* means of keeping a relevant promise. It will also be in the situation in which the *only* or *only satisfactory* means of putting the relying party in the position in which he would have been had the assumption never been induced, is the same as either the *only* or *only satisfactory* means of putting him in the position in which he would have been had the assumption proved justified. An example of the former may be found in MacCormick's illustration concerning Jones and MacDonald because the duty to ensure the reliability of induced assumptions may require the same response of MacDonald as a promise to assist Jones. An example of the latter may be found in situations, long familiar to lawyers, in which an award in the expectation measure is necessary to protect reliance because the expectation measure:

> "... offers the measure of recovery most likely to reimburse the plaintiff for the (often very numerous and very difficult to prove) individual acts and forbearances which make up his total reliance ..."[16]

It is critical to recognise, however, that the fact that the two duties sometimes might require the same practical response of the party on whom they fall does not mean that they cannot be, or ought not to be, distinguished.

To distinguish the duty under discussion from the duty not to lie is less complex than to distinguish it from the duty to keep promises. A lie is an untrue representation made by a person who has knowledge that the representation is untrue. It is clear that the duty under discussion is much broader. First, an induced assumption may be perfectly true and yet unreliable as a basis for action. Take the following example from Grice:

> "A is standing by an obviously immobilized car and is approached by B, and the following exchange takes place:

---

[16] L L Fuller and W R Perdue, "The Reliance Interest in Contract Damages", (1936–1937) 46 *Yale LJ* 52 and 373 at 60.

> A: 'I am out of petrol'
> B: 'There is a garage around the corner' "[17]

Assume that B's representation that there is a garage nearby is perfectly true. It seems artificial to claim that that representation involves an implied representation that the garage is open, has petrol to sell, and will continue to do so at least until such time as B is able to purchase some. However, unless the garage is indeed open, has petrol to sell, and will continue to do so, the representation will have induced an assumption that is unreliable as a basis for action on A's part. Similarly, an induced assumption regarding the future – including an induced assumption regarding intention – may be perfectly true in the only sense in which it is meaningful to speak of such an assumption as being true – that is, it accurately reflects the state of the inducing party's mind and depends upon no other false facts – and yet it may be protected by the duty to ensure the reliability of induced assumptions. Second, a party inducing an assumption may well fail to ensure the reliability of the assumption in circumstances in which he is under an obligation to do so even though he neither has knowledge that, nor is reckless about whether, the assumption is untrue. It is possible to break the duty under discussion without being in any sense deceitful.

It is clear that the duty under discussion is both distinguishable from, and much broader than, both the duty to keep promises and the duty not to lie. It is also clear, however, that any two of these duties might arise in a single fact situation. A legal system trying to give expression to these three moral duties in a coherent and defensible way, would face two tasks. First, it would have to determine when a breach of each duty should attract liability. Second, it would have to determine how liability should operate in situations in which more than one duty might apply. These are taxonomic questions of enormous potential difficulty.

3. SKETCHING A MAP OF THE LAW IN RELATION TO INDUCED ASSUMPTIONS

In fact, I would argue that the English and Australian law of obligations does include doctrines giving expression to all three of these moral duties. I would further argue that a failure to identify that the three duties are distinct and yet sometimes overlap has led to anxiety about both how those doctrines ought to operate and how they ought to operate together.

Such grand questions as the ideal taxonomy of the law of obligations are outside the scope of this book, but a sketch map of the law relating to induced assumptions would be helpful in considering the emergent doctrine of equitable estoppel. This map is not comprehensive[18] and I have no desire to defend it

---

[17] H P Grice, "Logic and Conversation" in D Davidson and G Harman (eds), *The Logic of Grammar* (Encino, Dickenson, 1975) at 70.

[18] See below at n.27.

against competing representations of the law. The focus of this book is on the doctrine emerging from *Waltons Stores* and *Verwayen* and not on the law relating to induced assumptions generally. The map is simply offered as a context for my understanding of the law of equitable estoppel.

First, a legal system protecting induced assumptions will need a doctrine giving effect to the duty to keep promises. The extent to which the common law of contract either does or should represent such a doctrine has, of course, been highly contested in the past twenty years.[19] However, given the continued centrality in the law of contract of remedies protecting the expectation interest, and the continued enforcement of contracts which have resulted in no benefit to the promisor and have caused no detriment to the promisee, the argument that promise is the moral heart of contract law has remained orthodoxy.

Of course, to claim that promise is the moral heart of contract law is to deny neither (i) that the award of remedies in the expectation measure, particularly in response to contracts that have caused no benefit or detriment, is sometimes difficult to justify,[20] nor (ii) that the law cannot, and should not, enforce all promises.[21] The legal enforcement of promises is constrained by an insistence upon requirements such as offer and acceptance, intention to enter legal relations, consideration and writing. The common law, then, seems equipped with a doctrine giving limited expression to the duty to keep promises and expressing an appropriate caution in the award, as of right, of remedies in the expectation measure.

Amongst the requirements for an enforceable contract, that of consideration is particularly pertinent to the discussion of equitable estoppel. The argument is presented in this book that equitable estoppel is, or ought to be, an independent cause of action designed to enforce the duty to ensure the reliability of induced assumptions. But the position has sometimes been advanced – recently by Gummow J in *Esanda Finance* v *Peat Marwick*[22] – that equitable estoppel is simply an alternative to consideration for the enforcement of contracts. This suggestion reflects an impatience with the doctrine of consideration, or at least with its effects in certain circumstances. This book is not the place for a developed apology for the doctrine of consideration, which has often been

---

[19] See G Gilmore, *The Death of Contract* (Columbus, Ohio UP, 1974), P S Atiyah, *The Rise and Fall of Freedom of Contract* (Oxford, Clarendon Press, 1979), P S Atiyah, *Promises, Morals and Law* (Oxford, Clarendon Press, 1981), C Fried, *Contract as Promise: A Theory of Contractual Obligation* (Cambridge, Harvard UP, 1981), J Raz, "Promises in Morality and Law", (1982) 95 *Harv L Rev* 916, A S Burrows, "Contract, Tort and Restitution: A Satisfactory Division or Not?", (1983) 99 *LQR* 217, R Birmingham, "Notes on the Reliance Interest, (1985) 60 *Washington L Rev* 217, W H Holmes, "The Freedom Not to Contract", (1986) 60 *Tulane L Rev* 751.

[20] See L L Fuller and W R Perdue, "The Reliance Interest in Contract Damages", (1936–1937) 46 *Yale LJ* 52 and 373 at 56–57, P S Atiyah, *Promises, Morals and Law* (Oxford, Clarendon Press, 1981) at 202–212 and P S Atiyah, *Essays on Contract* (Oxford, Clarendon Press, 1986) at 31–43.

[21] See M Cohen, "The Basis of Contract", (1933) 46 *Harv L Rev* 553 at 573 and L L Fuller, "Consideration and Form", (1941) 41 *Colum L Rev* 799 at 813.

[22] (1997) 188 CLR 241 at 299.

criticised.[23] Suffice it to say (i) that it seems a remarkably resilient intuition that there is a distinction between bargain and gratuitous promises, and that the law should only enforce bargain promises and promises made in the context of a solemn formality (such as the exchange of a peppercorn consideration or the execution of a deed),[24] and (ii) that if equitable estoppel does, in fact, give expression to the duty to ensure the reliability of induced assumptions, the imposition of a contract to protect those induced assumptions would be a quite inappropriate juridical response. This latter point will become clearer in the following chapters of this book when we consider (i) the issue of remedies in equitable estoppel, (ii) the possible co-existence of equitable estoppel and the existing law of contract and, (iii) the potential operation of equitable estoppel in four cases that have proved problematic to contract. At this point it is enough to emphasise that the enforcement of promises and the award of expectations is appropriately constrained by the law of contract and that consideration has had a vital rôle in this process.

Second, in addition to a doctrine giving expression to the duty to keep promises, a legal system protecting induced assumptions will require a doctrine giving expression to the duty not to lie. The common law has arguably fashioned such a doctrine in the tort of deceit. The tort of deceit applies only when a defendant either knows that an assumption he is inducing is false or is reckless as to its truthfulness.[25] However, just as not all promises are actionable, neither are all lies. The defendant must not only have knowingly made a misrepresentation of fact, he must also have intended that the plaintiff should act upon that misrepresentation and the plaintiff must have done so to his detriment. Perhaps as a reflection of the moral seriousness of lying, deceit gives rise to particularly

---

[23] See, for example, Lord Wright, "Ought the Doctrine of Consideration to be Abolished from the Common Law?" (1936) 49 *Harv L Rev* 1225 and Law Revision Committee *Sixth Interim Report (Statute of Frauds and the Doctrine of Consideration)* (1937) (Cmd 5449).

[24] See the comments of Handley JA in the equitable estoppel case *Hawker Pacific Pty Ltd* v *Helicopter Charter Pty Ltd* (1991) 22 NSWLR 298 at 307–308. In relation to the intuition that the law should prefer "bargain" promises, Patterson writes: "Reciprocal exchange is, then, a widely approved pattern of conduct in social relations outside of commerce and industry, and this makes the similar but narrower pattern required by consideration familiar and accessible to those who are unaware of legal consequences" (E W Patterson, "An Apology for Consideration", (1958) 58 *Colum L Rev* 929 at 946). Because this intuition is widespread, consideration arguably performs the "channelling function" of "[furnishing] a simple and external test of enforceability" (L L Fuller, "Consideration and Form", (1941) 41 *Colum L Rev* 798 at 801). However alternatives to consideration designed better to perform the same function are often proposed (see, for example, J D Gordon, "A Dialogue about the Doctrine of Consideration", (1990) 75 *Cornell L Rev* 987 at 1004–1005). In relation to the intuition that the law should prefer promises solemnly made, there is a long tradition of recognising the "cautionary" function of the doctrine of consideration (see L L Fuller, "Consideration and Form" (1941) 41 *Colum L Rev* 798 at 800), although many alternative means of better performing this function have also been proposed (see, for example, J D Gordon, "A Dialogue about the Doctrine of Consideration", (1990) 75 *Cornell L Rev* 987 at 1004–1005). Regarding the persistence of these intuitions, note the survival of the doctrine of consideration in the United States despite repeated academic attempts to announce its death (see M B Wesman, "Should we Fire the Gatekeeper? An Examination of the Doctrine of Consideration", (1993) 48 *U Miami L Rev* 45).

[25] *Derry* v *Peek* (1889) 14 App Cas 337.

harsh remedies. The defendant may be liable for all losses flowing from his misrepresentation and not merely those which are foreseeable.[26]

Third, if the duty outlined in this chapter is accepted, a legal system protecting assumptions needs, not only doctrines giving expression to the duties to keep promises and not to lie, but also a doctrine giving expression to the duty to ensure the reliability of induced assumptions. Perhaps because the application of this third duty is so fact sensitive, it is the proper legal treatment of this duty that has most vexed the common law. The doctrines that have arguably given it expression include[27] (i) the common law action to remedy negligent misstatement, (ii) the equitable action against a fiduciary who gives negligent advice in *Nocton* v *Lord Ashburton*,[28] and (iii) estoppel. Of course, it may surprise many jurists to see this group of doctrines linked together as giving expression to a unifying moral principle. Estoppel alone has been said to give expression to the promise principle,[29] to a desire to protect justified reliance,[30] and to a principle against unjust enrichment.[31] The notion that so seemingly disparate a group of doctrines might give expression to the same moral principle seems scandalously simplistic.

Yet, curiously, the application of each of these doctrines is triggered by the same fact scenario, the development of each of the doctrines has been plagued by the same difficulties, and the response to those difficulties provided by each doctrine is remarkably similar.

---

[26] *Doyle* v *Olby (Ironmongers) Ltd* [1969] 2 QB 158.

[27] This list of doctrines is obviously representative, rather than comprehensive. It excludes both some important statutory actions (for example, those contained in s 2(1) of the Misrepresentation Act 1967 (UK), ss 7(1) and 7(2) of the *Misrepresentation Act 1971–1972* (SA,) ss 4(1) and 4(2) of the *Law Reform (Misrepresentation) Act* 1977 (ACT), and s 52 of the *Trade Practices Act* 1974 (Cth)) and some important common law doctrines. Amongst these latter is, perhaps most significantly, the so-called "common intention" trust. The relationship between equitable estoppel and this doctrine is not explored in this book, but is ripe for examination as estoppel develops (see *Green* v *Green* (1989) 17 NSWLR 343, *Public Trustee* v *M. Kukula* (1990) 14 Fam LR 97, *Rasmussen* v *Rasmussen* [1995] 1 VR 613 and *W* v *G* (1996) 20 Fam LR 49). Other estoppel-related doctrines not a part of my sketch map include the equitable actions in *Burrowes* v *Lock* (1805) 10 Ves 470 and *Hammersley* v *De Biel*, (1845) 42 Cl & Fin 45 (see W T Barbour, "The History of Contract in Early English Equity" in P Vinogradoff (ed.), *Oxford Studies in Social and Legal History* vol iv (Oxford, Clarendon Press, 1914), I E Davidson, "The Equitable Remedy of Compensation", (1982) 3 *MULR* 349, F Dawson, "Making Representations Good", (1982) 1 *Canterbury L Rev* 329, I W Duncanson, "Equity and Obligations", (1976) 39 *MLR* 268, P D Finn, "Equitable Estoppel" in P D Finn (ed), *Essays in Equity* (Sydney, LBC, 1985), R P Meagher, W M C Gummow and J R F Lehane, *Equity: Doctrines and Remedies* 3rd edn (Sydney, Butterworths, 1992) at 422, O W Holmes, "Early English Equity", (1885) 1 *LQR* 162 at 171–174, D Jackson, "Estoppel as a Sword", (1965) 81 *LQR* 84, L A Sheridan, "Equitable Estoppel Today", (1952) 15 *MLR* 325).

[28] [1914] AC 398.

[29] See A S Burrows "*Contract, Tort and Restitution: A Satisfactory Division or Not?*" (1983) 99 *LQR* 217 at 239–244, S J Stoljar, "*Bargain and Non-Bargain Promises*" (1988) 18 *UWALR* 119, P Birks, *An Introduction to the Law of Restitution* revised edn (Oxford, Clarendon Press, 1989) at 47 and 290–293, S J Stoljar, "*Estoppel and Contract Theory*", (1990) 3 *JCL* 1.

[30] A S Burrows "*Contract, Tort and Restitution: A Satisfactory Division or Not?*" (1983) 99 *LQR* 217 at 239–244.

[31] P Birks, *An Introduction to the Law of Restitution* revised edn (Oxford, Clarendon Press, 1989) at 277–290.

The common law action in negligent misstatement, which was developed in *Hedley Byrne & Co.* v *Heller & Partners Ltd,*[32] compensates reliance upon negligently made representations of fact in contexts in which a duty of care can be established. Two concepts emerge from the decision of the House of Lords as determining the contexts in which a duty of care will be recognised. These are the concepts of a "voluntary assumption of responsibility" and of a "special relationship". These concepts remain the foundation of the law in England, but each has proved problematic. It has been argued that the notion of a "voluntary assumption of responsibility" fails to provide a clear test of when a duty of care will arise.[33] If a "voluntary assumption of responsibility" means that the defendant must have consciously accepted a duty of care, it is suggested that liability in negligence will rarely be proved; if it only means that the defendant must have given advice in circumstances in which he knew or ought to have known that reliance would eventuate,[34] it is suggested that it will provide too little constraint on the application of the doctrine. Similarly, it was unclear from the decision of *Hedley Byrne & Co* v *Heller and Partners Ltd,*[35] and remains unclear, whether a "special" relationship is one "equivalent to contract" (as Lord Devlin suggested in that case[36]), one that consists in knowledge of the likelihood of reliance by the other party (as Lord Reid seemed to suggest[37]), or simply the relationship of proximity known to the law of negligence generally (as Lord Morris and Lord Hodson seemed to claim[38]). In Australia, the issue of whether a duty of care arises in the context of negligent misstatement depends upon a variety of considerations that include the relative knowledge of the parties, whether there has been a voluntary assumption of responsibility, whether one party has invited the other to act on his advice and whether he had an interest in the other party so acting.[39] But how those considerations operate together has yet to be clearly enunciated and the law is no more settled in Australia than it is in England.

The action in *Nocton* v *Lord Ashburton*[40] imposes the obligation to compensate loss suffered, *inter alia*, because of reliance upon advice given by a fiduciary.

---

[32] [1964] AC 465.

[33] See, for example K Barker, "Unreliable Assumptions in the Modern Law of Negligence", (1993) 109 *LQR* 461 and K M Stanton, "Insurance, The Hedley Byrne Principle and Concurrent Liability" (1995) 3 *Tort L Rev* 85. See also *Hill* v *Van Erp* (1997) 188 CLR 159 at 228–231 *per* Gummow J. The concept is, however, enjoying some current judicial support. See the decisions of Lord Goff and Lord Browne-Wilkinson in *Henderson* v *Merrett Syndicates Ltd* [1995] 2 AC 145 and *White* v *Jones* [1995] 2 AC 207, of Lord Goff in *Spring* v *Guardian Assurance Plc* [1995] 2 AC 296 and of Lord Steyn in *Williams* v *Natural Life Health Foods* [1995] 2 All ER 577.

[34] See, for example, the judgment of Lord Browne-Wilkinson in *White* v *Jones* [1995] 2 AC 207 at 274.

[35] [1964] AC 465.

[36] Ibid. at 530.

[37] Ibid. at 486.

[38] Ibid. at 496 and 509 .

[39] *San Sebastian Pty Ltd* v *Minister Administering the Environmental Planning and Assessment Act 1979* (1986) 162 CLR 310 at 357 *per* Gibbs CJ and Mason, Wilson, Brennan and Dawson JJ.

[40] [1914] AC 932.

It has been argued that this duty is quite distinct from the tortious duty in negligent misstatement, and can only be relied upon when there is both a want of care and a conflict of duty and interest.[41] Lord Browne-Wilkinson has, however, recently claimed that "[t]he liability of a fiduciary for the negligent transaction of his duties is not a separate head of liability but the paradigm of the general duty to act with care imposed by law on those who take it upon themselves to act for or advise others."[42]

"Estoppel" may be taken to signify a rule ". . . which precludes a person from denying the truth of some statement formerly made by him, or the existence of facts which he has by words or conduct led others to believe in."[43] However, the term is rarely used alone or with so unqualified a meaning. It usually forms part of a longer tag such as "promissory estoppel", "proprietary estoppel", "estoppel by representation" or "estoppel *in pais*". These tags, and the categories of case to which they are attached, are beset with confusion. A rough categorisation of the estoppel cases before *Waltons* is adopted in Chapter Two, but it is sufficient for this sketch map of the law in relation to induced assumptions (i) to rely upon the broad definition of estoppel offered at the beginning of this paragraph and (ii) to note that in each category of estoppel, reliance upon an induced assumption by the party in whom the assumption was induced was key to preventing departure from that assumption by the party who had induced it.

The similar fact situation that triggers each of these doctrines, then, is that one party induces an assumption in the mind of another who relies upon it to his detriment, in the sense that he is worse off, because the assumption has proved unjustified than he would have been had it never been induced.

The difficulty that has plagued each of these doctrines is the difficulty, given that we all regularly induce assumptions in one another, of setting limits to the liability that might arise on the basis of induced assumptions. This difficulty is particularly acute in relation to potential reliance by third parties, that is, parties in whom the assumption was not directly induced but who have also come to rely upon it.

In response to this difficulty, a recurrent set of potential limits to liability runs through each of these categories of case. Three such limits have been particularly powerful. First, there has been an attempt to limit liability by focussing on particular categories of relationship. This concern with categories of relationship has been a concern of all three doctrines. The idea is that reliance is justified and ought to be compensated in some categories of relationship and not others and that the recognition of a limited class of relationships in which reliance is justified will constrain potential liability for reliance loss. Second, there has been an attempt to limit liability by focussing on the extent to which the inducing

---

[41] W M C Gummow, "Compensation for Breach of Fiduciary Duty" in T G Youdan (ed.), *Equity, Fiduciaries and Trusts* (Toronto, Carswell, 1989).

[42] *Henderson v Merrett Syndicates Ltd* [1995] 2 AC 145 at 205. See also the judgment of Lord Browne-Wilkinson in *White v Jones* [1995] 2 AC 207.

[43] J Burke, *Osborne's Concise Law Dictionary* 6th edn (London, Sweet & Maxwell, 1976) at 136.

party knew or ought to have known that the other party would rely upon the assumption. This is what sometimes lies behind the notion of a "voluntary assumption of responsibility" in negligent misstatement and was, as we shall see in Chapter Two, important to all the traditional categories of estoppel. Third, there has been an attempt to limit liability, and to preserve the rôle of contract in protecting reliance upon induced assumptions where those assumptions have been induced by a promise, by denying recovery for reliance upon an induced assumption regarding the inducing party's intentions, truthfully stated. This limitation has the appeal that the law divides neatly into liability for failing to keep promises and liability for untrue representations. It has had an important rôle in the law of negligent misstatement. It has also been important to all the traditional categories of estoppel save, significantly, "promissory" estoppel.

However, if the moral duty outlined in the opening sections of this chapter is, in fact, the heart of these different doctrines, it can be seen that each of these limitations to liability is potentially overstated, because each of the limitations – the issue of whether the party inducing the assumption and the party relying upon it enjoyed some special relationship of trust, the issue of whether reliance might have been expected and the issue of whether the assumption was one as to intention or fact – is merely one of a range of considerations going to determine whether, and how strongly, one party owes the duty to ensure the reliability of induced assumptions. What is needed is a doctrine that can handle this range of considerations with flexibility, and yet operate in only a limited and predictable range of circumstances. There is no suggestion that every breach of the duty to ensure the reliability of induced assumptions ought to be remedied by the law, any more than that every promise should be enforced or every lie give rise to liability.

If the remainder of this book is at all convincing, it may well be that equitable estoppel is emerging as a doctrine capable of filling this need. Equitable estoppel operates to enforce the duty to ensure reliability of induced assumptions, but does so only in those situations in which the duty applies most strongly. The strength of the duty and whether it has been broken is determined by an enquiry that the judges have called the "unconscionability" enquiry. If the doctrine described in Chapter Two can be accepted, then it may well give expression to the duty to ensure the reliability of induced assumptions in a way that is justifiable, predictable and constrained. How that doctrine interrelates with others giving expression to the duty to ensure the reliability of induced assumptions – and particularly the developing law of negligent misstatement – is a question that can be determined once estoppel itself is understood.

II

The Emergent Doctrine
of Equitable Estoppel

1. INTRODUCTION

Few would have predicted in 1987 that the High Court of Australia were about to launch "an exciting voyage of discovery . . . in . . . estoppel".[1] As late as 1986 the High Court had seemed antipathetic to any developments in this area. *Central London Property Trust Ltd v High Trees House Ltd*[2] was only accepted by the High Court in 1983[3] and then in a case in which the majority of their Honours declined to apply it.[4] Estoppel by representation and by convention had been defined in extremely conservative terms in the 1986 decision of *Con-Stan Industries of Australia v Norwich Winterthur Insurance (Australia) Ltd.*[5] The High Court hardly seemed likely to develop estoppel into a principle that could radically reorganise the law's approach to reliance upon induced assumptions.

Yet in 1987, unobserved though they may have been, the factors that were soon to encourage the development of equitable estoppel were already in place. First, an earlier curial tendency almost automatically to conform Australian to English law was beginning to break down. The High Court was eager to develop a distinctively Australian common law and, according to Sir Anthony Mason, felt English contract principles were too dominated by that country's position as an international commercial and maritime hub to be the centrepiece of Australian contract law.[6] Second, a rich source of material for the development of a new Australian doctrine of estoppel was being re-discovered in two High

---

[1] Sir Anthony Mason, "Themes and Prospects" in P D. Finn (ed.), *Essays in Equity* (Sydney, LBC, 1985) at 244–245.

[2] *Central London Property Trust Ltd v High Trees House Ltd* [1947] KB 130.

[3] *Legione v Hateley* (1983) 152 CLR 406.

[4] Mason, Brennan and Deane JJ (Gibbs CJ and Murphy J dissenting) .

[5] *Con-Stan Industries of Australia v Norwich Winterthur Insurance (Australia) Ltd* (1986) 160 CLR 226. For the current status of this decision see below at p.x.

[6] Sir Anthony Mason, "Future Directions in Australian Law: The Wilfred Fullagar Memorial Lecture" (1987) 13 *Mon LR* 149 at 153. This movement towards a distinctly Australian common law was also felt at the State court level after appeals to the Privy Council were abolished. Speaking of the *Australia Act*, 1986 (Cth) Priestley wrote: "This independence means that Australia can, like other nations, decide what its contract law is and is to be, free of the authority of any other country" (L J Priestley, "A Guide to a Comparison of Australian and United States Contract Law", (1989) 12 *UNSWLJ* 4 at 4). See also M P Ellinghaus, "An Australian Contract Law?", (1989) 2 *JCL* 13 and J L Toohey, "Towards an Australian Common Law" (1990) 6 *Aust Bar Rev* 1.

Court judgments by Dixon CJ, one in equity and one at common law.[7] Dixon CJ had been cited by Lord Denning MR as the early exponent of a radical understanding of estoppel, keen that estoppel develop into a broad "principle of justice and of equity" built upon assumptions "of fact or law, present or future".[8] Third, there had been a considerable amount of interest in estoppel in the first half of the 1980's. The *Australian Case Citator*[9] gives just seven references to these two Dixon CJ judgments for the forty five years prior to 1980. It gives none at all for the period 1960 to 1972. There are then sixteen references for the five year period between 1981 and 1986. Many of the State court decisions in this period reveal a readiness for the development of estoppel principles.[10] These factors eventually led to the radical developments of *Waltons* and *Verwayen*, developments which by 1989 were said to have had a "profound effect on the market place."[11]

Before considering the doctrine of equitable estoppel in detail, however, three preliminary tasks must be undertaken. First, the methodology of this chapter in expounding the doctrine developing from *Waltons* and *Verwayen* must be described. Second, an outline of the estoppel categories recognised in the period immediately preceding *Waltons* should be offered. Third, the facts of *Waltons* and *Verwayen* should be given. The reasoning in those cases – or as much of it as is important to the development of equitable estoppel – will be examined as the doctrine is expounded later in the chapter.

(a) Methodology

The methodology of this chapter in expounding the doctrine of equitable estoppel is necessitated by the current state of the Australian authorities.

At first glance, the significance of those authorities seems evident. The general shape and purpose of the emerging estoppel doctrine has been repeatedly

---

[7] *Thompson v Palmer* (1933) 49 CLR 507 and *Grundt v Great Boulder Pty Gold Mines Ltd* (1937) 59 CLR 641.

[8] *Moorgate Mercantile Co Ltd v Twitchings* [1976] QB 225 at 241–242. While the claims of Lord Denning MR may be somewhat overstated, it is surprising that at about the same time Starke and Higgins should have seen Dixon CJ as an opponent of promissory estoppel citing, incorrectly it is submitted, his lecture "Concerning Judicial Method" (1956) 29 *ALJ* 468. See J G Starke and P F P Higgins (eds), *Cheshire and Fifoot's The Law of Contract* 4th Australian edn (Sydney, Butterworths, 1974) at 674–675.

[9] This work claims to be ". . . a comprehensive case citator covering the entire period of Australian law reporting, based on material used in the *Australia Digest* service." *Australian Case Citator* (Sydney, LBC, 1988) at v.

[10] See, for example *Hexagon v Australian Broadcasting Commission* (1975) 7 ALR 233, *Offshore Oil NL v Southern Cross Exploration NL* (1985) 3 NSWLR 33, *Riches v Hogben* [1986] 1 Qd R 315 (cf. *Morris v Morris* [1982] 1 NSWLR 61), *Gollin & Co Ltd v Consolidated Fertilizer Sales Pty Ltd* [1982] Qd R 435.

[11] K Nicholson, "Two Recent Decisions Following Waltons Stores (Interstate) Ltd v Maher", (1989) 2 *Corp & Bus LJ* 195 at 197. Nicholson welcomed the "profound effect" of the *Waltons* decision which he said had lead to "commercially realistic resolutions . . . of various disputes".

described in decisions of both Federal and State courts. In *Verwayen* Mason CJ described the doctrine as:

> ". . . one doctrine of estoppel, which provides that a court of common law or equity can do what is required, but no more, to prevent a person who has relied upon an assumption as to a present, past or future state of affairs (including a legal state of affairs), which assumption the party estopped has induced him to hold, from suffering detriment in reliance upon the assumption as a result of the denial of its correctness."[12]

In the same case Brennan J said:

> "[E]stoppel yields a remedy in order to prevent unconscionable conduct on the part of the party who, having made a promise to another who acts on it to his detriment, seeks to resile from the promise . . . The remedy is to effect . . . 'the minimum equity to do justice' . . . The remedy is not designed to enforce the promise although, in some situations (of which *Waltons Stores v Maher* affords an example), the minimum equity will not be satisfied by anything short of enforcing the promise."[13]

The cases are full of passages that describe the emergent estoppel doctrine in these general terms.

Yet, although the significance of these recent authorities may seem clear, it is also clear that the Australian "law of estoppel is in a stage of development",[14] "a state of flux".[15] Passages such as those just quoted are cast in the most general terms and leave many questions open, both about the practical application of the new doctrine and its interrelation with other heads of liability. *Waltons* and *Verwayen* involved multiple judgments cast in differing terminology and little concerned to present a single coherent picture of the law. It was even submitted in *Commonwealth of Australia v Clark*[16] that *Verwayen* was incapable of yielding a *ratio* and, while none of the judges in the case expressly upheld that claim,[17] the difficulty which the judges had in applying *Verwayen* to an almost identical fact situation may well lend it some credibility.

---

[12] *Verwayen* at 413.

[13] Ibid. at 428–429. Similar passages include and *Waltons* at 404 *per* Mason CJ and Wilson J and *Austotel Pty Ltd v Franklins Selfserve Pty Ltd* (1989) 16 NSWLR 582 at 610 *per* Priestly JA.

[14] *Lorimer v State Bank of New South Wales* New South Wales Court of Appeal, 5 July 1991, unreported ([1991] ACL Rep NSW 95) *per* Kirby P.

[15] *PS Chellaram & Co Ltd v China Ocean Shipping Co Ltd* (1991) 1 Lloyd's Rep 493 at 502 *per* Kirby P.

[16] [1994] 2 VR 333.

[17] There were only two points in the judgments in *Commonwealth of Australia v Clark* [1994] 2 VR 333 in which the judges came close to accepting the submission that *Verwayen* yielded no *ratio*. These were (i) a passage in the judgment of Fullagar J (at 335) where he said that there was "no clearly binding *ratio decidendi*, either in the High Court's decision in *The Commonwealth v Verwayen* (1990) 170 CLR 394 or in any case so far, which relieves this court from its duty to follow its own prior decision" in *Verwayen v The Commonwealth (No 2)* [1989] VR 712, and (ii) a passage in the judgment of Ormiston J (at 374) in which he said that "there is a real difficulty in ascertaining the *ratio* of the High Court's decision on the question of estoppel and in particular on the question of detriment." However, it is clear that Fullagar J did not deny that there was a *ratio* in *Verwayen*, simply that there was a *ratio* which was not in line with the approach adopted by the Court of Appeal when it had heard the *Verwayen* case itself. Similarly, although Ormiston J claimed

The current state of the Australian estoppel authorities means that, while it is possible to argue for a particular formulation of the distinct doctrine that appears to be emerging, it is not possible to give a precise representation of equitable estoppel as it currently exists. The writers of one text claim that "[i]t would be a bold lawyer who would assert knowledge of what the law of estoppel was today in Australia."[18] The approach of this book is therefore not simply to "report" the present state of the doctrine. Such an approach would at best be dangerous and may in large part be impossible. Rather, the methodology adopted resembles that of an Australian judge faced with the many recent decisions concerning equitable estoppel, needing to extract from them a doctrinally coherent approach to the subject and then to justify it. In adopting this methodology, my goal is to be as faithful as possible to the existing case law and to develop the doctrine in a way that best equips it to give expression to the duty to ensure the reliability of induced assumptions.

In considering questions of methodology, an important issue concerning the use of older Australian and English authorities should also be emphasised. It has been said that questions of legal history and of the antecedents of the doctrine of equitable estoppel will not concern us in this book. As Ormiston J pointed out in *Commonwealth of Australia* v *Clark*,[19] it is not necessary for a judge applying the doctrine to concern himself with "the earlier cases for they provide no more than the background for the conclusions expressed by the present members of the High Court."[20] Nevertheless, earlier Australian and English judgments will be important to this exposition of equitable estoppel. While not compelled to assess the historical accuracy of the process by which equitable estoppel was formulated in *Waltons* and *Verwayen*, an Australian judge describing, explaining and refining the doctrine would be entitled to make use of English and older Australian cases in a way that might not have been envisaged before those cases. For example, the cases on the emergent estoppel doctrine claim that its antecedents lie, at least in part, in an amalgamation of "promissory" and "proprietary" estoppel principles. This purported derivation of the doctrine must entitle a judge to rely on both antecedent "promissory" and "proprietary" estoppel cases in explaining and refining the new Australian doctrine. This has in fact been the practice of the Australian lower courts in following doctrinal developments that have essentially been the work of the High Court. Many older English judgments are currently used in the Australian courts in ways in which their authors might have found quite remarkable.

---

that there was difficulty in ascertaining the *ratio* of *Verwayen*, he offered many pages of careful analysis of the judgments in the case attempting to do just that, because "what [had] been said by the High Court in *Verwayen's Case* [was] important and [could not] be properly ignored" (at 375). Ormiston J saw his task as being to "try to see what principles [could] be said to be common to [the] judgments" delivered in the High Court in *Verwayen* (at 375).

[18] R P Meagher, W M C Gummow, and J R F Lehane, *Equity: Doctrines and Remedies* 3rd edn (Sydney, Butterworths, 1992) at xi.

[19] *Commonwealth of Australia* v *Clark* [1994] 2 VR 333.

[20] Ibid. at 383.

Surprising as this may be, it reflects a practice with which the judges are familiar in the continual process of doctrinal development.[21]

(b) The Spencer Bower and Turner categories of estoppel

In order to consider the doctrine emerging from *Waltons* and *Verwayen* I shall need a taxonomy of the earlier estoppel cases and terminology with which to describe them. But as was suggested in Chapter One, an agreed taxonomy of those case is almost impossible to find. Take, for example, the use of the terms "promissory" and "proprietary" estoppel by Mason CJ and Wilson J in *Waltons*. These judges claim that the decision of the English Court of Appeal in *Crabb* v *Arun District Council*[22] involved the application of "promissory" estoppel.[23] But in *Crabb* v *Arun District Council* Lord Denning MR claimed to be applying the principle of "proprietary" estoppel.[24] He did, however, rely[25] on *Central London Property Trust Ltd* v *High Trees House Ltd*[26] – the *locus classicus* of "promissory" estoppel in English law – and it may have been that which confused the later judges. Mason CJ and Wilson J also emphasise that *Crabb* v *Arun District Council* – which they have just cited as an instance of "promissory" estoppel – is consistent with *Ramsden* v *Dyson*[27] – a decision they admit to be based in "proprietary" estoppel.[28] Terminological confusion like this abounds in the estoppel cases.

Given this confusion, I will adopt, without evaluation, the book *Spencer Bower and Turner: The Law Relating to Estoppel by Representation*[29] as an accurate statement of the law of estoppel in Australia in the period before *Waltons*. *Spencer Bower and Turner*, the third and most recent edition of which was published in 1977, was the only comprehensive published survey of the English and Australian law of estoppel at the time of the decisions in *Waltons* and *Verwayen*. It is cited in both those cases.[30] At the time, the book was treated

---

[21] In another area of the law, Young J once categorised a number of older authorities and then remarked: "Whilst it may be that some of the learned judges who decided the cases would be surprised to know that their decisions were included by me in this fourth category, it would seem to me that some of the cases that are cited in the textbooks fall into it . . . Again the classic case of *Craven-Ellis* v *Canons Ltd* [1936] 2 KB 403 may also be put into this category, even though it is quite obvious that the learned judges who decided that case may not themselves have so categorised it." (*Monks* v *Poynice Pty Ltd* (1987) 8 NSWLR 662 at 664).

[22] [1976] Ch 179.

[23] *Waltons* at 403.

[24] *Crabb* v *Arun District Council* [1976] Ch 179 at 187.

[25] Ibid. at 188.

[26] [1947] KB 130.

[27] (1866) LR 1 HL 129.

[28] *Waltons* at 404.

[29] A K Turner (ed.), *Spencer Bower and Turner: The Law Relating to Estoppel by Respresentation* 3rd edn (London, Butterworths, 1977) (hereafter "*Spencer Bower and Turner*").

[30] *Waltons* at 432 *per* Brennan J, *Verwayen* at 452 *per* Dawson J, 470 and 472 *per* Toohey J and 481 *per* Gaudron J.

in both the courts and in academic texts as the major work of reference in the area.[31] It was referred to in most of the important English and Australian estoppel decisions in the twenty years before *Verwayen*.[32] The book was an important part of the legal culture out of which *Waltons* and *Verwayen* emerged and it is therefore appropriate to rely upon its categorisation of the estoppel cases and corresponding terminology.

Spencer Bower and Turner opened their book with a division of estoppel into two categories, estoppel by representation and estoppel *per rem judicatam*. The second of these they put to one side as involving considerations essentially different to those upon which the ordinary private law doctrine of estoppel was built. The first they saw as consisting in three sub-categories, estoppel by representation proper, estoppel by convention or deed, and the doctrine of encouragement or acquiescence, often called "proprietary" estoppel. To these categories of estoppel were added "two quasi-estoppels, in which while some significant departure is made from one or more of the general propositions . . . governing true estoppels, yet the principles generally relating to estoppels are seen for the most part to be applicable."[33] These "quasi-estoppels" were election and "promissory" estoppel.

Spencer Bower and Turner defined estoppel by representation in the following terms:

> ". . . where one person ('the representor') has made a representation to another person ('the representee') in words or by acts or conduct, or (being under a duty to the representee to speak or act) by silence or inaction, with the intention (actual or presumptive), and with the result, of inducing the representee on the faith of such representation to alter his position to his detriment, the representor, in any litigation which may afterwards take place between him and the representee, is estopped, as against the representee, from making, or attempting to establish by evidence, any averment substantially at variance with his former representation, if the representee at the proper time, and in the proper manner, objects thereto."[34]

Within this framework, estoppel by convention was distinguished from estoppel by representation proper, in that it was founded:

---

[31] For example, in relation to estoppel by convention, one author claims that "[t]he frequency with which passages in this chapter [of the book] have been approved by various judges indicates the strong influence this chapter has exerted over the understanding of this doctrine" (M N Harvey, "Estoppel by Convention: An Old Doctrine with New Potential", (1995) 23 *ABLR* 45 at 45 n 7).

[32] These include *Kammins Ballrooms Co Ltd v Zenith Investments (Torquay) Ltd* [1971] AC 850, *Hexagon Pty Ltd v Australian Broadcasting Commission* (1975) 7 ALR 233, *Evenden v Guildford City Association Football Club Ltd* [1975] 1 QB 917, *Crabb v Arun District Council* [1976] Ch 1790, *Moorgate Mercantile Co Ltd v Twitchings* [1976] QB 225, *Brikom Investments Ltd v Carr* [1979] QB 467, *Amalgamated Investment and Property Co v Texas Commerce International Bank* [1982] 2 QB 84, *Taylors Fashions Ltd v Liverpool Victoria Trustees Co Ltd* [1982] QB 133, *Legione v Hateley* (1983) 152 CLR 406, *Con-Stan Industries of Australia Pty Ltd v Norwich Winterthur Insurance (Australia) Ltd* (1986) 160 CLR 226.

[33] *Spencer Bower and Turner* at 313.

[34] Ibid. at 4.

"... not on a representation of fact made by a representor and believed by a representee, but on an agreed state of facts the truth of which has been assumed, by convention of the parties, as the basis of a transaction into which they are about to enter."[35]

Further, for estoppel by convention, the party relying upon the assumed state of facts did not need to have believed in them. It would be sufficient if he had assumed that they were to be treated as true as between the parties themselves.[36]

Estoppel by acquiescence or encouragement was said to operate in the following circumstances:

"... A has a right or title which B is in fact infringing under a mistaken belief that his acts are not acts of infringement at all, and A is aware of his own title or right and also of B's invasion of that title or right, and of his erroneous belief that he is not encroaching thereon, but is lawfully exercising rights of his own, and yet, with that knowledge, A so conducts himself, or so abstains from objection, protest, warning or action as to foster and maintain the delusion under which he knows that B is labouring, and induce B to act to his prejudice on the faith of the acknowledgment to be implied from such conduct or inaction, [then] A is not permitted afterwards to assert his own rights against B, or contest B's rights against himself."[37]

This type of estoppel was distinguished from the others in that, whereas the latter were merely rules of evidence incapable of founding a cause of action, under this type an action could be brought. Further, a party relying upon this type of estoppel was ordinarily required to establish a greater degree of knowledge in the party against whom the estoppel was sought than was a party relying upon any other type of estoppel by representation. He was required to show that the representor had actual knowledge, not only of his own rights, but also of the fact that the other party was acting under a mistaken assumption.[38] Spencer Bower and Turner did not distinguish proprietary estoppel on the basis that it applied only to establishing title to land as some writers have suggested.[39]

According to Spencer Bower and Turner, promissory estoppel could only ever be established between the parties to a contract or "that kind of relationship."[40] Where a promise was made between such parties which was "intended to create legal relations, [was] to the knowledge of the promisor to be acted upon by the promisee, and [was] in fact so acted upon by the promisee,"[41] it would be given legal effect by the courts. The principal difference between promissory estoppel and estoppel by representation was therefore that the former could be built upon a promise and not merely a representation of fact. Like estoppel by

---

[35] Ibid. at 157.
[36] Ibid. at 159–160.
[37] Ibid. at 283–284.
[38] Ibid. at 288.
[39] For example, A S Burrows, "Contract, Tort and Restitution: A Satisfactory Division or Not?", (1983) 99 *LQR* 217 at 240.
[40] *Spencer Bower and Turner* at 380.
[41] Ibid. at 369.

representation proper and estoppel by convention, promissory estoppel gave rise to no new cause of action, but could provide a defence against the enforcement of otherwise enforceable rights.

There had been debate as to whether "detriment" of the type necessary to found an estoppel by representation was also necessary to found a promissory estoppel. Spencer Bower and Turner claimed that this debate flowed from a misunderstanding of the term detriment in estoppel cases generally. It was sometimes argued that estoppel by representation required proof of detriment in the very acts undertaken in reliance upon the representation, for example, proof of expenditure incurred.[42] Spencer Bower and Turner claimed that the detriment needed for both promissory estoppel and estoppel by representation consisted in any "injustice to the promisee which would result if the promisor were allowed to recede from his promise."[43] Detriment was therefore to be judged at the moment at which the promisor/representor proposed to resile from his promise/representation.[44] Gauging detriment involved comparing the position of the promisee/representee before and after the proposed withdrawal by the promisor/representor and not before and after his reliance upon the promise/representation. In support of such a position Spencer Bower and Turner cited the judgment of Dixon J in *Grundt* v *Great Boulder Pty Gold Mines Ltd*.[45]

Finally, it was emphasised in Spencer Bower and Turner's book that promissory estoppel did not modify rights *per se*. The promisor could revoke his promise with notice as long as he could restore the other party to a position equivalent to that which he originally occupied. This was also a position about which there was some, albeit limited, debate.[46]

(c) The facts of Waltons and Verwayen

The facts of *Waltons* involved negotiations for the lease of retail premises in a New South Wales country town. The apparent terms of the lease were that the lessor, Maher, would demolish an old factory on a certain site and build a retail store to suit the requirements of the lessee, Waltons. Waltons required that the

---

[42] For example, this position is still adopted in G H Treitel, *The Law of Contract* 9th edn (London, Sweet & Maxwell, 1995) at 105.

[43] *Spencer Bower and Turner* at 390.

[44] Ibid. at 110.

[45] Dixon J said: ". . . the real detriment or harm from which the law seeks to give protection is that which would flow from the change of position if the assumption were deserted that led to it. So long as the assumption is adhered to, the party who altered his situation upon the faith of it cannot complain. His complaint is that when afterwards the other party makes a different state of affairs the basis of an assertion of right against him then, if it is allowed, his own original change of position will operate as a detriment" (*Grundt* v *Great Boulder Pty Gold Mines Ltd* (1938) 59 CLR 641 at 675).

[46] For an outline of this debate see A S Burrows, "Contract, Tort and Restitution: A Satisfactory Division or Not?", (1983) 99 *LQR* 217 at 240.

new premises be ready for them as a matter of urgency. Maher's solicitor communicated his client's reluctance to begin demolition of the existing premises until it was certain that the agreement to lease was concluded. When the terms of the agreement had been settled by the solicitors and Waltons' solicitors had notified the other side that they had received verbal instructions that the terms were acceptable, contract documents were sent to Maher's solicitors. A cover letter dated 7 November included the following paragraph:

> "You should note that we have not yet obtained our client's specific instructions to each amendment requested, but we believe that approval will be forthcoming. We shall let you know tomorrow if any amendments are not agreed to."

There was no communication between the parties on the following day. On 10 November Waltons became aware that demolition of the factory had begun in order to meet a contract deadline of 5 February. On 11 November Maher's solicitors sent Waltons' solicitors the executed documents "by way of exchange". However, Waltons were reconsidering their position and waited until 19 January – by which time about 40 per cent of the retail store was complete – to inform Maher that they no longer wanted to proceed with the lease. Maher brought an action for specific performance of that lease.

The trial judge and the New South Wales Court of Appeal both found for the lessor. The trial judge held that at the time he commenced demolition of the factory, Maher believed that a valid lease was in existence by way of exchange, that this belief was caused by Waltons' conduct and that they were estopped from denying it. The New South Wales Court of Appeal held (i) that, at the time he commenced demolition, Maher believed that there was a binding agreement with Waltons, though not necessarily by way of exchange of contract, (ii) that this belief was caused by Waltons' conduct, and (iii) that they were estopped from denying it. Further, each court held that Maher had been entitled to specific performance of that lease at the time at which proceedings had been instituted but that such an award was no longer appropriate at the time of the first instance judgment. Each court held that Maher was therefore entitled to damages in lieu of specific performance, presumably under the *Supreme Court Act* 1970 (NSW) section 68. The trial court had ordered an inquiry into damages but the case went on appeal before the inquiry was ever instituted.

Waltons appealed to the High Court who dismissed the appeal. Deane and Gaudron JJ accepted that Maher had believed that a valid lease existed at the time he began demolition, Gaudron J accepting that Maher had believed that an exchange had taken place. These judges therefore dealt with the case as one of estoppel on an assumption of existing fact.[47] Mason CJ, Wilson and Brennan JJ dealt with the case as one concerned with the expectation that contracts would in the future be exchanged and applied the doctrine of equitable estoppel.[48]

---

[47] *Waltons* at 443 *per* Deane J and at 460 *per* Gaudron J.
[48] Ibid. at 398 *per* Mason CJ and Wilson J and at 430–431 *per* Brennan J.

Verwayen involved undertakings made by the Commonwealth of Australia as defendant in an action relating to a collision between two naval vessels. The collision, in which the plaintiff Verwayen was injured, occurred in 1964, approximately twenty years before proceedings in the case were commenced. At the time of the collision, it had been thought that negligence actions could not be brought between members of the armed forces for injuries sustained in the course of duty. However, this position was disapproved in a decision of the High Court of Australia delivered just two years before Verwayen, and several others, brought proceedings against the Commonwealth for negligence.

By its defence, dated 14 March 1985, the Commonwealth admitted liability and put only the question of damages in issue. It did not raise the public policy defence concerning members of the armed forces sustaining injury in the course of duty, nor did it plead the relevant statute of limitation. Indeed, throughout the period November 1983 to November 1985 the Commonwealth made repeated representations both to Verwayen and to others that it would not rely on either defence in actions based on the collision. On several occasions after filing its defence, the Commonwealth joined with Verwayen's solicitors in requesting an expedited hearing of the damages question on the basis that liability was not in issue.

However, in about November 1985, the Commonwealth changed its position in relation to the limitation and public policy defences. Leave to amend was sought and granted, and a new defence was delivered on 29 May 1986 in which both defences were relied on. The plaintiff delivered a reply in which he disputed the existence of the public policy defence, claimed that the *Limitation of Actions Act* 1958 (Vict) did not apply to the Commonwealth and, in the alternative, asserted that the defendant had either waived or was estopped from relying upon either defence.

The trial judge having found for the defendant on the basis of the limitation defence and the Full Court of the Supreme Court of Victoria having overturned his decision on the ground of estoppel, the Commonwealth appealed to the High Court which by a majority of four to three dismissed the appeal. Of the majority, two of the judges, Deane and Dawson JJ, found for Verwayen on the basis of estoppel, and two of the judges, Toohey and Gaudron JJ, dealt with the appeal on the basis of waiver. Two of the minority judges, Mason CJ and McHugh J, rejected the waiver arguments and found that any equity the plaintiff could establish on the basis of estoppel had been satisfied by an order for costs. The third minority judge, Brennan J, also rejected the waiver arguments and held that in the circumstances estoppel did not require that the Commonwealth be kept to its promise, but would have remitted the matter to the trial judge so that the plaintiff could show what detriment was suffered in continuing with the action until the defence was amended.

The importance of this decision can only be seen in the context of recent developments in the Australian law of estoppel. No single understanding of the so-called doctrine of "waiver" receives support across the seven judgments.

Indeed, at least one judge has been prepared to hold that "the reasons of the majority of the High Court in *Verwayen* . . . support the view that there is no independent doctrine of waiver."[49] A fairly coherent picture of the developing Australian law of estoppel does emerge, however, and it is this aspect of the case which is important to this chapter.[50]

Incidentally, the importance of this case to the development of the law of estoppel in Australia is in one sense surprising. *Verwayen* need not have been handled as an estoppel case at all. The case might just have easily been categorised as one about issues relating to the abuse of process, in particular to a judge's discretion to grant or refuse leave to amend a defence. A similar fact situation has been treated by the House of Lords on the grounds of when a judge may exercise his discretion to strike out a claim. In this latter case, *Roebuck* v *Mungovin*,[51] Lord Browne-Wilkinson said that the introduction of concepts of waiver, acquiescence or estoppel into cases essentially concerned with process issues was "merely confusing".[52] That *Verwayen* was argued and decided as an estoppel case, is a sign of how important the doctrine had become in Australia.

2. THE ELEMENTS OF EQUITABLE ESTOPPEL

The formulation of equitable estoppel to be offered here can be summarised in fourteen points, each of which will be considered in turn. They are that:

(a) Equitable estoppel is a single doctrine of common law and equity,

(b) able to be used as either a cause of action or defence,

(c) between two parties not necessarily in any kind of pre-existing relationship.

(d) To establish an estoppel one party, A, (or his privy?),

(e) must show that he has held an assumption

(f) regarding the present or the future, of fact or of law,

(g) and that he has acted or refrained from acting,

(h) in reliance upon that assumption,

(i) to his detriment. The detriment which A must show is that he is in a worse position, because the assumption upon which he has relied has proved unjustified, than he would have been had he never held it.

---

[49] *Mowie Fisheries Pty Ltd* v *Switzerland Insurance Australia Ltd* (1996) 140 ALR 57 at 80 *per* Tamberlin J.

[50] Of course, "waiver" may well not be an independent doctrine at all (see J Ewart, *Waiver Distributed* (Cambridge, Harvard UP, 1917)). I have suggested elsewhere that at common law "waiver" primarily refers to the situation in which a right or remedy has been lost or dispensed with under the doctrine of estoppel or common law election and that in equity it primarily refers to the situation in which a right or remedy has been lost or dispensed with under the doctrine of estoppel or release (see M Spence, "Equitable Defences" in P Parkinson, (ed.), *The Principles of Equity* (Sydney, LBC, 1996) at 940–941). For the argument that "waiver" is a discrete doctrine see K Arjunan, "Waiver and Estoppel – A Distinction Without a Difference?", (1993) 21 *ABLR* 86.

[51] [1994] 2 AC 224.

[52] Ibid. at 236 *per* Lord Browne-Wilkinson.

(j)   A must also show that the other party, B, (or his privy?),

(k)   induced the relevant assumption

(l)   and that, having regard to a number of specified considerations, it would be unconscionable for B not to remedy the detriment that A has suffered by relying upon the assumption.

(m) When these things are established, the court may award a remedy sufficient to reverse the detriment that A has shown.

(n)   Defences.

(a) Equitable estoppel is a single doctrine of Common Law and Equity . . .

The recent development of the doctrine of estoppel in Australia has occurred in two stages.

First, in *Waltons* the various categories of estoppel were merged into just two. These were called "common law" and "equitable" estoppel, although this nomenclature was far from historically unproblematic.[53] "Equitable" and "common law" estoppel were described by Priestley JA in *Silovi v Barbaro*:[54]

"The following can I think be distilled from the reasons in *Waltons* notwithstanding the somewhat different language used by different judges. (1) Common law and equitable estoppel are separate categories, although they have many ideas in common. (2) Common law estoppel operates upon a representation of existing fact, and when certain conditions are fulfilled, establishes a state of affairs by reference to which the legal relation between the parties is to be decided. This estoppel does not itself create a right against the party estopped. The right flows from the court's decision on the state of affairs established by the estoppel. (3) Equitable estoppel operates upon representations or promises as to future conduct, including promises about legal relations. When certain conditions are fulfilled, this kind of estoppel is itself an equity, a source of legal obligation. (4) Cases described as estoppel by encouragement, estoppel by acquiescence, proprietary estoppel and promissory estoppel are all species of equitable estoppel. (5) For equitable estoppel to operate in circumstances such as those of the present case there must be the creation or encouragement by the defendant in the plaintiff of an assumption that a contract will come into existence or a promise be performed, and reliance on that by the plaintiff, in circumstances where departure from the assumption by the defendant would be unconscionable.[55] (6) Equitable estoppel may lead to

[53]   See above at n. 7.

[54]   *Silovi v Barbaro* (1988) 13 NSWLR 466 at 472. Priestley JA concedes that his summary does not refer to the reasoning of Deane J in *Waltons*.

[55]   Priestley JA was subsequently to amend point (5) by reading the Privy Council case *Attorney-General of Hong Kong v Humphrey's Estate (Queen's Gardens)* [1987] AC 114 alongside *Waltons*. He held this approach to be permissible because of the treatment that the Privy Council case received in *Waltons* and re-expressed point (5) in the following terms: "For equitable estoppel to operate there must be the creation or encouragement by the defendant in the plaintiff of an assumption that a contract will come into existence or a promise be performed or an interest granted to the plaintiff by the defendant, and reliance on that by the plaintiff in circumstances where departure from the assumption by the defendant would be unconscionable." *Austotel Pty Ltd v Franklins Selfserve Pty Ltd* (1989) 16 NSWLR 582 at 610.

the plaintiff acquiring an estate or interest in land; that is, in the common metaphor, it may be a sword. (7) The remedy granted to satisfy the equity (which either is the estoppel or created by it) will be what is necessary to prevent detriment resulting from the unconscionable conduct."

From this summary of the majority approach in *Waltons*, it can be seen that "common law estoppel" was equivalent to Spencer Bower and Turner's "estoppel by representation". "Equitable estoppel", however, represented an amalgam of their "estoppel by acquiescence or encouragement" and "promissory estoppel", a doctrine that Spencer Bower and Turner did not classify as a species of estoppel at all.[56] Like "estoppel by acquiescence", equitable estoppel could be a "sword" as well as a "shield", and gave rise to the "minimum equity to do justice" to the party relying upon it. Yet, like "promissory estoppel", it could be built upon a representation as to the future and could give rise to remedies in the expectation measure.

Some question might be raised about the status of estoppel by convention in the *Waltons* taxonomy of estoppel. This doctrine was referred to explicitly at only three points in the judgments in *Waltons* and then only very obliquely.[57] However two of these references[58] seem to assume that estoppel by convention was to be included as a type of common law estoppel of the type outlined in *Silovi v Barbaro*.[59] This also seems to have been the approach of Dixon CJ in *Thompson v Palmer*[60] and *Grundt v Great Boulder Pty Gold Mines Ltd*,[61] the two authorities most central to the developments in *Waltons*. Further, this approach seems to be assumed in at least the judgment of Deane J in *Verwayen*.[62] To treat estoppel by convention in this way is effectively to treat it as a sub-category of estoppel by representation in the way suggested by Spencer Bower and Turner.[63] This would not be possible if estoppel by convention applied in situations in which the party estopped was in no way responsible for the other party's adopting, or continuing in, the assumption which was the basis of their relationship, a suggestion that has sometimes been made.[64] However, the better position is that estoppel by convention did not apply in such situations. It is submitted, therefore, that estoppel by convention was intended by the judges in *Waltons* to be treated as a type of common law estoppel.

Athough, after *Waltons*, Australian law recognised just two categories of estoppel, distinguishing those categories was still considered quite important. At that time, it was stressed that common law and equitable estoppel were bound by different limitations. While common law estoppel was capable of

---

[56] See above at pp. 21–22.
[57] *Waltons* at 403 *per* Mason CJ and Wilson J, at 427 *per* Brennan J and at 463 *per* Gaudron J.
[58] Ibid. at 403 *per* Mason CJ and Wilson J and at 427 *per* Brennan J.
[59] *Silovi v Barbaro* (1988) 13 NSWLR 466 at 472 *per* Priestley JA.
[60] *Thompson v Palmer* (1933) 49 CLR at 547 *per* Dixon CJ.
[61] *Grundt v Great Boulder Pty Gold Mines Ltd* (1937) 59 CLR 641 at 675 *per* Dixon CJ.
[62] *Verwayen* at 560 *per* Deane J.
[63] See above at p. 21.
[64] See below at p. 50.

preventing departure from an induced assumption, it only operated in relation to assumptions of existing fact and could not be used as a cause of action. Similarly, while equitable estoppel could apply to induced assumptions regarding the future and could found a cause of action, it would only "permit a court to do what [was] required in order to prevent detriment to the party who [had] relied on the assumption induced by the party estopped but no more".[65] These different limitations were said to be a means of preventing either doctrine from becoming a generalised source of liability for representations and usurping the traditional function of contract law. It was thought that

> "[a] distinction between contract and the operation of estoppel would . . . be much more difficult to maintain if the distinction between common law and equitable estoppel is obscured."[66]

Notwithstanding these fears however, a second stage in the development of the doctrine of estoppel came with the decision in *Verwayen*. In this decision three of the judges – Mason CJ, Deane and Gaudron JJ – argued that common law and equitable estoppel should themselves be merged into just one "single overarching doctrine".[67] It was argued that common law estoppel should be collapsed into equitable estoppel and effectively disappear. As Kirby P pointed out in the decision of *Lorimer v State Bank of New South Wales*, "no clear majority has yet emerged in the High Court for a unified doctrine of estoppel and no holding of that Court so requires."[68] Yet neither was there a clear majority in *Verwayen* for a continued distinction between equitable and common law estoppel, and the trend of Australian opinion seems to be that a unified doctrine would be "conceptually simpler and easier of application".[69]

It is submitted that the move towards a unified doctrine of estoppel in Australia is a desirable one and the term "equitable estoppel" is used in this

---

[65] *Verwayen* at 412 *per* Mason CJ.

[66] P Parkinson, "Equitable Estoppel: Developments after *Waltons Stores (Interstate) Ltd* v *Maher*", (1990) 3 JCL 50 at 60.

[67] *Verwayen* at 411 *per* Mason CJ. Deane J had already rejected the distinction between equitable and common law estoppel in *Waltons* at 155 and in *Foran* v *Wight* (1989) 168 CLR 385 at 434–436. *Quaere* whether Mason CJ had also arrived at this point in *Foran* v *Wight* at 411–412.

[68] *Lorimer* v *State Bank of New South Wales*, New South Wales Court of Appeal, 5 July 1991, unreported ([1991] ACL Rep 325 NSW 95). In *Avtex Airservice Pty Ltd* v *Bartsch* (1992) 107 ALR 539 at 563, Hill J claimed that two problems were abundantly clear: "The first is that there is confusion in the case law as to the precise distinction, if any, between concepts of election, waiver and estoppel; the second is that there is, as yet, no unanimous view as to whether there is a unified doctrine of estoppel applicable both to estoppel by conduct and equitable or promissory estoppel, and including perhaps as well, the doctrine of waiver and election." Three cases drawn almost at random can illustrate this confusion. In *McCraith* v *Fraser* (1991) 104 FLR 227 it was held that common law estoppel remains an independent doctrine. In *Henderson* v *Amadio Pty Ltd [No 1]* it was simply assumed that common law and equitable estoppel had been merged. In *DTR Securities Pty Ltd* v *Sutherland Shire Council* (1993) 79 LGERA 88 at 98 Talbot J expressly claimed that it now "appears safe to say" that there is one overarching doctrine of estoppel in Australia.

[69] *Lorimer* v *State Bank of New South Wales*, New South Wales Court of Appeal, 5 July 1991, unreported ([1991] ACL Rep 325 NSW 95) *per* Kirby P. Lunney is right to call the move to a unified estoppel a "logical advance in this area of the law" (M Lunney, "Towards a Unified Estoppel – The Long and Winding Road" (1992) 56 *Conv* 239 at 250).

book to refer to that unified doctrine.[70] The issue of whether a unified doctrine will usurp the function of contract law will be considered at the beginning of Chapter Three. At this point, two reasons for welcoming the unification of common law and equitable estoppel should be emphasised.

The first of these reasons concerns the distinction between assumptions induced by representations of present fact and assumptions induced by representations as to the future, so important to the claimed distinction between the two doctrines. It is doubtful whether this distinction, first drawn in *Jorden* v *Money*,[71] has been a part of Australian law since *Foran* v *Wight*.[72] In *Verwayen*, Mason CJ described the distinction as "unsatisfactory"[73] and took the existing law to be "that an assumption as to future fact may ground an estoppel by conduct at common law as well as in equity".[74] Moreover, if the doctrine of equitable estoppel is to develop as a vehicle for the duty to ensure the reliability of induced assumptions, it is desirable that this distinction be lessened in importance. As explained in Chapter One, that duty can apply both where an assumption of fact is induced and where an assumption as to the future is induced. Once this distinction between assumptions as to fact and assumptions as to the future has been abandoned, a central distinction between the *Waltons* categories of equitable and common law estoppel will have been given up and a step taken towards justifying their unification.

A second reason to welcome the unification of common law and equitable estoppel is that "it is anomalous and potentially unjust to allow the two doctrines to inhabit the same territory and yet produce different results".[75] As described in *Waltons*, equitable and common law estoppel would often apply in the same fact situations. The question of the remedy to be applied in those situations, and whether effect ought to be given automatically to assumed states of affairs or some more flexible approach taken, is an important matter of remedies that by the time of *Verwayen* was being considered directly. To hide this important question, and others like it,[76] behind artificial categorisations of estoppel as "equitable" or "common law" serves no purpose in a fused legal system. As Deane J said in *Waltons* it is

"... unduly to preserve the importance of past separation and continuing distinctness as a barrier against the orderly development of a simplified and unified legal system which fusion was intended to advance."[77]

---

[70] The term "equitable" estoppel is admittedly a somewhat confusing tag for the unified doctrine. I have elsewhere used the term "Australian " estoppel for the unified doctrine, but have here adopted "equitable" estoppel because of its apparent general acceptance. See M Spence, "Australian Estoppel and the Protection of Reliance" (1997) 11 *JCL* 203.

[71] (1854) 5 HLC 185.

[72] *Foran* v *Wight* (1989) 168 CLR 385 at 411 *per* Mason CJ and 435 *per* Deane J.

[73] *Verwayen* at 410.

[74] Ibid. at 412.

[75] Ibid. at 412 *per* Mason CJ.

[76] Such as whether terms may be imposed on a plaintiff in the award of a remedy. See below at p. 67.

[77] *Waltons* at 447. See also L Kirk, "Confronting the Forms of Action: The Emergence of Substantive Estoppel", (1991) 13 *Adel LR* 225.

For these two reasons, the trend of Australian law towards a unified law of estoppel is to be welcomed and the first element of the doctrine of equitable estoppel is that it is "One single doctrine of common law and equity . . ."

(b) Able to be used as either a cause of action or defence . . .

One of the limitations upon all the categories of estoppel outlined by Spencer Bower and Turner, except proprietary estoppel, was that they were only rules of evidence and incapable of founding a cause of action. Estoppel was a "shield" and not a "sword", though in the quaint phraseology of one case, plaintiffs could often be seen "thrusting forward with [their] shield handing out some incidental buffeting"![78] Once again this limitation grew out of a fear that estoppel might prove a rival to contract and overthrow consideration "by a side wind",[79] a danger that is considered in Chapter Three.

However, this potential limitation of equitable estoppel is logically incoherent and ought not to be imposed upon the doctrine. In *Waltons* Brennan J said:

> "[T]here is a logical difficulty in limiting the principle so that it applies only to promises to suspend or extinguish existing rights. If a promise by A not to enforce an existing right against B is to confer an equitable right on B to compel fulfilment of the promise, why should B be denied the same protection in similar circumstances if the promise is intended to create in B a new right against A? There is no logical distinction to be drawn between a change in legal relationships affected by a promise which extinguishes a right and a change in legal relationships effected by a promise which creates one. Why should an equity of the kind to which *Combe* v *Combe* refers be regarded as a shield but not a sword?"[80]

This logical difficulty will obviously arise wherever estoppel is allowed to affect the enforcement of legal rights and provides good justification for the abandonment of the distinction between estoppel as a sword and as a shield.

Perhaps for this reason, and notwithstanding the doubts of two of the judges of the High Court in *Verwayen*,[81] the trend of the equitable estoppel authorities seems to be towards the abandonment of the distinction. This trend arguably began with *Waltons* in which at least three judges openly allowed the doctrine as a "sword".[82] The growth of the trend can be demonstrated in two separate aspects of the *Verwayen* decision.

Ironically, the first occurs in the judgment of Deane J in a passage in which His Honour was purportedly illustrating the operation of the distinction. Deane J argued that where A is the owner of Blackacre and promises to transfer it to B but later refuses to do so, B can sometimes use estoppel to prevent A denying the

---

[78] *Stevens* v *Standard Chartered Bank* (1988) 53 SASR 323 at 344 *per* Bollen J.
[79] *Combe* v *Combe* [1951] 2 KB 215 at 220 *per* Denning LJ.
[80] *Waltons* at 425–426.
[81] See *Verwayen* at 437–440 *per* Deane J and 459–460 *per* Dawson J.
[82] *Waltons* at 406 *per* Mason CJ and Wilson J and at 425–426 *per* Brennan J.

existence of a trust of the land, for breach of which he can bring an action. Deane J claimed that in such a situation the action is essentially "the ordinary one of a beneficiary against a trustee for actual or threatened breach of trust"[83] and that the estoppel is merely being used as a defence. However, it is clear that A's promise to transfer and B's consequent reliance are being used as the factual basis of the rights that actually give rise to the remedy. It is estoppel and not breach of trust that gives rise to the liability.

Second, *Verwayen* as a whole provides an example of a case in which it may seem that equitable estoppel was only used as a "shield" and yet in which at least some of the judges went out of their way to ensure that it took effect as a "sword". In this case the plaintiff had argued that the defendant was estopped from raising particular defences to a negligence action, *viz.* the denial of a duty of care and the pleading of a statute of limitations. This would have meant that the fact of negligence was still in issue but that certain defences had been removed by means of estoppel. Yet, significantly, the majority encouraged the plaintiff to amend his reply so as to raise estoppel in relation to any denial of liability by the defendant at all[84] and then two of the majority found for the plaintiff on the basis of this doctrine. Thus, for at least those two judges, the defendant's liability effectively arose out of the estoppel and not its negligence.

It is thus becoming clear that equitable estoppel is able to be used both as a "shield" and a "sword", both as a cause of action and defence. Indeed in *The News Corporation Ltd* v *Lenfest Communications Inc*[85] equitable estoppel was specifically classified as a cause of action for the purpose of certain rules of court. There is no sense in maintaining the fiction, as two judges of the High Court seem prepared to do, that the doctrine is only being used defensively.

(c) Between two parties not necessarily in any kind of pre-existing relationship

Despite the importance of promissory estoppel in the development of equitable estoppel, and despite the Spencer Bower and Turner claim that parties between whom a promissory estoppel might operate must be bound by a pre-existing contractual relationship, this requirement is not a part of the new Australian doctrine. The plaintiff and defendant in *Waltons* were not in any kind of contractual relationship but were merely parties to unsuccessful contractual negotiations. Moreover, subsequent decisions have assumed that this possible limitation on the application of the doctrine no longer applies.[86]

What is slightly less clear, however, is whether some other type of legal relationship between the parties might be a necessary pre-condition to the

---

[83] *Verwayen* at 437.

[84] Ibid. at 462–463 *per* Dawson J speaking for the majority.

[85] (1996) 21 ACSR 553.

[86] See, for example, point (5) of Priestley JA's influential summary of estoppel doctrine in *Silovi Pty Ltd* v *Barbaro* (1988) 13 NSWLR 466 at 472, amended in *Austotel Pty Ltd* v *Franklins Selfserve Pty Ltd* (1989) 16 NSWLR 582 at 610 *per* Priestley JA.

application of equitable estoppel. The court in *Waltons* seemed to deny that any type of legal relationship was necessary. It was understood by both judges and academic commentators that the case had abolished this requirement,[87] that it had driven "promissory estoppel one step further by enforcing [a non-contractual promise] directly in the absence of a pre-existing relationship of any kind."[88] However, in *Verwayen*, the question of whether a pre-existing relationship was necessary was treated as still open by at least two of the judges, Mason CJ and Dawson J. Their judgments might be seen as raising a doubt that the requirement is not altogether abolished.

The better view is that no pre-existing legal relationship should be required for the application of equitable estoppel. Significantly, the two judges for whom the requirement still seemed a live issue in *Verwayen* also treated it in a way which rendered it almost meaningless. Each of them suggested that the requirement might be satisfied by proof of a relationship of plaintiff and defendant[89] and Dawson J[90] even suggested that the relationship of tortfeasor and victim might be enough. If these views are right, it is hard to see what value is being given to the term "legal" in the requirement that the parties enjoy a "pre-existing legal relationship".[91]

Moreover, in policy terms, it "is not easy to see why such a relationship should be necessary."[92] While this requirement might have made sense in the context in which promissory estoppel could only be used defensively, its primary justification must have disappeared with the abolition of that restriction on the doctrine. If it is accepted that the doctrine might be developed as a vehicle for the duty to ensure the reliability of induced assumptions, then any relationship that might be discovered between the parties becomes relevant only as one consideration in determining whether liability should arise. The parties' relationship becomes a part of the unconscionability enquiry. After all, there is no suggestion that Jones and MacDonald enjoyed any type of pre-existing relationship in MacCormick's paradigm.[93] It is therefore suggested that the pre-existing legal relationship requirement ought to be abandoned.

---

[87] See, for example, *Collin v Holden* [1989] VR 510 at 517 and E Clark, "The Swordbearer has Arrived: Promissory Estoppel and Walton Stores (Interstate) Ltd v Maher", (1987) 9 *U Tasmania L Rev* 68 at 73–74.

[88] *Waltons* at 400 *per* Mason CJ and Wilson J. It is surprising, given that Mason CJ seems to imply that this is the effect of *Waltons*, that he expresses doubt about the point in *Verwayen* at 403.

[89] *Verwayen* at 403 *per* Mason CJ and at 454–456 *per* Dawson J.

[90] Ibid. at 455.

[91] These judges were not the first to arrive at this rather curious conclusion, however. Tadgell J formed a similar view of the plaintiff-defendant relationship in *Collin v Holden* [1989] VR 510 at 517–518. His Honour relied on the authority of Fullagar J in *Bobko v Commonwealth of Australia* Supreme Court of Victoria, 22 April 1988, unreported, who in turn was said to have relied upon the authority of Donaldson J in *Durham Fancy Goods Ltd v Michael Jackson (Fancy Goods) Ltd* [1968] 2 QB 839.

[92] T E Cain, "Estoppel and Waiver: *The Commonwealth v Verwayen* in the High Court", (1990) 2 *Bond L Rev* 241 at 245.

[93] See above at pp. 4–5.

(d) To establish an estoppel one party, A, (or his privy?) . . .

The question of whether privies may take the *benefit* of an estoppel is obviously related to two further questions, each of which is considered below. First, it is related to the issue of whether B's privies may be *bound* by an estoppel, even though they did not themselves induce the original assumption.[94] Second, it is related to the issue of whether a party in whom an assumption has been induced only indirectly can protect reliance upon it by means of estoppel.[95]

In *Verwayen* Deane J said:

> "The persons who may be bound by or who may take the benefit of such an estoppel extend beyond the immediate parties to it, to their privies, whether by blood, by estate or by contract."[96]

This proposition, however, is clearly in need of some refinement.

There are two ways in which one of A's privies might attempt to rely upon an equitable estoppel. Both of these have to do with situations in which it is argued that equitable estoppel ought to give rise to a proprietary remedy.[97] This is why, in the sentence following that just cited from *Verwayen*, Deane J emphasised that equitable estoppel "can be the origin of primary rights of property."[98]

First, one of A's privies might claim that an estoppel which could have been argued between the original inducing and relying party has changed the nature of rights in a particular piece of property to which he is successor in title and that he ought therefore to be able to rely directly upon that estoppel. This line of argument would presuppose that a change in the rights relating to a particular piece of property has arisen out of the circumstances giving rise to the estoppel themselves and not just from the compensatory award of a court. If this line of reasoning can be accepted (and the passage cited above seems to lend it support) then third parties ought to be able to rely upon an equitable estoppel directly.

Second, one of A's privies might show that the original relying party has himself been awarded compensation from a court in the nature of a proprietary remedy and claim that the award of the court has changed the nature of the rights in a particular piece of property to which he is successor in title. This is no more than a claim that an equitable estoppel is capable of giving rise to a remedy of full proprietary rights, a change *in perpetuum* to rights in a particular piece of property. For example, under an award in equitable estoppel, title to a particular piece of land may be increased by the award of a right of access over a neighbouring piece of property. A successor in title to that land might want to show that the original award was in the nature of a proprietary right capable of running with the land.

[94] See below at pp. 47–50.
[95] See below at p. 52.
[96] *Verwayen* at 444.
[97] For the availability of such remedies see below at p.x.
[98] *Verwayen* at 444.

The issue of which of these two arguments might prove successful in the Australian courts is a vexed one.[99] There have been some suggestions in the recent cases that the former argument is the one that will prevail, that the circumstances giving rise to an equitable estoppel will sometimes be seen as themselves effecting a change in the rights relating to a particular piece of property.[100]

However, I would argue that it is appropriate to allow one of A's privies to rely upon an equitable estoppel only to the extent entailed in the second of the two arguments outlined above. There is no *prima facie* reason why a party who is not the party who has acted in reliance upon the original assumption ought to be able to argue an equitable estoppel directly against the original inducing party. It would not be compatible with the compensatory nature of equitable estoppel to allow him to do so. This would be particularly true if the doctrine can be seen as giving expression to the duty to ensure the reliability of induced assumptions. The duty is owed to a particular party, the party in whom the assumption has been induced. It is therefore that party, and no other, who ought to benefit from the doctrine.

(e) Must show that he has held an assumption . . .

I come, then, to the first of the elements of the doctrine of equitable estoppel that must be established by a party seeking to invoke it. A party seeking to rely upon equitable estoppel must show that he has held the particular assumption upon which the estoppel is to be based.[101] This requirement raises two important questions.

(i) How specific must the relevant assumption be?

It is important to distinguish this issue from the issue of how unequivocally a party to be estopped must have induced the relevant assumption.[102] As an example, a party against whom an estoppel is sought may have induced an assumption that a lease would be granted over certain property. Another party may have induced an assumption that a lease would be granted for a period of three years and at a rent of £200 *per* month, subject to the condition that the property only be used as a hair salon. In either case the assumption may have been

---

[99] It parallels a debate in England as to the extent to which proprietary estoppel and the common intention constructive trust are identical. See D J Hayton, "Equitable Rights of Cohabitees", [1990] *Conv* 370, P Ferguson, "Constructive Trusts – A Note of Caution" (1993) 109 *LQR* 114, D J Hayton, "Constructive Trusts of Homes – A Bold Approach" (1993) 109 *LQR* 485.

[100] See below at p.x.

[101] See, for example, *Gallagher* v *Pioneer Concrete (NSW) Pty Ltd* (1993) 113 ALR 159 at 192 in which a party seeking to rely on equitable estoppel failed because he could not establish that a relevant assumption had ever been held.

[102] See below at pp. 51–52.

unequivocally induced. Yet one of these assumptions is cast in far more general terms than the other.

The question of how specific an assumption must be to found an equitable estoppel was addressed in the decision of the New South Wales Court of Appeal in *Austotel Pty Ltd* v *Franklins Selfserve Pty Ltd*.[103] In that case a party against whom an estoppel was sought relied upon a passage from the judgment of Priestley JA in *Silovi* v *Barbaro*:

> "For equitable estoppel to operate in circumstances such as those of the present case there must be the creation or encouragement by the defendant in the plaintiff of an assumption that a contract will come into existence or a promise be performed . . ."[104]

In *Austotel Pty Ltd* v *Franklins Selfserve Pty Ltd* it was argued that this passage referred to a contract or promise "the content of which was known", containing "precise terms describing what [the party seeking to establish the estoppel] expected from the defendant".[105] It was submitted that such a party would be unable to raise an equitable estoppel unless he were able to point to precise details in the assumption induced.

However, this argument was rejected in *Austotel Pty Ltd* v *Franklins Selfserve Pty Ltd*. Priestly JA claimed that the passage cited from *Silovi* v *Barbaro* did not purport fully to "cover the field" of equitable estoppel.[106] Rather, he divided the existing estoppel cases into two types, those he called "*Waltons* type" cases and those he called "*Plimmer* type" cases. He demonstrated that, while in the former category of case the induced assumption was often cast in very specific terms, in the latter category of case it was framed much more generally, usually taking the form that "an interest" in certain property would be granted to the party raising the estoppel. Into this latter category of case he put many of the decisions traditionally discussed under the label "proprietary" estoppel such as *Plimmer* v *The Mayor of Wellington*,[107] *Ramsden* v *Dyson*,[108] *Inwards* v *Baker*,[109] and *Crabb* v *Arun District Council*.[110] Priestley JA then claimed that equitable estoppel covers both these categories of case and can usually be built upon a general, as well as a specific, assumption. He claimed that the generality of the relevant assumption is in many cases no obstacle to applying a doctrine that gives the courts:

> ". . . a wide, albeit of course judicial, discretion as to what extent relief should be given and what form it should take."[111]

This judicial discretion to fashion relief will be more fully discussed below.

---

[103] (1989) 16 NSWR 582.

[104] *Silovi* v *Barbaro* (1988) 13 NSWLR 466 at 472.

[105] *Austotel Pty Ltd* v *Franklins Selfserve Pty Ltd* (1989) 16 NSWLR 582 at 604.

[106] Ibid. at 604.

[107] (1884) LR 9 App Cas 699.

[108] (1866) LR 1 HL 129.

[109] [1965] 2 QB 29.

[110] [1976] Ch 179.

[111] *Austotel Pty Ltd* v *Franklins Selfserve Pty Ltd* (1989) 16 NSWLR 582 at 608. Compare *Holiday Inns Inc* v *Broadhead* (1974) 232 EG 961 and 1087 at 1087 *per* Goff J.

The approach adopted by Priestley JA has been followed in subsequent decisions. Equitable estoppels have been founded upon some very general assumptions. Thus in *Blazely* v *Whiley*[112] an estoppel was founded on an assumption that a house would be sold to a particular party even though no purchase price had been agreed. In *W* v *G*[113] an estoppel was founded upon the assumption that one partner to a lesbian relationship would "accept the role of parent" to children born to the other partner "and would in so doing accept responsibility for the material and general welfare of both children, and would support [their mother] in providing for the needs of both children and [herself]."[114]

However the issue arises whether – though generality may usually be no bar – there might ever be a case in which the assumption proved is so general that equitable estoppel will not be applied. This is an issue which Priestley JA failed to address directly in *Austotel Pty Ltd* v *Franklins Selfserve Pty Ltd* and in relation to which there exists no other authority.

The answer to this problem may well emerge, not from any requirement as to the nature of an assumption that can found an equitable estoppel, but from two other pre-conditions to the application of the doctrine discussed below. The first is the requirement alluded to earlier that the inducement of the relevant assumption be unequivocal. The more detailed an assumption can be shown to be, the easier it will be to show that it was induced unequivocally. The second is the requirement of unconscionability. On the basis of the criteria set out below, withdrawal from an extremely general induced assumption is less likely to be unconscionable than is withdrawal from a very narrowly framed assumption. Thus, while in theory there may be no limit determined by the cases as to the generality of an assumption capable of founding an equitable estoppel, in practice the requirements that the assumption be unequivocally induced and that withdrawal from it be unconscionable will usually operate to preclude the most generally framed assumptions from the ambit of the doctrine.

(ii) Must the party holding the relevant assumption honestly have believed its truth?

According to Spencer Bower and Turner, application of the various categories of estoppel, except estoppel by convention, required proof that the party seeking to establish the estoppel believed in the truth of the representation upon which it was to be based. Estoppel was not available where there was knowledge, actual or imputed, that the representation was false.[115] In relation to proprietary estoppel this requirement was often expressed in terms of the first of Fry

---

[112] (1995) 5 Tas R 254.
[113] (1996) 20 Fam LR 49.
[114] Ibid. at 56–57.
[115] *Spencer Bower and Turner* at 92 and 130.

J's *probanda* from *Willmott v Barber*,[116] that a party seeking to establish an estoppel must have made a mistake as to his legal rights.[117]

Yet in whatever terms it was expressed, the requirement was an obvious consequence of the centrality of the reliance element of estoppel. A party cannot be said to have relied upon a particular representation or assumption if he knew that it was false.[118] This is presumably also the reason why the requirement was not a part of the law of estoppel by convention. In the context in which estoppel by convention applied it would be possible sincerely to rely upon a version of affairs known to be false, if it were honestly believed that all parties involved would treat that particular version as true. For a similar reason, and in practice if not in theory, the belief requirement for proprietary estoppel often applied in a way similar to that in which it did for estoppel by convention, rather than in the way it did for estoppel by representation generally.[119] The proprietary estoppel cases often involved the creation or encouragement of an assumption that a right would either be granted or not insisted upon in the future. In such situations, the only real sense in which belief in the truth of the assumption could be relevant was once again in the sense of belief that a particular state of affairs would be treated as true as between the parties. Thus Goff J held that a mistake as to rights was not an essential element of a claim to relief under proprietary estoppel.[120] But, again, even if the requirement of honest belief for proprietary estoppel was treated simply as a requirement of honest belief that a particular assumption would be treated as true as between the parties, and not as a requirement of belief that it was in fact true, the requirement would still have served to buttress the reliance element of estoppel.

Given the centrality of reliance to the doctrine of equitable estoppel, there is no doubt that some type of requirement of honest belief should be part of the doctrine. But the question remains as to the form which that requirement should take. Should it be the requirement of estoppel by representation proper that the party seeking to establish the estoppel should genuinely have believed in the truth of the assumption upon which it is to be based, or the estoppel by convention and proprietary estoppel requirement that he must have believed it would be treated as true as between the parties? It is submitted that the requirement of honest belief to be adopted for equitable estoppel, capable as it is of being built upon assumptions regarding the future as well as the present and regarding law as well as fact, should be that requirement traditionally applied to estoppel by convention. *Grundt v Great Boulder Pty Gold Mines Ltd*,[121] a

---

[116] (1880) 15 Ch D 96.

[117] Spencer Bower and Turner claim that this *probandum* is "identical with or a corollary of, the general rule that no representee can claim to have been misled who knows the general facts" (*Spencer Bower and Turner* at 287).

[118] *Canadian & Dominion Sugar Co Ltd v Canadian National (West Indies) Steamships Ltd* [1947] AC 46 at 56 *per* Lord Wright.

[119] P D Finn, "Equitable Estoppel" in P D Finn (ed.), *Essays in Equity* (Sydney, LBC, 1985) at 69

[120] *Holiday Inns Inc v Broadhead* (1974) 232 EG 961 and 1087 at 1087.

[121] *Grundt v Great Boulder Pty Gold Mines Ltd* (1937) 59 CLR 641 at 676 *per* Dixon J.

case that has already proved a rich store of material for the development of the doctrine of equitable estoppel in the High Court, contains a classic statement of the estoppel by convention requirement and would provide ample authority for its application to the developing doctrine.

Incidentally, whatever the belief requirement for equitable estoppel, it is unlikely that the concept of constructive notice of falsehood will play a part in the application of the doctrine. The question of whether the plaintiff ought not to have believed that the representation was true, or ought not to have believed that it would be treated as true as between the parties, will be dealt with as a part of the unconscionability issue discussed below.[122]

Having thus considered both the requisite specificity of an assumption upon which an equitable estoppel may be built and the extent to which the party seeking to rely upon it must have believed it to be true, I turn to its possible content.

(f) Regarding the present or the future, fact or law . . .

In dealing above with the issue of whether equitable and common law estoppel have been subsumed into the single doctrine of equitable estoppel, it was explained that the concept of equitable estoppel, as used in the recent Australian cases, does not recognise a distinction between assumptions regarding the present and assumptions regarding the future. Further, it was shown that this distinction does not, and arguably ought not, to form a part of the doctrine of equitable estoppel as it seems to be developing. These issues, therefore, do not require further discussion and it will be assumed that an equitable estoppel can be built upon an assumption as to the future as well as the present.

A similar issue that does deserve attention here, however, is the claim that estoppel can only be built upon assumptions of fact and not of law. According to Spencer Bower and Turner, the antecedent law of estoppel by representation distinguished two types of situation in which the distinction between representations of fact and law could potentially become an issue. First, there were statements of "fact accompanied by, or involving, an inference or proposition of law, where such inference or proposition [was] not distinct or severable from the statement of fact".[123] In these situations the fact that the relevant statement was one of combined fact and law did not prevent the application of estoppel by representation. Second, there were statements of "a rule, principle, or proposition of the general law"[124] or statements of the legal effects of facts which formed the subject matter of quite separate statements. These were treated as essentially statements of opinion and could therefore only be used as statements of fact to

---

[122] See *Standard Chartered Bank Australia* v *Bank of China* (1991) 23 NSWLR 164 at 177–181 *per* Giles J and *Australian Securities Commission* v *Marlborough Gold Mines Ltd* (1993) 177 CLR 485 at 506 *per* Mason CJ and Brennan, Dawson, Toohey and Gaudron JJ.

[123] *Spencer Bower and Turner* at 38.

[124] Ibid. at 38–39.

found an estoppel by representation in as much as they represented an implied statement of fact concerning the present state of the speakers mind, "an implied statement by the representor of the fact that the opinion expressed as to the law [was] actually entertained by him, or by the person to whom it [was] attributed."[125]

In *Con-Stan Industries of Australia* v *Norwich Winterthur Insurance (Australia) Ltd*[126] the High Court of Australia seemed to narrow this formulation of the law by providing that estoppel could not be built upon a mixed representation of fact and law. This decision was subsequently criticised by Samuels JA in *Eslea Holdings Ltd* v *Butts* where it was pointed out that

> ". . . the authorities to which the judgment in *Con-Stan* refers are not inconsistent with the proposition that a conventional estoppel might rest upon a foundation of assumed law as well as assumed fact."[127]

Thus, in the period immediately preceding *Waltons*, the Australian law of estoppel seemed to hover between the position outlined by Spencer Bower and Turner and Samuels JA in *Eslea Holdings Ltd* v *Butts*, and the more restrictive position in *Con-Stan Industries of Australia* v *Norwich Winterthur Insurance (Australia) Ltd.*

It is therefore a sign of how sudden and radical the recent transformation of Australian estoppel law has been, that just four years later a High Court judgment in *Verwayen* could include this passage concerning the distinction between assumptions of fact and law:

> "The assumption may be one as to legal as well as to a factual state of affairs. There is simply no reason to restrict the assumption to a factual matter as there was at the time when the rules of estoppel by conduct were evidentiary. It has already been recognised that an equitable estoppel may relate at least to a matter of mixed fact and law: see *Waltons Stores*, at 415–416, 420–421, 452; *Foran* v *Wight*, at 433–435. Moreover, the distinction between assumptions as to fact and assumptions as to law is artificial and elusive; see the discussion of Oliver J in *Taylors Fashions Ltd* v *Liverpool Trustees Co.* [*sic*] at 150–151. So it would be productive only of confusion and arid technicality to restrict the operation of the doctrine so as to exclude from its scope an assumption as to a purely legal state of affairs."[128]

Further, in this same decision, Deane J declared that the assumption founding an equitable estoppel "may be of fact or law, present or future",[129] a position that he had adopted in *Foran* v *Wight*,[130] and that has since been repeated.[131] In

---

[125] Ibid. at 39.
[126] *Con-Stan Industries of Australia* v *Norwich Winterthur Insurance (Australia) Ltd* (1986) 160 CLR 226 at 244–245.
[127] *Eslea Holdings Ltd* v *Butts* (1986) 6 NSWLR 175 at 188.
[128] *Verwayen* at 413 *per* Mason CJ.
[129] Ibid. at 445.
[130] *Foran* v *Wight* (1989) 168 CLR 385 at 435.
[131] See, for example, *Forbes* v *Australian Yachting Federation* (1996) 131 FLR 241 at 287 and *Cukeric* v *David Jones (Australia) Pty Ltd* (1996) 70 IR 26 at 44.

Foran v *Wight* Deane J called the distinction between fact and law "essentially illusory".[132]

It would seem that, far from its earlier position in *Con-Stan Industries of Australia* v *Norwich Winterthur Insurance (Australia) Ltd*, the High Court is developing an equitable estoppel altogether free of the distinction between assumptions of fact and law. It is true that this development is not yet complete. Indeed, the decision in *Con-Stan Industries of Australia* v *Norwich Winterthur Insurance (Australia) Ltd* has never been overruled on this point. The decision was not even cited in *Waltons, Verwayen* or *Foran* v *Wight*. Nevertheless, the abandonment of the distinction between assumptions of fact and law has been readily accepted by other Australian courts,[133] has also occurred in the context of the restitution of mistaken payments,[134] and can arguably be justified in two ways, each reflecting one of the two traditional reasons for excluding statements of law from estoppel.

The first reason for excluding statements of law from estoppel is, according to Spencer Bower and Turner, that statements of law are statements of opinion.[135] However, it is not immediately apparent that this is true. A statement of "fact" is a statement presenting itself as a verifiable truth. A statement of "opinion" is expressly the statement of a "judgement or belief based on grounds short of proof."[136] Legal theorists such as MacCormick have shown that statements of law are often capable of clear cut deductive justification[137] and at least in such straightforward cases there may be no real sense in which the relevant statement of law is a statement of less verifiable fact than a statement about the physical world.

In any case, even if statements of law are, in fact, statements of opinion it is still not clear why statements of opinion should not be able to give rise to an assumption founding an equitable estoppel. If equitable estoppel is to be developed into a legal vehicle for the duty to ensure the reliability of induced assumptions, the distinction between assumptions of fact and opinion cannot be given dispositive force in determining when the doctrine will apply. It is clearly possible that a party expressing an opinion might have broken this duty. Inducing reliance upon an assumption regarding opinion can be just as much as source of preventible harm as inducing reliance upon an assumption regarding fact.

---

[132] *Foran* v *Wight* (1989) 168 CLR 385 at 435.

[133] See, for example, *Burnside Sub-Branch RSSILA Inc* v *Burnside Memorial Bowling Club Inc* (1992) 58 SASR 324 at 344, *Inn Leisure Industries Pty Ltd* v *D F McCloy Pty Ltd* (1991) 100 ALR 447 at 463 *per* French J, and *Lorimer* v *State Bank of New South Wales* New South Wales Court of Appeal, 5 July 1991, unreported ([1991] ACL Rep 325 NSW 95).

[134] *David Securities Pty Ltd* v *Commonwealth Bank of Australia* (1992) 175 CLR 353. See also in England, Law Commission, *Consultation Paper No.120: Restitution of Payments Made Under a Mistake of Law* (1991).

[135] *Spencer Bower and Turner* at 38–39.

[136] H W Fowler and F G Fowler, (eds), *The Concise Oxford Dictionary of Current English* 5th edn (Oxford, Clarendon Press, 1964) at 848.

[137] N MacCormick, *Legal Reasoning and Legal Theory* (Oxford, Clarendon Press, 1978) Ch II

The second reason traditionally advanced for the exclusion of assumptions of law from the operation of estoppel is that an assumption of law is equally verifiable by both parties. However, arguments of, and thus statements regarding, law are not equally accessible to all. At least in some circumstances, it must be justifiable to rely upon an assumption as to law induced by another person. That other person ought to be regarded as subject to the duty to ensure the reliability of induced assumptions and not exempted from liability giving it legal expression.

Deane J would seem justified, therefore, in his claim that equitable estoppel can be built upon assumptions of "fact or law, present or future".

(g) And that he has acted or refrained from acting . . .

This seventh element in the establishment of an estoppel is obviously closely related to the eighth (the element of reliance) and the ninth (the element of detriment). If a person seeking to establish an estoppel has not in any way acted or refrained from acting since the relevant assumption was induced, then he can be said neither to have relied upon that assumption, nor to be in any worse position should it prove unjustified than he would have been had it never been held.

But an initial question arises before the elements of detriment or reliance can be discussed. This is the question of what will count as refraining from action for the purposes of equitable estoppel. A clue to answering this question may be found in an English case, *Fontana N V v Mautner*. In that case Balcombe J said:

> "I am quite positive in my mind on the evidence I have heard that Mr Mautner did nothing, either by action or inaction, in reliance on the representation made by Mr Isaac Sofair."[138]

While perhaps clumsy, the phrase "did nothing . . . by . . . inaction" points to an important distinction between *refraining or forbearing from acting* and merely *not acting*. The antecedent categories of estoppel apply in at least certain circumstances when the party seeking to establish the estoppel can show that he has refrained from adopting a particular course of action.[139] Merely not acting, however, has often been cited as a reason for not recognising a particular estoppel, including an equitable estoppel.[140]

The difference seems to be between (i) situations in which the party seeking to establish the estoppel has been in a position to adopt a new course of action

---

[138] (1980) 254 EG 199 at 207.

[139] See *Spencer Bower and Turner* at 106.

[140] For examples drawn from the traditional categories see *Newbon v City Mutual Life Assurance Society Ltd* (1935) 52 CLR 723, *Fontana N V v Mautner* (1980) 254 EG 199, *Cook Industries Inc v Meunerie Liegeois S A* [1981] 1 Lloyd's Rep 359, *Raiffeisen Hauptgenossenschaft v Louis Dreyfus & Co* [1981] 1 Lloyds Rep 345, *Bremer Handelsgesellschaft mbH v Deutsche Contihandelsgesellschaft mbH* [1983] 1 Lloyd's Rep 689. For an equitable estoppel example see *Windrum v Rejilo* (1988) 87 ANZ Convey Rep 491 at 495.

and has addressed his mind to the possibility of doing so, but, on the basis of the assumption that he has been induced to hold, has not adopted the new course of action, and (ii) situations in which the party seeking to establish the estoppel has either had no opportunity or not addressed his mind to the possibility of adopting any course of action different from that to which he had already been committed. The former of these situations – that of refraining from action – could sometimes clearly be a situation of reliance. The latter – that of mere inaction – equally clearly could not.

It would appear, then, that equitable estoppel – like the various antecedent categories – ought only to be applied when the party seeking to establish the estoppel has somehow acted or refrained from acting following the inducement of the assumption upon which the estoppel is to be built. Only such a requirement is consonant with the purpose of the doctrine in protecting reliance upon induced assumptions.

(h) In reliance upon that assumption . . .

Once again, it is important to distinguish this element of equitable estoppel from another with which it might be confused, that of detriment discussed below.[141] This distinction between reliance and detriment is also a part of the antecedent categories of estoppel and was set out by Jonathan Parker QC in *Coombes v Smith*:

> "Two questions have, it seems to me, to be asked in relation to each of [the plaintiff's actions]: (1) was it done in reliance on the defendant's assurances or, in other words, on the faith of the plaintiff's mistaken belief, the existence of which I have, for present purposes, to assume? and (2) by doing it, did the plaintiff prejudice herself or otherwise act to her detriment?"[142]

Given the underlying purpose of equitable estoppel in protecting reliance upon induced assumptions, the element of reliance is obviously very important to the operation of the doctrine. Only such detriment as flows from reliance upon the induced assumption can be remedied.

Because of the centrality of this requirement, it might seem surprising to suggest that a party seeking to establish an equitable estoppel ought not always to be required to prove reliance. However, in relation to promissory and proprietary estoppel, there was a rebuttable presumption that any action, or refraining from action, subsequent to the inducement of the assumption, was undertaken in reliance upon the assumption,[143] although it is probable that this

---

[141] As an example of a situation in which these two elements of estoppel were confused, see the arguments of counsel in *Coombes v Smith* [1986] 1 WLR 808 summarised at 829.

[142] Ibid. at 820.

[143] *Brikom Investments v Carr* [1979] QB 467, *Greasley v Cooke* [1980] 1 WLR 1306, *Re Basham* [1986] 1 WLR 1498, *Coombes v Smith* [1986] 1 WLR 808.

presumption only arose when the relevant action or inaction was the "natural consequence" of the assumption induced.[144] As regards equitable estoppel this question of the burden of proving reliance has not yet been determined. Yet in as much as cases concerning the antecedent estoppel categories have repeatedly been used as a guide in the development of the new doctrine, it is likely that the presumption will also be held to apply in this context. The issue is whether it should.

It is submitted on grounds of convenience that, notwithstanding the centrality of reliance, the presumption of reliance should be allowed to operate in the context of equitable estoppel. Proving reliance would be an almost impossible task for a party seeking to plead equitable estoppel. Both English and Australian courts have dealt with the issue of reliance for estoppel by asking the question: "Despite any other contributing factors, would the party seeking to establish the estoppel have adopted a different course (of either action or refraining from action) to that which he did had the relevant assumption not been induced?"[145] Except for his own personal testimony – which, as Lord Denning MR has pointed out, "must be mere speculation"[146] – it is difficult to imagine what type of evidence the party seeking to establish the estoppel could offer to answer such a question in the affirmative.

On the other hand, once reliance has been presumed, there are a number of different ways in which the party against whom an estoppel is sought can rebut the presumption and answer this relevant question in the negative. In particular, he can show (i) that it was impossible for the other party to adopt any course of action or inaction than that which he did adopt, or (ii) that it is improbable that the other party would have adopted a different course to that which he did adopt.

Thus there are cases in which it was shown to be impossible that a party seeking to establish an estoppel relied upon the relevant assumption, because at the time of the supposed reliance the assumption had either not yet been induced[147] or could no longer have been held.[148]

Similarly, it is not difficult to imagine situations in which it would not be impossible, but rather highly improbable, that there had been reliance. In

---

[144] *Newbon v City Mutual Life Assurance Society Ltd* (1935) 52 CLR 723.

[145] For examples of English cases see *United Overseas Bank v Jiwani* [1976] 1 WLR 964, *Et Soules & Cie v International Trade Development Co Ltd* [1980] 1 Lloyd's Rep 129, *The Scaptrade* [1983] 2 AC 694. For an example of an equitable estoppel case that raised this issue see *Windrum v Rejilo* (1988) 87 ANZ Convey Rep 491. The approach of the United States promissory estoppel cases is similar. See, for example, *Floyd v Christian Church Widows & Orphans Home* 176 SW 2d 128 (1948).

[146] *Brikom Investments v Carr* [1979] QB 467 at 482.

[147] For an equitable estoppel case, see *Australian Broadcasting Commission v XIV Commonwealth Games Ltd* (1988) 2 BR 318. For an earlier Australian case, see *Hocking v Western Australian Bank* (1909) 9 CLR 738. For analogous English estoppel cases, see *Hewlett v London County Council* (1908) 24 TLR 331 and *Mac Fisheries v Harrison* (1924) 93 KBD 811. Another example of factual impossibility can be found in *Morrison v Universal Marine Insurance Co* (1873) LR 8 Ex 197.

[148] *Milchas Investments Pty Ltd v Larkin* (1989) ATPR ¶40–956 at 50,439.

Milchas Investments Pty Ltd v *Larkin* it was shown that reliance had most probably been upon an assumption different to that induced by the party against whom the estoppel was sought.[149] In *Budmore Pty Ltd* v *Johnson*[150] the fact that a party seeking to establish an estoppel had been prepared to "bluff along" and take considerable risks in relation to a transaction under negotiation was used to show that he was not relying on any induced assumption that the negotiations would be successful. In *Austotel Pty Ltd* v *Franklins Selfserve Pty Ltd* parties negotiating a lease were involved in what the defendant called a "cat and mouse" game in which each was "trying to secure the best position for themselves, obtain the commitment of the other parties, but leave an escape route open for themselves."[151] Although the argument was unsuccessful in *Austotel Pty Ltd* v *Franklins Selfserve Pty Ltd* itself, there must often be commercial situations in which the competitive and uncertain atmosphere in which a particular assumption is induced makes reliance highly improbable.

Largely on grounds of convenience, therefore, it is submitted that the rebuttable presumption of reliance that assists parties seeking to establish either promissory or proprietary estoppel should also operate in relation to equitable estoppel. This eighth element would then become less of a potential limitation upon the application of the doctrine than it might otherwise be.

(i) To his detriment

The requirement of detriment was a controversial one in each of the categories of estoppel before *Waltons* and *Verwayen*.[152] Spencer Bower and Turner argued that proof of detriment was requisite for all the categories of estoppel (including promissory estoppel). However "detriment" was defined broadly. It consisted in any loss that the party arguing the estoppel suffered because the assumption upon which he had relied proved unjustified (but not including, where the relevant assumption was that a particular benefit would be granted, the loss of the expected benefit *per se*). In other words, the party seeking to establish the estoppel was required to show that he was in a worse position because the relevant assumption had proved unjustified than he would have been had it never been induced. Other writers agreed that detriment was a necessary ingredient of estoppel. But they argued that the detriment necessary to found an estoppel by representation was detriment in the narrower sense of a loss suffered even before the relevant assumption had proved unjustified, detriment flowing from the action or inaction in reliance itself. The detriment required to found a promissory estoppel was said to be detriment in the sense intended by Spencer Bower and Turner.

---

[149] *Milchas Investments Pty Ltd* v *Larkin* (1989) ATPR ¶40–956 at 50,439.
[150] (1993) 6 BPR 13,574.
[151] *Austotel Pty Ltd* v *Franklins Selfserve Pty Ltd* (1989) 16 NSWLR 582 at 614 *per* Priestley JA.
[152] See above at p. 22.

It is now clear that the Spencer Bower and Turner approach to detriment – the "broader" approach – is to be applied in the context of equitable estoppel. The Spencer Bower and Turner approach finds strong support in *Thompson v Palmer*[153] and *Grundt v Great Boulder Pty Gold Mines Ltd*,[154] the two Dixon CJ judgments that were very heavily relied upon in both *Waltons* and *Verwayen*. Further, the existing equitable estoppel authorities plainly prefer the broader approach. For example, in *Verwayen* Mason CJ drew a distinction between two types of detriment, in approximate terms the two envisaged by prior theory: "detriment which would result from the denial of the correctness of the assumption upon which the person has relied" and "detriment which the person has suffered as a result of his relying on the correctness of the assumption."[155] While Mason CJ envisaged that the remedy to be awarded under an equitable estoppel would usually be shaped by the second, narrower, sense of detriment, he claimed that detriment in the broader sense would be sufficient to establish the estoppel.[156] That detriment in the broader sense is sufficient to found an equitable estoppel is also clear from the other judgments delivered in *Verwayen*,[157] from *Waltons*[158] and from various State court authorities.[159] The burden of proving such detriment lies with the party seeking to establish the estoppel.[160]

If equitable estoppel is to be developed as a vehicle for the duty to ensure the reliability of induced assumptions, the adoption of this "broader" concept of detriment is to be welcomed. Ensuring the "reliability" of an induced assumption means ensuring that a party who relies upon it is not worse off if the assumption proves unjustified than he would have been had it never been induced. Mason CJ implicitly acknowledged this purpose of the detriment

---

[153] *Thompson v Palmer* (1933) 49 CLR 507 at 547 *per* Dixon J.

[154] *Grundt v Great Boulder Pty Gold Mines Ltd* (1937) 59 CLR 641 at 674–675 *per* Dixon J.

[155] *Verwayen* at 415–416.

[156] Ibid. at 415–416.

[157] At 429–430 *per* Brennan J, 455–456 *per* Dawson J, 487–488 *per* Gaudron J, and 501 *per* McHugh J. Deane J adopted a similar approach at 448–449. Note that Brennan J also underlined that the broad approach to detriment "does not consist in a loss merely attributable to non-fulfilment of the promise" (at 429 and see also *Berno v Green's Steel Constructions Pty Ltd* (1991) 103 FLR 133 at 143). It is submitted that, for this reason, the formulation of the detriment requirement approved by Murray J in *Reg Russell & Son Pty Ltd v Buxton Meats Pty Ltd* (1996) ATPR ¶41–476 at 41,851 is wrong. Murray J claimed that ". . .detriment will be found . . . by comparing the appellant's position brought about by their reliance upon the assumption with their position if they had so acted and the assumptions had been made good."

[158] At 404 *per* Mason CJ and Wilson J and at 416, 423, 424 and 429 *per* Brennan J.

[159] See, for example, *Citra Constructions v Allied Asphalt Co Pty Ltd* Supreme Court of NewSouth Wales, 28 March 1990, unreported, *Lorimer v State Bank of New South Wales* New South Wales Court of Appeal, 5 July 1991, unreported ([1991] ACL Rep 325 NSW 95), *Commonwealth of Australia v Clark* [1994] 2 VR 333, *Austral Standard Cables Pty Ltd v Walker Nominees Pty Ltd* (1992) 26 NSWLR 524. Further, it should be noted that the Spencer Bower and Turner approach to detriment has a long history of acceptance in Australia in relation to all the various orthodox categories of estoppel. For a list of Australian decisions to this effect see K Lindgren, "Estoppel in Contract", (1989) 12 *UNSWLJ* 153 at 175.

[160] *Thompson v Palmer* (1933) 49 CLR 507 at 549 *per* Dixon J.

requirement when he said in *Verwayen* that the broader definition of detriment "makes it clear that the detriment must flow from the reliance upon the assumption."[161]

Certainly, some have claimed that this broad concept of detriment can hardly be a limitation on the application of estoppel at all.[162] And it is true that, at its limits, the concept may seem like meagre limitation on the application of the doctrine. For example, in *Austral Standard Cables Pty Ltd v Walker Nominees Pty Ltd*[163] a vendor was able to estop a purchaser from rescinding a contract for the sale of land, for failure by the vendor to give vacant possession on the day fixed for completion, on the basis that the purchaser had induced an assumption that completion would not take place on that day. At the trial the vendor had not established that it would have been able to give vacant possession of the land in any case. However, on a successful appeal at least one judge, Handley JA, was prepared to find that the loss of a real chance of avoiding detriment – in this case the loss of a real chance of providing vacant possession – constituted detriment for the purposes of equitable estoppel.[164] It is submitted that so attenuated a concept of detriment constitutes almost no detriment at all.

Nevertheless, the broad concept of detriment does not necessarily imply as attenuated a concept of detriment as that recognised by Handley JA. The courts have stressed that the detriment upon which an equitable estoppel is grounded must involve "material" or "significant" disadvantage.[165] Further, the utility of the broad concept in distinguishing between situations that are more or less deserving of relief is highlighted in Chapter Three. In that chapter, the application of the doctrine to the facts of *Williams v Roffey Brothers Contractors Ltd*[166] and *Citra Constructions Ltd v Allied Asphalt Co Pty Ltd*[167] is contrasted. In the first case, detriment could most probably be established by a party seeking to rely on equitable estoppel and in the second it could not. The broad concept of detriment has more explanatory power than many would allow.

Three final points concerning the detriment requirement deserve emphasis. First, the detriment must, of course, be detriment to the party seeking to establish the estoppel and not to a third party. In *Cairns Festival Faire Pty Ltd v AEFC Ltd*[168] a shopping centre project was in financial difficulty and a bank agreed to

---

[161] *Verwayen* at 417.

[162] See, for example, R P Meagher, W M C Gummow, and J R F Lehane *Equity: Doctrines and Remedies* 2nd edn (Sydney, Butterworths, 1984) at 399.

[163] *Austral Standard Cables Pty Ltd v Walker Nominees Pty Ltd* (1992) 26 NSWLR 524 (cited with approval in *S & E Promotions v Tobin Brothers Pty Ltd* (1994) 122 ALR 637 at 654).

[164] Ibid. at 540.

[165] *Thompson v Palmer* (1933) 49 CLR 507 at 547 *per* Dixon J, *Newbon v City Mutual Life Assurance Society Ltd* (1935) 52 CLR 723 at 734 *per* Rich, Dixon and Evatt JJ, *Verwayen* at 420 *per* Brennan J and 444 *per* Deane J, *Hawker Pacific Pty Ltd v Helicopter Charter Pty Ltd* (1991) 22 NSWLR 298 and *Territory Insurance Office v Adlington* (1992) 84 NTR 7.

[166] *Williams v Roffey Brothers & Nicholls Contractors Ltd* [1991] 1 QB 1.

[167] *Citra Constructions Ltd v Allied Asphalt Co Pty Ltd*, Supreme Court of New South Wales, 28 March 1990, unreported.

[168] Federal Court of Australia, 3 September 1993, unreported ([1993] ACL Rep 110 FC 7).

extend a credit facility if certain other parties invested in the project. The other parties invested in the project but the bank withdrew its credit facility. The owners of the shopping centre brought an action in estoppel seeking damages to remedy the consequences of the bank's withdrawing its credit facility. However, it was held that the only relevant detriment was detriment to the investors and not the owners of the shopping centre who could therefore not succeed in estoppel.

Second, the detriment that must be proved for equitable estoppel is detriment flowing from the activity of the party estopped in inducing an assumption and reliance upon it. Proof of such detriment may be particularly difficult in situations in which one party has induced the other to continue with, and to rely upon, an assumption already held. In such situations the courts will need to be sure that they remedy detriment arising only as a result of the activities of the party against whom the estoppel is sought and not detriment which would have arisen in any case.[169]

Third, the relevant detriment need not be pecuniary in nature. In *Verwayen*, Deane J said:

> "Equity has never adopted the approach that relief should be framed on the basis that the only relevant detriment or injury is that which is compensable by an award of monetary damages."[170]

His Honour then found for Verwayen on the basis that, had the Commonwealth been allowed to resile from the assumption it had induced, he would have suffered aggravated psychiatric damage. In other words, he would have been in a worse position than had the assumption never been induced, not financially, but in terms of his mental health. The anticipated deterioration of a plaintiff's mental health was also counted as detriment in *Commonwealth of Australia* v *Clark*.[171] Thus, not only is the detriment necessary to establish an equitable estoppel a broad concept in the sense outlined earlier in this section, but it also can be built upon non-pecuniary as well as pecuniary detriment.[172]

(j) A must also show that the other party, B,[173] (or his privy?) . . .

I have already argued that an equitable estoppel should only be available to a party who has himself relied upon an induced assumption and not to his privies

---

[169] It has been suggested that tort law concepts of causation might prove useful in this context, see J Munro, "The New Law of Estoppel", (1993) 23 *Victoria U Wellington L Rev* 273 at 295.

[170] *Verwayen* at 448. See also *Verwayen* at 416 *per* Mason CJ, at 461–462 *per* Dawson J and at 504 *per* McHugh J and *Lorimer* v *State Bank of New South Wales* New South Wales Court of Appeal, 5 July 1991, unreported ([1991] ACL Rep 325 NSW 95).

[171] *Commonwealth of Australia* v *Clark* [1994] 2 VR 333.

[172] See also *Lucas* v *McNaughton* (1990) 14 Fam L R 347 at 349 and 351 and *Public Trustee* v *Wadley* (1997) 7 Tas R 35 at 139 *per* Wright J (dissenting).

[173] Here "B" is taken to include "B's" agents, see *Milchas Investments Pty Ltd* v *Larkin* (1989) ATPR ¶40–956 at 50,437.

(unless an award made to the original relying party or in his name has already altered rights in relation to a particular piece of property). But what of the complementary suggestion that privies of the party inducing the assumption ought to be subject to the burden of the estoppel if they take from the original inducing party with knowledge of the circumstances in which the assumption was induced?[174]

This question arose in the decision in *Silovi v Barbaro*. In this case the owners of land entered into a ten year lease for a part of their property on which the tenants planted Cocos palms at a cost of $90,500. Cocos palms take approximately ten years to mature. The lease could not be registered because it was for only a part of a lot and for more than five years but the new tenants lodged a caveat to protect their interest and the owners of the land assured them that they would not break their lease. They later repeated these assurances. However the owners of the land then entered into an agreement to sell the property to a third party, a rival nurseryman, subject to the tenant's lease. The vendors and purchasers instructed the same solicitors and, at least before completion, the owner knew that the purchasers would evict the tenants. The tenants brought proceedings against both the owners of the land and its purchasers.

Priestley JA, with whom Hope and McHugh JJA agreed, found that the conduct of the owners in entering into a contract which would permit the exclusion of the tenants was unconscionable. This unconscionable conduct founded an equitable estoppel, the finding of which was not prevented by the relevant statutory provisions that excluded registration of a lease over part of a lot for more that five years. Moreover, they held that the equitable interest which arose was a personal licence coupled with a *profit à prendre* and was sufficient to prevent the later equitable interests of the purchaser, acquired under a contract of sale and with knowledge of the circumstances giving rise to the estoppel, from prevailing.

What is interesting in *Silovi v Barbaro* is that the equitable interest in the property of the party in whom the assumption was induced is treated as an earlier interest than the interest of the purchaser under the contract of sale: that is, it is seen as having arisen at the time of the events giving rise to the estoppel and as having run with the land to affect whomever took with notice.[175] In fact Priestley JA distinguished between common law and equitable estoppel in that rights under the former were said to flow "from the courts decision on the state of affairs",[176] while rights under the latter were said to flow from the facts giving rise to the estoppel themselves.[177] This is especially interesting because the original inducing party was in fact a party to the action and still registered proprietor of the property, so it may have been that the same result could have been achieved even by recognising that the interest in the land arose later from the

---

174 *Verwayen* at 444 *per* Deane J.
175 *Silovi* v *Barbaro* (1988) 13 NSWLR 466 at 475 *per* Priestley JA.
176 Ibid. at 472.
177 Ibid. at 472.

compensatory award of the court. The reasoning in *Silovi v Barbaro* would thus seem to contradict the understanding of how estoppel operates proposed above.

I would argue, however, that an award in equitable estoppel is always an award of a compensatory nature and that any proprietary interest to which an equitable estoppel might give rise flows from the award of the court. On this basis, I would suggest that *Silovi v Barbaro* might have been better approached by asking (i) whether the tenant could establish a case in equitable estoppel against the registered proprietor of the land, and (ii) whether an award of a proprietary nature should have been made against that registered proprietor. If an award of a proprietary nature had been made, then the party taking the land by contract would have taken it subject to the tenant's proprietary rights, and have been left to seek compensation from the registered proprietor in contract. If it had not been possible by the time of the award to remedy the detriment suffered by the party in whom the assumption was induced by means of a proprietary award, then the court would have needed to fashion some other remedy to compensate that party. A third party ought not to become liable for an original inducing party's breach of the duty to ensure the reliability of induced assumptions simply because he has knowledge of that breach.

Cases subsequent to *Silovi v Barbaro* have been unclear as to which of these approaches to equitable estoppel might be adopted. On the one hand, in *Kintominas v Secretary, Department of Social Security*[178] circumstances giving rise to an estoppel were said to create a beneficial interest in the property in a party who could have, but had not, brought an action in estoppel, such that the legal owner of the property could be assessed under a social security assets test as holding the property subject to that interest. In *Lee v Ferno Holdings Pty Ltd*,[179] Meagher JA assumes without comment that a party who has taken an assignment of a lease from a party who has induced an assumption regarding its operation can be bound by an estoppel founded on that assumption. On the other hand, the approach advocated in this section finds some support in the decision of Spender J in *Dixon Projects Pty Ltd v Masterton Homes Pty Ltd*.[180] In this case a party sought to assert equitable ownership of copyright in certain architectural plans. That ownership was said to arise from an estoppel which would operate to prevent the legal owner from assigning his interest in the copyright, an assignment which he had promised to make. However, there was no suggestion that the legal owner had attempted to resile from his promise to assign, there had been no detriment to the party seeking to rely upon the estoppel and, Spender J implies, even if there had been circumstances potentially giving rise to an estoppel between the legal owner of the copyright and the party to whom assignment had been promised, any proprietary award made would have been to correct an "inequity" between those parties. Equitable ownership could

---

[178] (1991) 103 ALR 82 at 93 *per* Einfeld J.
[179] (1993) 33 NSWLR 404 at 408.
[180] (1996) 36 IPR 136.

not be established simply because circumstances that might have given rise to an estoppel could be proved.

If equitable estoppel is to be developed as a vehicle for the duty to ensure the reliability of induced assumptions, it is to be hoped that *Silovi* v *Barbaro* will not be followed.

(k) Induced the relevant assumption . . .

An inducement of an assumption consists in either the creation or the encouragement of that assumption in the mind of the other party.[181] Only if the party against whom an estoppel is sought induced the assumption upon which it is founded, can he be said to have caused preventible harm by failing to ensure its reliability. For this reason, all the pre-*Waltons* categories of estoppel included a requirement that the relevant assumption had been induced by the party against whom the estoppel was sought. This was even true of estoppel by convention. Given that estoppel by convention operated in the area of common but mistaken assumptions, it might have been thought that the party seeking to establish the estoppel did not need to prove a representation inducing him to adopt or continue in the relevant assumption. In fact, this was not the case. As Parkinson has demonstrated,[182] although Lord Denning MR sought to argue for a doctrine of estoppel by convention which would apply wherever the parties to a contract were "both under a common mistake as to the meaning or effect of it – and thereafter embark[ed] on a course of dealing on the footing of that mistake",[183] this approach was explicitly rejected in both England and Australia.[184] Moreover, such an approach would have been entirely at odds with the rationale for estoppel by convention laid down in *Grundt* v *Great Boulder Pty Gold Mines Ltd* that a person has "*played such a part in the adoption of the assumption* that it would be unfair or unjust if he were left free to ignore it."[185] It is clear that even under the doctrine of estoppel by convention the party to be estopped had somehow to be causally responsible for the other party's adoption of or continuation in the assumption upon which it was sought to found the estoppel.

[181] See, for example, *Waltons* at 406 *per* Mason CJ and Wilson J and at 427 *per* Brennan J and *Verwayen* at 422 *per* Brennan J.

[182] Parkinson, P, "Estoppel" in P Parkinson (ed.), *The Principles of Equity* (Sydney, LBC, 1996) at 265–270.

[183] *Amalgamated Investment & Property Co Ltd* v *Texas Commerce International Bank Ltd* [1982] 2 QB 84 at 121 *per* Lord Denning MR. See also the judgment of Lord Goff in *Kenneth Allison Ltd* v *A E Limehouse & Co* [1992] 2 AC 105 at 127.

[184] *Keen* v *Holland* [1984] 1 All ER 75, *K Lokumal & Sons (London) Ltd* v *Lotte Shipping Co Pty Ltd* [1985] 2 Lloyd's Rep 28, *Coghlan* v *S H Lock (Aust) Ltd* (1985) 4 NSWLR 158. In *Lee* v *Ferno Holdings Pty Ltd* (1993) 33 NSWLR 404 at 408 Meagher JA specifically speaks of a requirement for estoppel by convention that one party "caused" the other to adopt the relevant assumption. This approach is also implicit in many other decisions see, for example, *Pacific Pty Ltd ALH Australia* v *McGlinn* (1996) 7 BPR 15,179 at 15,185–15,186.

[185] *Grundt* v *Great Boulder Pty Gold Mines Ltd* (1937) 59 CLR 641 at 675 *per* Dixon J (emphasis added).

An assumption may be induced by "any of the means available for the expression and communication of thought".[186] It may be induced by words, by some type of writing not involving words,[187] or by conduct (including "a nod, or a wink, or a shake of the head, or a smile").[188] It is possible that it can even be induced by silence.[189]

To found an equitable estoppel, an assumption must have been induced in sufficiently unequivocal terms.[190] But it is unclear precisely how unequivocal the inducement must have been. On the one hand, it has been warned that the courts ought not to interpret statements inducing assumptions with too much "pedantry".[191] There has been the suggestion in the cases,[192] and in the academic literature,[193] that a particular inducement need only to be *a* cause and not *the* cause of a party's adoption of or continuation in a particular assumption. On the other hand, there has been the suggestion that the inducement of an assumption for equitable estoppel must be more unequivocal than the making of an offer for contract.[194] Such a requirement would be consistent with the suggestions made by Mahoney JA in *Green v Green*[195] and MacLelland J in *Tie Rack (Aust) Pty Ltd v Inglon Pty Ltd*[196] that the inducement must unequivocally have evinced an intention to effect legal rights. It might be thought that such analogies with the law of contract are inappropriate and that the preferred approach is that of Priestley JA in *Austotel Pty Ltd v Franklins Selfserve Pty Ltd*[197] who emphasises that issues relating to contractual intent have no *prima facie* relevance to the application of equitable estoppel. Nevertheless, these contractual analogies show just how unequivocal some of the judges think an inducement needs to be to found an equitable estoppel.

[186] *Spencer Bower and Turner* at 45.

[187] For example, by a map or plan, see *Espley v Wilkes* (1872) LR 7 Ex 298 and *Dabbs v Seaman* (1925) 36 CLR 538.

[188] *Walters v Morgan* (1861) 3 De G F & J 718 at 724 *per* Lord Campbell LC.

[189] See below at pp. 52–54.

[190] *Nepean District Tennis Association Inc v Penrith City Council* (1988) 66 LGRA 440, *Sterns Trading Pty Ltd v Steinman & Ors* (1988) ANZ Convey Rep 493, *Windrum v Rejilo* (1988) 87 ANZ Convey Rep 491, *Roy v Waterton* (1989) ANZ Convey Rep 528, *Powprop Pty Ltd v Valbirn Pty Ltd* (1990) ANZ Convey Rep 529, *McPhillips v Ampol Petroleum (Victoria) Pty Ltd* (1990) ATPR ¶41-014, *P S Chellaram & Co Ltd v China Ocean Shipping Co Ltd* (1991) 1 Lloyd's Rep 493, *Amann Aviation Pty Ltd v Commonwealth of Australia* (1991) 100 ALR 267 (affirmed on other grounds (1991) 174 CLR 64), *R W Miller & Co Pty Ltd v Krupp (Australia) Pty Ltd* (1992) 11 BCL 74, *Gobblers Inc Pty Ltd v Steven* (1993) 6 BPR 13,591, *Furness v Adrium Industries Pty Ltd* (1993) Aust Torts Reports ¶81-245, *Elkhoury v Farrow Mortgage Services Pty Ltd* (1993) 114 ALR 541, *Hollier v The Australian Maritime Safety Authority* (1998) V Conv R ¶54,581, *Mobil Oil Australia Ltd v Lyndel Nominees Pty Ltd* (1998) 153 ALR 198.

[191] *Morris v FAI General Insurance Co. Ltd* (1995) 8 ANZ Insurance Cases ¶61-258 at 75,882 *per* Fitzgerald P.

[192] *Austral Standard Cables Pty Ltd v Walker Nominees Pty Ltd* (1992) 26 NSWLR 524 at 540 *per* Handley JA.

[193] J Munro, "The New Law of Estoppel", (1993) 23 *Victoria U Wellington L Rev* 273 at 295

[194] *Windrum v Rejilo* (1988) 87 ANZ Convey Rep 491.

[195] (1989) 17 NSWLR 343 at 370.

[196] (1989) Convey Rep ¶55-456.

[197] (1989) 16 NSWLR 582 at 614 *per* Priestley JA.

An appropriate test for whether an inducement of an assumption was sufficiently unequivocal to found an equitable estoppel would focus directly on the issue of whether the inducement caused the other party to adopt, or continue in, the relevant assumption. In this context the application of the "but-for" limb of the tort law rules as to causation would have much to recommend it.[198] Only if it can be shown that the party in whom the assumption was induced would not have held or continued to have held the relevant assumption had the other party not induced him to do so, ought liability in equitable estoppel to arise. Of course, like reliance, this causation would be more difficult to prove than to disprove, and it may well be that a presumption of causation would be appropriate in this area. It is clear, however, that much remains about the causal link between the inducement and the assumption that needs to be teased out as the case law on equitable estoppel develops.

Two issues may prove of particular difficulty. First, the question needs to be resolved whether an inducement can be indirect as well as direct. That is, if B intends to induce an assumption in A and unwittingly also induces that assumption in C, can he be held liable for the consequences to C of holding that assumption? This issue parallels that which has confronted courts in determining whether, for example, auditors owe a duty of care in negligent misstatement to potential investors in a company.[199] I would argue that, as a matter of causation, it is clearly possible indirectly to induce an assumption in C and that there ought to be no bar to establishing an equitable estoppel on that basis alone. Indeed, in one equitable estoppel case, *Winterton Constructions Pty Ltd v Hambros Australia Ltd*,[200] it is implied that equitable estoppel might sometimes be available in this situation, although on the facts the party against whom the estoppel was sought was held not to have induced the relevant assumption. To suggest that equitable estoppel might sometimes be available in these circumstances is not to suggest that a party in the position of B has necessarily broken a duty to ensure the reliability of induced assumptions, and far less to suggest that liability ought to arise. Whether B is, or ought to be, aware of C's likely reliance will be relevant to these further issues, and therefore will be an important part of the determination of the question whether it would be unconscionable for B not to remedy any detriment that C has suffered by his reliance. But these are issues going to the determination of unconscionability and not the determination of whether the assumption has been induced.

Second, the question needs to be resolved whether silence can ever constitute the inducement of an assumption founding an equitable estoppel. There is no doubt that silence, as much as any smile or wink, is capable of communicating meaning. But silence is notoriously difficult to interpret. The difficulty for the

---

[198] For a general summary of the causal inquiry in tort see B S Markesinis and S F Deakin, *Tort Law* (Oxford, Clarendon Press, 1994) at 163–192.

[199] See *Caparo Industries Plc v Dickman* [1990] 2 AC 605 and *Esanda Finance Corporation Ltd v Peat Marwick Hungerfords (Reg)* (1997) 188 CLR 241.

[200] (1992) 111 ALR 649 at 668–669 *per* Hill J.

courts is knowing when silence is so communicative that it can fairly be treated as having induced a particular assumption.

As a response to this problem the courts have limited the situations in which silence may give rise to an estoppel (including, so far, an equitable estoppel) to those in which there is a duty to speak.[201] At first sight, this response to the problem of estoppel and silence seems satisfactory. If one party is under a duty to inform another that a particular state of affairs has arisen and he remains silent, then his silence may well be taken to communicate that the particular state of affairs has not yet come about.

However, for those who would wish to see equitable estoppel develop around the duty to ensure the reliability of induced assumptions, this approach to estoppel and silence is fundamentally flawed. This is because there is no necessary nexus between a duty to speak and the question of whether silence in any given case has induced a particular assumption.

Thus, an assumption may have been induced by silence and no duty to speak apply. The common law has always demonstrated a reluctance to recognise duties to speak. The equitable estoppel cases have not remedied this situation. They have been very unclear as to when such a duty might arise. *Waltons* was a case in which precisely this problem was central and yet no useful test emerges from the decision. In *Verwayen*, Deane J spoke elusively of a requirement that the party against whom the estoppel is sought should speak when "it [is] his duty in conscience to do so"![202]

Conversely, a duty to speak may sometimes impose an obligation even in contexts in which no assumption has been induced in one party by another. An example to illustrate this point may be found in the line of cases beginning with *Ramsden* v *Dyson*. These cases impose a duty to speak upon a party, A, who knows that another party, B, is building upon A's land in the mistaken belief that the land either already does, or will soon, belong to B. As Birks points out, these cases, although classified under orthodox theory as cases involving an estoppel, fail to distinguish between "inducing" and "not undeceiving".[203] A can stand by and watch B building in silence and yet effectively communicate his approval of B's work or he can hide from B's sight and fail to inform B that the land in question is in fact his own. Only such of the *Ramsden* v *Dyson* cases as involve inducing an assumption – that is, those involving the former situation – can correctly be classified as cases involving liability of the type envisaged by equitable estoppel. If liability is to be imposed in the latter situation it is liability flowing from a duty to speak and not from a duty to remedy detriment

---

[201] See, for example, *Greenwood* v *Martins Bank* [1933] AC 51 at 57 *per* Lord Tomlin, *Thompson* v *Palmer* (1933) 49 CLR 507 at 547 *per* Dixon J, *Grundt* v *Great Boulder Pty Gold Mines Ltd* (1937) 59 CLR 641 at 677, *Waltons* at 397–398 *per* Mason CJ and Wilson J and 427–428 *per* Brennan J, at 444 *per* Deane J and at 461 *per* Gaudron J, *Verwayen* at 444 *per* Deane J, *KMA Corporation Pty Ltd* v *G & F Productions Pty Ltd* (1997) 381 IPR 243 at 249 *per* Eames J.

[202] *Verwayen* at 444.

[203] P Birks, *An Introduction to the Law of Restitution* revised edn (Oxford, Clarendon Press, 1989) at 290–293.

caused by reliance upon an induced assumption. Once again, we can see that there is no necessary nexus between a duty to speak and the question of whether silence in any given case has induced a particular assumption. Thus, an approach to the question of estoppel and silence fashioned around a duty to speak can only be of limited helpfulness.

It is suggested that a better test for determining when silence might give rise to an equitable estoppel is whether, in all the circumstances, B's silence can be taken to have indicated endorsement of a particular assumption. Only if it can, could the party who has remained silent have been causally responsible for the adoption of, or continuance in, the assumption by the other party. Whether or not B's silence indicated endorsement of a particular assumption is capable of objective assessment, as in this example from Grice:

> A is writing a testimonial about a pupil who is a candidate for a philosophy job, and his letter reads as follows: "Dear Sir, X's command of English is excellent, and his attendance at tutorials has been regular, Yours etc." . . . A cannot be opting out, since if he wished to be uncooperative, why write at all? He cannot be unable, through ignorance to say more, since the man is his pupil; moreover, he knows that more information is wanted. He must therefore, be wishing to impart information which he is reluctant to write down. This supposition is only tenable on the assumption that he thinks Mr. X is no good at philosophy. This, then, is what he is implicating.[204]

This test of whether silence has indicated endorsement of a particular assumption is appropriate because it focuses upon the central concern of the inducement requirement, *viz.* the causation of the assumption.[205] It is also a test that finds some support in the cases. In *Waltons* Deane J claimed that Waltons had, by their silence, "effectively *caused* the Mahers to adopt the mistaken belief"[206] and Gaudron J claimed that their silence was a "proximate *cause*"[207] of the adoption of the assumption. In *S & E Promotions* v *Tobin Brothers Pty Ltd*[208] an equitable estoppel was established because one party had, by its silence "lulled" the other "into a false sense of security" and a parallel is drawn with the possibility of engaging in misleading or deceptive conduct by remaining silent.[209] It is suggested that this test, focussing on causal responsibility for the adoption or continuance in, the relevant assumption will not lead to unbridled liability, because liability for silence will still be constrained by the unconscionability requirement.

---

[204] H P Grice, "Logic and Conversation" in D Davidson and G Harman (eds), *The Logic of Grammar* (Encino, Dickenson, 1975) at 71.

[205] Compare the approach adopted by Robertson that focuses upon the inducing party's knowledge that the assumption would be adopted and relied upon (A Robertson, "Knowledge and Unconscionability in a Unified Estoppel", (1998) 24 *Mon LR* 115).

[206] *Waltons* at 441 (emphasis added).

[207] Ibid. at 463 (emphasis added).

[208] (1994) 122 ALR 637.

[209] Ibid. at 656.

(l) And that, having regard to a number of specified considerations, it would be unconscionable for B not to remedy the detriment that A has suffered by relying upon the assumption.

In the equitable estoppel cases "unconscionability" operates as a factor limiting compensation for detrimental reliance, although alternatives have been proposed. In particular, Robertson has proposed "reasonable reliance" as a limiting factor.[210] This approach is unsatisfactory because, as Robertson himself admits, equitable estoppel operates as an action to correct a civil wrong.[211] But if liability is to arise, as Robertson claims, wherever the requirements of assumption, inducement, detrimental reliance and reasonableness of reliance have been made out,[212] it may well arise where no identifiable wrong has been committed. The focus of the doctrine must be, not on the conduct of the party seeking to establish the estoppel as Robertson claims,[213] but on the wrongfulness of the behaviour of the party against whom the estoppel is sought. It is precisely such wrongfulness that a concept of unconscionability, built upon the duty to ensure the reliability of induced assumptions, can identify. Perhaps for this reason, reasonableness of reliance has not, as Robertson admits, been an important part of the discussion of estoppel in Australia,[214] while "the prevailing wisdom . . . is that "unconscionability" is a key element" of equitable estoppel.[215]

Whether it would be unconscionable for a party who has induced an assumption to resile from it is determined by a range of criteria. Each of these criteria is focussed on the issues of (i) whether, and if so how strongly, the duty to ensure the reliability of induced assumptions arose between this plaintiff and defendant, and (ii) whether the duty has been broken and preventible harm caused. Liability will only attach to a breach of the duty to ensure the reliability of induced assumptions in situations in which that duty is plain and plainly broken.

In that it involves balancing a range of criteria to determine whether or not relief ought to be available on this basis, the concept of "unconscionability", and therefore the doctrine of equitable estoppel, might be described as "discretionary". The criteria that determine unconscionability are outlined below but,

---

[210] A Robertson, "Towards a Unifying Purpose for Estoppel", (1996) 22 *Mon LR* 1.

[211] A Robertson, "Situating Equitable Estoppel within the Law of Obligations" (1997) 19 *SLR* 32.

[212] A Robertson, "Knowledge and Unconscionability in a Unified Estoppel" (1998) 24 *Mon LR* 115 at 117.

[213] A Robertson, "Towards a Unifying Purpose for Estoppel" (1996) 22 *Mon LR* 1 at 2.

[214] Ibid. at 16. I reject Robertson's rather strained reading of *Australian Securities Commission* v *Marlborough Gold Mines Ltd* (1993) 177 CLR 485. The court in this case did not accept that the party claiming the estoppel could have believed the relevant assumption, a factor clearly counting against a finding of unconscionability (see below at p. 62). The court did not introduce a general requirement of reasonable reliance.

[215] A Robertson, "Knowledge and Unconscionability in a Unified Estoppel" (1998) 24 *Mon LR* 115 at 115.

first, the nature of equitable estoppel as a "discretionary" doctrine ought to be addressed. Lawyers are naturally suspicious of discretionary doctrines. Some even see them as incompatible with the rule of law. Equitable estoppel has not escaped criticism on this ground.

(i) Equitable estoppel as "discretionary"

The terms "discretion" and "discretionary" are ubiquitous, but extremely difficult to define.[216] Two possible meanings of the term are not intended in this book. First, "discretion" is not intended to signify the freedom Hart[217] claims that judges have, and Dworkin claims that they do not,[218] in "hard cases". The discretion envisaged is similar to that which Loughlan[219] and Plater[220] describe in their accounts of the work of the equity judges or that which Williams[221] describes in his account of how judges deal with criminal confessions. In Dworkin's terminology, this is "weak" and not "strong" discretion.[222] Second, "discretion" is not intended to imply immunity from appeal.[223] This sense of the term "discretion" – a sense focused upon the institutional status of certain types of decision – is not helpful in describing equitable estoppel because there has been no suggestion that the application of the doctrine should be less subject to appeal than the application of any other ground of legal liability.

Instead, the terms "discretion" and "discretionary" are intended to signify a particular pattern of judicial reasoning. The doctrine of equitable estoppel does not involve a judge in the application of legal rules of the type outlined by MacCormick in the first chapters of *Legal Reasoning and Legal Theory*.[224] That is, the doctrine does not take the form "If conditions A and B are satisfied then the result is Z". Rather, the application of the doctrine involves the judge turning his mind to a fixed range of criteria, choosing to accord each a relative

---

[216] As Christie has put it: "Few terms have as important a place in legal discourse as "discretion". Despite the importance of the term, however, those who use it do not agree on its meaning. It is universally accepted that discretion has something to do with choice; beyond this, the consensus breaks down" (G C Christie, "An Essay on Discretion", [1986] *Duke LJ* 747 at 747). Similarly, Yablon writes: "Legal thought has always had difficulty developing a satisfactory criterion for distinguishing rule bound judicial actions from discretionary ones and, in turn, distinguishing appropriate exercises of discretion from abuses" (C M Yablon, "Justifying the Judge's Hunch: An Essay on Discretion", (1990) 41 *Hastings LJ* 231 at 233).

[217] H L A Hart, *The Concept of Law* (Oxford, Clarendon Press, 1961).

[218] R Dworkin, *Taking Rights Seriously* (London, Duckworth, 1977) and *Law's Empire* (London, Fontana, 1982).

[219] P Loughlan, "No Right to a Remedy? An Analysis of Judicial Discretion in the Imposition of Equitable Remedies", (1989) 17 *MULR* 132.

[220] Z Plater, "Statutory Violations and Equitable Discretion", (1982) 70 *California L Rev* 524.

[221] C R Williams, "Judicial Discretion in Relation to Confessions", (1983) 3 *OJLS* 222 at 234–237

[222] R Dworkin, "The Model of Rules", (1967) 35 *U Chi L Rev* 14.

[223] See D J Galligan, *Discretionary Powers: A Legal Study of Official Discretion* (Oxford, Clarendon Press, 1990) at 12, G C Christie, "An Essay on Discretion", [1986] *Duke LJ* 747 at 747, K C Davis, *Discretionary Justice: A Preliminary Enquiry* (Urbana, U Illinois Press, 1971) at 4.

[224] N MacCormick, *Legal Reasoning and Legal Theory* (Oxford, Clarendon Press, 1978) Ch's II and III.

importance in the fact situation at hand, and thus justifying a particular result. It will take the form, "Having regard to the range of considerations A to G, and in this case laying particular emphasis upon considerations A, D and F, I determine that the result is X". While these two forms of rule may not be distinguishable in terms of theoretical logic, in practice they represent two different ways of framing a legal argument.

The advantage of structuring the doctrine of equitable estoppel in this way is that it is then equipped to give expression to the duty to ensure the reliability of induced assumptions. As described in Chapter One, the issues of whether that duty might arise in a particular situation will depend upon a range of considerations each of which needs carefully to be taken into account. A discretionary ground of liability of the type envisaged gives a judge the freedom to balance various criteria in fixing liability under the section. In this way it is well suited to the legal expression of the duty.

However, discretionary grounds of liability, in this as in other areas, have met with precisely the complaint that they offer a judge too much freedom in imposing liability. In this sense, the greatest potential strength of equitable estoppel – its flexibility as a discretionary doctrine – is also its greatest potential weakness. The flexibility of a discretionary doctrine may be bought at too high a cost in terms of predictability of result. According to one Australian judge, the courts must be very careful that equitable estoppel does not become:

> ". . . a kind of 'palm tree justice' according to which the answer to the critical question in every future case will reside only in the breast of the judge."[225]

Treitel is wary of attempts to unite promissory and proprietary estoppel into a doctrine built upon concepts of unconscionability, claiming that:

> "Attempts to unite [promissory and proprietary estoppel] by posing 'simply' the question whether it would be 'unconscionable' for the promisor to go back on his promise are, it is submitted, unhelpful as they provide no basis on which a legal doctrine capable of yielding predictable results can be developed."[226]

Spencer Bower and Turner claim that such a process of unification is one of "robust over-simplification" and may lead, if followed far enough, to palm-tree justice.[227]

Some of the recent equitable estoppel cases contain comments that must aggravate the fears of those frightened by the prospect of unbridled discretion. To take one example, consider the following comments from *P S Chellaram & Co Ltd* v *China Ocean Shipping Co Ltd*:

> "[T]he decision [whether or not to allow an estoppel], being founded upon an appeal to conscience, is partly impressionistic. It represents a reaction to the facts as

---

[225] *Bobko* v *Commonwealth of Australia* (1988) Supreme Court of Victoria, 22 April 1988, unreported, *per* Fullagar J.
[226] G H Treitel, *The Law of Contract* 9th edn (London, Sweet & Maxwell, 1995) at 136.
[227] *Spencer Bower and Turner* at 309.

elaborated. The reaction to the same facts will necessarily differ from one judge to another, as the dissenting opinions in many cases of estoppel show. Such difference may reflect the different experiences of judges, some of whom will evidence a conscience more tender than others."[228]

It would, indeed, be alarming if the outcome of a legal decision should depend upon the extent to which the conscience of any given judge may or may not be described as "tender".

Fortunately, however, such comments do not dominate the recent equitable estoppel decisions. Most of the judgments – including the same judgment from *P S Chellaram & Co Ltd* v *China Ocean Shipping Co Ltd* in a passage following – emphasise that the decision of a judge whether or not to allow an equitable estoppel "is not at large" and that "[t]here are rules to lay down the criteria and the approach that must be taken by" such a judge.[229] As Dorney puts it, the judges are keen to emphasise that:

> The new equitable estoppel is a carefully confined doctrine which is in no way an invitation to open-ended discretion in the enforcement of promises.[230]

Discretionary doctrines of this particular type – in which there is a clear range of criteria to be taken into account in determining whether or not to apply the doctrine – are widely recognised as capable of yielding predictable results. For example, Lord Denning MR claims that predictability can be achieved in discretionary decision-making if "the courts . . . set out the considerations which should guide the judges in the normal exercise of their discretion."[231] DeMott claims it is in this way that the equity courts yielded predictable results.[232] Sir Thomas Bingham assumes that a discretionary decision bound by guidelines is one in which the "dragon of arbitrary discretion . . . has been domesticated and put on a short leash"[233] and Galligan claims that it is often "a reasonable compromise between certainty and justice".[234] Williams demonstrates that a discretionary decision based upon predetermined considerations is "governed by law just as much as a decision as to the application of a legal rule"[235] and McNicol

---

[228] *P S Chellaram & Co Ltd* v *China Ocean Shipping Co Ltd* (1991) 1 Lloyd's Rep 493 at 512 *per* Kirby P.

[229] Ibid. at 512.

[230] M Dorney, "The New Estoppel", (1991) 7 *Aust Bar Rev* 19 at 46.

[231] *Ward* v *James* [1966] 1 QB 273 at 293.

[232] D A DeMott, "Modern Equity: Forward", (1993) 56 *Law & Contemp Probs* 1 at 1.

[233] Sir Thomas Bingham, "The Discretion of the Judge", *The Royal Bank of Scotland Law Lecture* (1990) at 2.

[234] D J Galligan, *Discretionary Powers: A Legal Study of Official Discretion* (Oxford, Clarendon Press, 1990) at 42.

[235] C R Williams, "Judicial Discretion in Relation to Confessions", (1983) 3 *OJLS* 222 at 252. See, similarly, the proposal of guidelines as a way of controlling untrammelled discretion in P H Robinson, "Legality and Discretion in the Distribution of Criminal Sanctions", (1988) 25 *Harv J Legis* 393 at 421. Guidelines will be particularly effective if supported by a clear goal such as the legal expression of the duty to ensure the reliability of induced assumptions; see J J Berman, "Sentencing Reform of s 1437: Will Guidelines Work?", (1980) 17 *Harv J Legis* 98. On this type of discretion and the danger of uncertainty, see also Sir Gordon Borrie, "Trading Malpractices and Legislative Policy", (1991) 107 *LQR* 559 at 569.

and Maher believe it to be almost analogous to a decision applying a "rule of law".[236] Section 51AB of the *Trade Practices Act* 1974 (Cth), which lists criteria for consideration in assessing "unconscionability" in a way not dissimilar to that envisaged under equitable estoppel, has been commended precisely for the relatively predictable results it is believed it will yield.[237]

It is at least arguable that judges are more anxious to ensure that their decisions are predictable when they reach decisions based upon the open balancing of criteria to guide discretion than they are where their decisions are more specifically rule-based.[238] Moreover, as the judges exercise their discretion in the cases, particular patterns of fact will be recognised as almost always involving unconscionable conduct, and the recognition of those patterns of fact will lend even greater predictability to the application of the doctrine.

(ii) The criteria for determining unconscionability

Assuming, therefore, that the problem of predictability is not insurmountable, there are eight aspects of the parties' dealings and relationship that a judge must consider in determining whether or not it would be unconscionable for a party who has induced an assumption simply to resile from it.

Three features of this list of criteria ought to be underscored. First, the criteria outlined in this section are those which most consistently determine when unconscionable behaviour is actually found in the existing equitable estoppel cases. Second, they are the criteria most directly relevant to the issues of whether the duty to ensure the reliability of induced assumptions arises, how strongly it applies and whether it has been broken. Thus the first seven aspects of the parties' dealings and relationship are the same as those that were identified in Chapter One as determining when the duty to ensure the reliability of induced assumptions arises. The eighth relates to any action already taken by the party upon whom the duty rests to ensure that he has not, by inducing reliance, caused preventible harm. Third, the courts seem to be treating these eight aspects of the parties' dealings and relationship in a way that shows a sensitivity to the duty to ensure the reliability of induced assumptions. It will be recalled that each of the first seven aspects of the parties' dealings and relationship can be used to show that one party has more or less strongly induced reliance and that the duty therefore applies with greater or lesser force. The courts seem to have recognised this in their application of equitable estoppel. Thus, as each aspect of the parties' dealings or relationship is outlined below, a range of circumstances is identified

---

[236] S B McNicol and F K H Maher, "The Range and Limits of Judicial Discretion", (1987) 73 *ArchRSozPhil* 37 at 38.

[237] See, for example, Sir Gordon Borrie, "Trading Malpractices and Legislative Policy", (1991) 107 *LQR* 559 at 569 and J Goldring, "Certainty in Contracts, Unconscionability and the TPA: The Effect of Section 52A", (1988) 11 *SLR* 514 at 535. Section 52A was renumbered section 51AB in 1992.

[238] Yablon demonstrates that judges are at least keen to appear more cautious in this context, C M Yablon, "Justifying the Judges Hunch: An Essay on Discretion", (1990) 41 *Hastings LJ* 231 at 271–272.

in which the duty applies with a greater or lesser force and in which, correspondingly, the courts are more or less likely to give it legal effect.

The first aspect of the parties' dealings that a court must consider in determining whether departure from an induced assumption would be unconscionable is that of how the assumption and reliance upon it were induced.

In relation to the issue of how the assumption was induced, Giles J has claimed that;

> "[T]he precise means whereby the assumption was induced is part . . . of assessing the part taken in occasioning the adoption of the assumption and whether or not departure from the assumption would be 'unjust and inadmissible'."[239]

Although an equitable estoppel can be founded upon an assumption induced by any means of communication, whether unconscionability is likely to be found will, to a certain extent, depend upon the precise mode of inducement. A court determining whether an equitable estoppel can be found must carefully consider the part the inducing party has played in the adoption of the assumption.[240]

For example, consideration of the other criteria being equal, the courts seem far more ready to intervene in circumstances in which the assumption has been induced by express representation than they are in contexts in which the assumption has arisen because of the inducing party's conduct or silence. The more passive the party against whom the estoppel is sought has been, the less credible the claim that he has induced reliance. A preference for express modes of inducement seems to be have been implicitly identified in *Verwayen* itself. Deane J sets out the major categories of situation in which the conduct of a party to be estopped might be regarded as unconscionable. These are situations where the party against whom the estoppel is sought:

(a) has induced the assumption by express or implied representation;
(b) has entered into contractual or other material relations with the other party on the conventional basis of the assumption;
(c) has exercised against the other party rights which would exist only if the assumption were correct;
(d) knew that the other party laboured under the assumption and refrained from correcting him when it was his duty in conscience to do so.[241]

Deane J then goes on to say:

> "Ultimately, however, the question whether departure from the assumption would be unconscionable must be resolved not by reference to some preconceived formula

---

[239] *Les Edwards & Son Pty Ltd v Commonwealth Bank of Australia* Supreme Court of NSW, 14 June 1990, unreported.
[240] See, for example, *Waltons* at 404 *per* Mason CJ and Wilson J, at 427 *per* Brennan J, at 445 *per* Deane J and at 460 *per* Gaudron J all relying upon Dixon J in *Thompson v Palmer* (1933) 49 CLR 507 at 547 and in *Grundt v Great Boulder Pty Gold Mines Ltd* (1937) 59 CLR 641 at 675–676.
[241] *Verwayen* at 444.

framed to serve as a universal yardstick but by reference to all the circumstances of the case . . ."[242]

This passage seems to move from the central case of inducement – the express representation – to modes of inducement which the courts will be less likely in "all the circumstances of the case" to see as founding an estoppel. It moves from the explicit to the more implicit modes of inducement in a way which implies that the courts should be more cautious in dealing with these latter categories.

In relation to the issue of how reliance upon the assumption was induced, an express invitation to rely will ordinarily lend support to the claim that reliance was strongly induced. It will not, however, conclusively determine that it was. Reliance may be expressly invited upon an assumption of such a type, and in the context of such a relationship, that it is implausible to say that reliance has been strongly induced. A pop star who invites radio listeners to rely, by coming to hear him, upon the assumption that he will, at a future time, sing in a particular place, can hardly be said to have strongly induced any individual listener's reliance. Even an express invitation to rely may not constitute a strong inducement.

The second aspect of the parties dealings' and relationship that a court must consider in determining whether departure from an induced assumption would be unconscionable, is that of the content of the relevant assumption. An equitable estoppel can be founded on an induced assumption regarding a wide variety of matters, including an assumption regarding fact and an assumption regarding the future. However, once again the courts are less willing to found an equitable estoppel in some circumstances than they are in others.

For example, the courts seem less willing to found an equitable estoppel upon an induced assumption as to the future than they are to found an estoppel upon an induced assumption as to present fact. It is repeatedly said in the cases that "failure to fulfil a promise does not of itself amount to unconscionable conduct" and that even if the promise has been relied upon "something more would be required".[243] This is because a "promisee may reasonably be expected to appreciate that he [could not] safely rely upon [a voluntary promise]."[244] In addition, it is less likely that the harm arising from reliance upon an induced assumption as to the future will be preventible, than will be harm arising from reliance upon an induced assumption as to fact. Unforeseeable changes of circumstance may render it impossible to prevent harm to the relying party, especially given that the inducing party need only to prevent such harm *in so far as he is reasonably able*. An equitable estoppel may be based upon a "promise" or, in the expression that the courts use interchangeably with the term "promise", an "assumption as to future fact."[245] Yet a party seeking to establish an estoppel upon the

---

[242] Ibid. at 445.
[243] *Waltons* at 406 *per* Mason CJ and Wilson J.
[244] Ibid. at 406.
[245] See, for example, *Verwayen* at 412 *per* Mason CJ.

basis of an assumption of this type will be less likely to succeed than a party seeking to establish an estoppel on the basis of an assumption as to existing fact.

Third, a court considering the application of equitable estoppel must consider the relative knowledge of the parties. Thus, it is clear from the cases that unconscionability is more likely to be found when the inducing party knew that the other party would rely upon the relevant assumption,[246] or suffer harm thereby. Thus, there have been equitable estoppel cases where the fact that the inducing party knew that reliance and harm were likely has counted towards a finding of unconscionability.[247] There have been cases where the fact that the inducing party knew or ought to have known that the induced assumption was unreliable counted towards a finding of unconscionability.[248] Finally, there have been cases where the inducing party's ignorance of the circumstances surrounding the creation of an assumption have counted against a finding of unconscionability. In one case, a party who was ignorant of a breach of contract could not be estopped from relying upon it simply because of his silence.[249] Again each of these categories of case seems to reflect a sensitivity to the strength of the duty to ensure the reliability of induced assumptions in different contexts.

Fourth, a court considering unconscionability for equitable estoppel must consider the parties' relative interest in the relevant activities in reliance. The importance of this issue was stressed in *Waltons* itself. In *Waltons* one party had induced another to believe that it would, as a matter of due course, complete formalities for the lease of premises that it required to be built to certain specifications. It was important to a finding of equitable estoppel that it was strongly in the inducing party's interest that the relying party act upon this assumption before the relevant formalities had, in fact, been completed.[250] This result may be contrasted with other equitable estoppel decisions in which the greater interest of the relying party in the relevant activities in reliance clearly weighed against a finding of unconscionability. For example, *Powprop Pty Ltd v Valbirn Pty Ltd*[251] is a case which, like *Waltons*, involved construction work undertaken in anticipation of a prospective lease. However in this case the court found that the construction work was not undertaken primarily in the interests of the prospective lessee, the party who, it was alleged, had induced the assumption that the lease would go ahead, but because the lessor "was extremely anxious to enter into a lease with the [lessee], and was 'prepared to risk the expense

---

[246] See, for example, *Waltons* at 402 *per* Mason CJ and Wilson J and at 423 *per* Brennan J.

[247] See, for example, *Waltons* at 407 *per* Mason CJ and Wilson J, at 411 *per* Brennan J, at 442 *per* Deane J, and at 461 *per* Gaudron J and *Marvon Pty Ltd* v *Yulara Development Co* (1989) 98 FLR 348.

[248] See, for example, *Doubikin Holdings Pty Ltd* v *Grail Pty Ltd* (1991) 5 WAR 563 at 578, *Standard Chartered Bank Australia* v *Bank of China* (1991) 23 NSWLR 164, *Avtex Airservice Pty Ltd* v *Bartsch* (1992) 107 ALR 539 at 566, *Australian Securities Commission* v *Marlborough Gold Mines Ltd* (1993) 177 CLR 485 and *Kirton* v *Nethery* [1997] ANZ Convey R 53 at 55.

[249] *Berry* v *Hodson* [1989] 1 Qd R 361. See also *Pan Foods Co* v *ANZ Banking Group* (1996) 14 ACLC 698 at 713–714.

[250] See, for example, *Waltons* at 407 *per* Mason CJ and Wilson J.

[251] [1990] ANZ Conv Rep 529.

of the alterations in the hope that it might achieve what it wanted.'"[252] This issue is relevant to a finding of unconscionability because, it is suggested, the greater the interest of the party against whom the estoppel is sought in the other party's reliance, the more likely it is that he induced it. Further, if one must "accept the bitter with the sweet", having accepted the benefit of reliance must reinforce a party's duty to ensure that it does not cause preventible harm.

Fifth, a court applying the doctrine of equitable estoppel must pay attention to the nature and context of the parties' relationship. The Australian judges have revealed an awareness that there are contexts in which it is difficult to argue that one party has induced reliance. Thus it has been stressed that the judges should be more reluctant to find unconscionability in commercial, than in consumer, contexts because a higher degree of self-reliance might be expected in the former than in the latter.[253] Compare, for example, the cases *Stefanou v Fairfield Chase Pty Ltd*[254] and *Weiss v Barker Gosling*.[255] In the former case, the client of a legal firm was estopped from resiling from an agreement that the firm would be retained on particular terms *inter alia* because it was "an experienced company". In the latter case and on similar facts, a client's status as an individual consumer of legal services was thought to count in his favour in assessing whether, had the issue arisen, he would have been estopped from resiling from such an agreement. The judges again seem to be identifying an issue relevant to the question of whether the duty to ensure the reliability of induced assumptions arises and to be handling that issue appropriately.

Sixth, another issue relevant to a finding of unconscionability for equitable estoppel is the parties' relative strength of position. Consider the following passage from the judgment of Deane J in *Verwayen*:

> "[The rationale of the doctrine of estoppel by conduct] is that it is right and expedient to save [people] from being victimized by other people . . . In this as in other areas of equity-related doctrine, conduct which is 'unconscionable' will commonly involve the use or insistence upon legal entitlement to take advantage of another's special vulnerability or misadventure."[256]

This passage is interesting because it assumes a connection between the concept of unconscionable conduct for equitable estoppel and the concept for which the same label is used under the doctrine of unconscionable or "catching" bargains.[257] Indeed, Deane J subsequently relied upon this passage in the

---

[252] Ibid. at 530.

[253] See, for example, *Austotel Pty Ltd v Franklins Selfserve Pty Ltd* (1989) 16 NSWLR 582 at 585–586 *per* Kirby P.

[254] Federal Court of Australia, 10 December 1993, unreported.

[255] (1993) 16 Fam LR 728.

[256] *Verwayen* at 440–441.

[257] This is a connection which has also been made by others: for example, by Sir Anthony Mason in "Future Directions in Australian Law: The Wilfred Fullagar Memorial Lecture", (1987) 13 *Mon LR* 149 at 152. In the course of that lecture, Sir Anthony Mason linked the unconscionable conduct for estoppel described in *Legione v Hateley* (1983) 152 CLR 406 with the unconscionable conduct for "catching bargains" described in *Commercial Bank of Australia v Amadio* (1983) 151 CLR

unconscionable bargain case of *Louth* v *Diprose*[258] and it has been relied upon in the application of section 51AAA of the *Trade Practices Act* 1974 (Cth) prohibiting conduct which is "unconscionable within the meaning of the unwritten law". Under the doctrine of unconscionable bargains, relief from binding contractual obligations will be granted where:

> "... a party makes unconscientious use of his superior position or bargaining power to the detriment of the party who suffers from some special disability or is placed in some special situation of disadvantage eg, a catching bargain with an expectant heir ..."[259]

The particular idea which unites the doctrines of Australian estoppel and unconscionable bargains is that of a "special vulnerability", "special disability" or inequality of bargaining power as between the parties. Like those granting relief against unconscionable bargains, the High Court decisions so far applying equitable estoppel have involved either dealings between two relatively "small" players or between one party with considerable, and another with more limited, resources or access to legal advice. The relative strength of the parties is important because it is far easier to induce reliance, and far easier to cause preventible harm thereby, when dealing with a weaker party.

Seventh, the history of the parties' relationship is also relevant to a finding of equitable estoppel. This may be demonstrated in two ways. First, it is apparent that the doctrine of estoppel by convention is being subsumed into the doctrine of equitable estoppel,[260] and it is submitted that the intuition that reliance is more likely in long-standing relationships is an intuition important to estoppel by convention. Second, there are cases in which the length of the parties' relationship was a factor counting towards a finding of unconscionability. In *Hill* v *A W J Moore and Co Pty Ltd*[261] two neighbours had enjoyed a relationship of co-operation in the building and maintenance of a private road for some fifteen years. One of those parties had induced an assumption in the other that they were, and would continue to be, entitled to use the road. The length of the parties' dealings with one another counted towards a finding that it would have been unconscionable for the party who had induced the assumption to resile from it without compensating the other party's detriment. Once again, reliance will more readily be induced, and thus the duty not to cause preventible harm stronger, in contexts of longstanding relationships.

The eighth and final factor that a judge must consider in the application of equitable estoppel is whether the party who has induced the relevant assumption has already taken any steps to ensure that he has not caused preventible harm. A party may be able to show that he has done all that was reasonably

---

447. For an equitable estoppel case that treats the two doctrines as closely related see *Re Ferdinando: Ex p ANZ Banking Group Ltd* v *Official Trustee in Bankruptcy* (1993) 42 FCR 243.

[258] (1992) 175 CLR 621.

[259] *Commercial Bank of Australia* v *Amadio* (1983) 151 CLR 447 at 461 *per* Mason CJ.

[260] *Waltons* at 403 *per* Mason CJ and Wilson J and at 427 *per* Brennan J, *Verwayen* at 560 *per* Deane J.

[261] Supreme Court of New South Wales, 31 August 1991, unreported.

within his power to ensure that the assumption was reliable or to ensure that the other party did not suffer harm by relying upon it.

One important issue which arises in relation to this eighth factor is whether harm to the party in whom the assumption is induced can be prevented by giving notice that the assumption is not to be relied upon. It is submitted that, provided that such notice is communicated unequivocally and effectively and provided that the party in whom the assumption is induced has not already relied upon it to his detriment, it is unlikely that the induced assumption could be used as the basis of an equitable estoppel.

For example, in the context of pre-contractual negotiations, a party may well make it clear that there is to be no reliance upon any induced assumption until the relevant contract is finalised and reduced to writing. This freedom to avoid liability is important and must be respected.[262] In this matter the Australian courts are likely to be influenced by the decision of the Privy Council in *Attorney General of Hong Kong* v *Humphrey's Estate (Queen's Gardens) Ltd* in which it was said:

> "It is possible but unlikely that in circumstances at present unforeseeable a party to negotiations set out in a document expressed to be 'subject to contract' would be able to satisfy the court that . . . some form of estoppel had arisen to prevent the parties from refusing to proceed with the transactions envisaged in the document."[263]

Thus, in *Australian Broadcasting Commission* v *XIVth Commonwealth Games*,[264] a television station had been negotiating for Australian television rights for the 1990 Commonwealth Games. Agreement in principle had been achieved and the Australian Broadcasting Commission had paid half of the agreed fees when the defendant granted the rights to a third party. The judge held both that all of the parties "confidently anticipated ultimate agreement and . . . proceeded on this basis" and that "[i]t is well established that an estoppel . . . may be constituted by silence."[265] Nevertheless, the defendant had made it clear all along that a formal contract would need to be finalised and this was also understood to have been the case by the plaintiff. Therefore the plaintiff's activities in reliance had been taken at its own risk. No estoppel was established.

This case may be contrasted, of course, with the decision in *Waltons* itself. In this case the parties also intended that their dealings be incorporated in a contract expressed in writing. In *Waltons*, however, the party against whom the estoppel was sought had done nothing to ensure that the assumption induced – that is, the assumption that the relevant contractual formalities would be completed in due course – did not cause preventible harm. Indeed, that party had

---

[262] See W H Holmes, "The Freedom Not to Contract", (1986) 60 *Tulane L Rev* 751.

[263] *Attorney-General of Hong Kong* v *Humphrey's Estate (Queen's Gardens) Ltd* [1987] 1 AC 114 at 127–128.

[264] *Australian Broadcasting Commission* v *XIVth Commonwealth Games Ltd* (1988) 2 BR 318

[265] Ibid. at 337 *per* Kearney J.

strongly encouraged the relevant activities in reliance even though it knew both that the other party believed that those formalities were certainly to be completed and that there was a real risk that they would not be.

A parallel situation emerges in which a contract is expressed to constitute the whole of the legal relationship between the parties, but, after the contract is completed, one party relies upon an assumption induced during pre-contractual negotiations which is contrary to its written terms. While it is clear that an equitable estoppel can be founded on an assumption induced during pre-contractual negotiations, even one varying the terms of the written agreement, it is also clear that the courts will pay great heed to the parties' attempt to reduce their relationship to writing.[266]

While simple phrases such as "subject to contract" or "this agreement constitutes the whole relationship between the parties" ought not to be allowed to oust the courts' jurisdiction in every case, they ought not to be lightly ignored. A comparison of cases such as *Australian Broadcasting Commission* v *XIV Commonwealth Games* and *Waltons* shows the courts distinguishing circumstances in which these words amounted to a genuine attempt to ensure that the induced assumption did not cause preventible harm from those in which they did not. Once again the courts seem able to handle the question of whether the party has done all he can to ensure the reliability of induced assumptions with a considerable degree of subtlety.

I have thus outlined the eight principal considerations which a judge must take into account in looking for unconscionable conduct to found an equitable estoppel. Each of these must be carefully balanced against the others and each involves a sliding scale moving from circumstances in which an estoppel is less likely, to circumstances in which an estoppel is more likely, to be found. That it is these eight aspects of the parties' dealings and relationship that determine unconscionability, and the way in which those aspects of the parties' dealings and relationship are being handled by the courts, show that the duty to ensure the reliability of induced assumptions could form a useful basis in principle for the emergent doctrine.

(m) When these things are established, the court may award a remedy sufficient to reverse the detriment that A has shown.

In *Silovi* v *Barbaro* Priestley JA summarised the decision of the High Court in *Waltons*. In his summary, he explained that the remedy to which a finding of equitable estoppel will give rise "will be what is necessary to prevent detriment resulting from the unconscionable conduct."[267] Relief under equitable estoppel

---

[266] *Liangis Investments Pty Ltd* v *Daplyn Pty Ltd* (1994) FLR 28, *Skywest Aviation* v *Commonwealth of Australia* (1995) 126 FLR 61.
[267] *Silovi* v *Barbaro* (1988) 13 NSWLR 466 at 472 *per* Priestley JA.

will be whatever is necessary, by way of personal or proprietary relief,[268] to put the relying party in the position in which he would have been had the assumption never been induced. Despite doubts about the point expressed by Marks J in *Commonwealth* v *Clark*[269] it is clear that this can include monetary relief.[270] It is also clear that it can include specific and proprietary relief.[271]

In awarding remedies on this basis, the courts should exercise caution and be strongly influenced by the concept of the "minimum equity to do justice between the parties."[272] Thus, there may arise situations in which "to do justice between the parties" it is appropriate that a conditional award be made to a party whose claim is founded in equitable estoppel. It is submitted that the flexibility of the concept of the "minimum equity" and its derivation in equity mean that the courts ought to be able to make such conditional awards, even when the party who can establish the estoppel is seeking monetary compensation. Examples of such conditional awards may be found in the existing equitable estoppel decisions.[273]

It is important to emphasise that the function of remedies in equitable estoppel is to compensate reliance and neither to enforce expectations *per se*, nor to reverse an unjust enrichment. However, the availability of remedies in the expectation and restitution measures ought briefly to be considered.

---

[268] On the possibility of an equitable estoppel giving rise to the award of an interest in property see, for example, the summary of *Waltons* offered in *Silovi* v *Barbaro* (1988) 13 NSWLR 466 at 472. Of course, the courts will not always be prepared to award relief of this type. Thus, in a New Zealand case heavily reliant upon *Waltons* in which it might have been expected that the plaintiff would be granted a promised renewal of his lease he was, instead, awarded damages (see *Dowell* v *Tower Corp* [1991] ANZ Conv Rep 177). Where an interest in property is awarded that interest may be transferable (see *Hill* v *Moore* Supreme Court of New South Wales, 31 August 1990, unreported) and able to be the subject of a caveat (as in *Bond Brewing New South Wales Ltd* v *Reffell Party Ice Supplies Pty Ltd* Supreme Court of New South Wales, 9 September 1987, unreported).

[269] [1994] 2 VR 333 at 342.

[270] See, for example, *Verwayen* at 417 *per* Mason CJ, at 431 *per* Brennan J, at 441–442 *per* Deane J and at 476 *per* Toohey J. See also A Robertson, "Satisfying the Minimum Equity: Equitable Remedies After *Verwayen*" (1996) 20 *MULR* 805 at 842–843.

[271] See, for example, *Verwayen* at 412 *per* Mason CJ, at 429 *per* Brennan J and at 444 *per* Deane J.

[272] *Verwayen* at 413 and 416 *per* Mason CJ, at 429 *per* Brennan J and at 442 *per* Deane J. Mason CJ speaks of "proportionality" between the remedy and the detriment which it is designed to avoid (*Verwayen* at 413) and this language has been picked up in subsequent cases. See, for example, *Re Neal; Ex p Neal* v *Duncan Properties Pty Ltd* (1993) 114 ALR 659 at 669 *per* Drummond J, *Woodson (Sales) Pty Ltd* v *Woodson (Australia) Pty Ltd* (1996) 7 BPR 14,685, *Mobil Oil (Australia) Ltd* v *Lyndel Nominees* (1998) 153 ALR 198 at 238–239.

[273] See, for example, *Austotel Pty Ltd* v *Franklins Selfserve Pty Ltd* (1989) 16 NSWLR 582 at 603; *Quach* v *Marrickville Municipal Council (No's 1 &2)* (1991) 22 NSWLR 55 at 71 in which it was suggested *in obiter* that an appropriate award might have been to require the defendants to give up any interest they had in certain land, subject to a right to drain; *S & E Promotions* v *Tobin Brothers Pty Ltd* (1994) 122 ALR 637 at 653 in which the potentially conditional nature of relief under equitable estoppel was affirmed; and *Callaghan* v *Callaghan* (1995) 64 SASR 396 in which a conditional award was justified by reference to the concept of the "minimum equity to do justice."

(i) Remedies in the expectation measure

On the basis of the duty to ensure the reliability of induced assumptions, it may sometimes be appropriate that equitable estoppel gives rise to an award in the expectation measure. This will be where such an award is the *only* or *only satisfactory* way in which to put the relying party in the position in which he would have been had the assumption never been induced. It will be where an award in the expectation measure is the *only* or *only satisfactory* way to protect reliance and to "prevent detriment resulting from the unconscionable conduct." The High Court has been quite clear that this is an acceptable approach to remedy. The technique of awarding relief in the expectation measure to protect reliance was apparently adopted in *Waltons*, although it might be argued that this was because the case was for damages in lieu of specific performance and that the issue of alternative approaches to remedy was not directly addressed. The technique of awarding relief in the expectation measure to protect reliance was also an approach adopted in several of the judgments in *Verwayen*.

However, the courts have also been at pains to stress that "the substantive doctrine of estoppel permits a court to do what is required to avoid detriment and does not, in every case, require the making good of the assumption."[274] Expectations ought only to be enforced in situations in which this is the "minimum equity to do justice."

A problem emerges, therefore, as to when a court applying the doctrine of equitable estoppel will in fact enforce the expectations of the party in whom the assumption has been induced. As Young J pointed out in *Eagle Star Trustees Ltd v Tai Ping Trading Pty Ltd (No 2)*,[275] this was essentially the matter which divided the High Court in *Verwayen*. Three of the judges in that case appear to have believed that equitable estoppel did require that the plaintiff's expectations be enforced,[276] three of the judges indicated that it did not,[277] and one was only prepared to remit the case for consideration of the point.[278]

From *Verwayen*, two competing presumptions as to when expectations will be enforced seem to have emerged. The first depends upon a distinction between detriment in a "broader" and in a "narrower" sense drawn by Mason CJ. Detriment in the "broader" sense is that "detriment which would result from the denial of the correctness of the assumption upon which the person has relied."[279] Detriment in the "narrower" sense "is the detriment which the person has suffered as a result of his reliance upon the assumption".[280] Mason CJ claimed that the remedy to be granted under equitable estoppel "will often be

---

[274] *Verwayen* at 487–488 *per* Gaudron J.
[275] Supreme Court of New South Wales, 30 October 1990, unreported.
[276] Deane, Dawson and Gaudron JJ.
[277] Mason CJ and Tooohey and McHugh JJ.
[278] Brennan J.
[279] *Verwayen* at 415 *per* Mason CJ.
[280] Ibid. at 415.

closer in scope to the detriment suffered in the narrower sense".[281] In other words, Mason CJ was setting up a presumption that compensating actual loss incurred in reliance will put the party who has relied in the position in which he would have been had the assumption not been induced and thereby adequately compensate him for a breach of the duty to ensure the reliability of induced assumptions. Deane and Gaudron JJ, however, seem to have favoured the opposite presumption.[282] Gaudron J said:

> ". . . it may be that an assumption should be made good unless it is clear that no detriment will be suffered other than that which can be compensated by some other remedy."[283]

Thus the enforcement of expectations would be the remedy to which equitable estoppel would *prima facie* give rise.

It is suggested that, of these two approaches, it is that of Mason CJ which is to be preferred. It must be admitted that, since *Verwayen*, the Australian courts have been perhaps too ready to enforce expectations. Robertson has demonstrated this in a study of twenty four cases in the period 1991 to 1996.[284] However, equitable estoppel is not centrally concerned with the enforcement of expectations – the domain of contract – but rather with the duty to ensure the reliability of induced assumptions and with the consequent protection of reliance. Enforcing expectations is sometimes the only satisfactory way of protecting reliance, but should be done only as a last resort. It ought first to be presumed that compensating loss already incurred will put the relying party into the position in which he would have been had the assumption not been induced. The burden of proving that this is not so, and that the enforcement of expectations is necessary to protect reliance in the instant case, ought then to fall upon the party claiming the estoppel.

(ii) Remedies in the restitution measure

There is no suggestion in the equitable estoppel cases that the doctrine should give rise to remedies in the restitution measure. This is not surprising, as remedies in the restitution measure are increasingly associated with the reversal of unjust enrichment[285] and the purpose of equitable estoppel is the compensation of harm resulting from reliance. What are surprising, however, are two comments made by members of the court that decided *Waltons* and *Verwayen*. These comments, which suggested a muddying of the distinction between

---

[281] Ibid. at 416.

[282] Ibid. at 445–446 and 487.

[283] Ibid. at 487. Indeed Dorney considers this presumption to be the "express basis of decision of the majority in *Verwayen*" (M Dorney, "The New Estoppel", (1991) 7 *Aust Bar Rev* 19 at 38).

[284] A Robertson, "Satisfying the Minimum Equity: Equitable Estoppel Remedies After *Verwayen*" (1996) 20 *MULR* 804.

[285] See P Birks, *An Introduction to the Law of Restitution* revised edn (Oxford, Clarendon Press, 1989).

equitable estoppel and the actions in unjust enrichment, ought briefly to be considered.

The first of the two comments was made by Deane J in the course of his judgment in *Waltons*:

> Notions of good conscience and fair dealing, enforced by the rationale of legal doctrines precluding unjust enrichment, point towards a conclusion that, in such circumstances, the prospective lessee should be precluded from departing from the mistaken assumption about his future conduct.[286]

It is not immediately plain what effect His Honour intended to give this passage except, perhaps, that enrichment might be another indicator of unconscionability.[287] It ought not to be taken as advocating some type of merger of estoppel with unjust enrichment principles.

The second of the two comments occurs in a review by Sir Anthony Mason[288] of Birks' *Introduction to the Law of Restitution*. In this book Birks discusses the doctrine that he calls the "doctrine in *Ramsden v Dyson*", and which Spencer Bower and Turner know as "proprietary" estoppel. Birks deplores the "remedial uncertainty" of that estoppel doctrine. He claims that it has been used to remedy two quite different ills and that some of the *Ramsden v Dyson* doctrine cases are best explained on the basis of restitution for unjust enrichment and some are best explained on the basis of promissory estoppel.[289] Further, Birks pays little attention to the distinction between contract and estoppel claiming that only "[l]ocal difficulties may for a time obscure the fact that contracts, like roses, remain the same under all names."[290] Thus the classic estoppel cases come to be seen as an amalgam of restitution for unjust enrichment and the contractual enforcement of expectations, with virtually no room for the reliance base attributed to them in cases such as *Waltons*. What is surprising is that in his review of Birks' book, Sir Anthony Mason cites with apparent approval a passage at odds with the reliance based approach. He then claims that:

> *Waltons Stores (Interstate) v Maher* . . . would provide a stimulating vehicle for the discussion of these propositions.[291]

Once again the purpose of these comments is not clear. It is unlikely that Sir Anthony Mason, the advocate of the reliance based approach to estoppel, was suggesting a Birksean division of the estoppel cases into contract and unjust enrichment. However, if he was, then two points must be made. First, it is important to underscore the differences of principle dividing these three doc-

---

[286] *Waltons* at 453 (emphasis added).

[287] Compare the factor of the parties' relative interest in the activities undertaken in reliance discussed above at pp. 62–63.

[288] Sir Anthony Mason, "An Introduction to the Law of Restitution", (1989) 1 *JCL* 265.

[289] P Birks, *An Introduction to the Law of Restitution* revised edn (Oxford, Clarendon Press, 1989) at 291.

[290] Ibid. at 47.

[291] Sir Anthony Mason, "An Introduction to the Law of Restitution", (1989) 1 *JCL* 265 at 266.

trines. The principles that promises should be kept, that enrichments unjustly made at another's expense should not be retained, and that harm ought sometimes to be prevented by ensuring the reliability of induced assumptions, are distinct. To claim that a line of cases concerned with the third of these principles can be explained away on the basis of the first two would not make for coherence in charting the law of obligations. Second, the recent estoppel cases have not supported a division of the doctrine into contract and unjust enrichment. Nor have they spoken of enrichment as a necessary corollary of unconscionable conduct. Rather, they continue to stress reliance as the basis of estoppel. In *Foran* v *Wight*, for example, a line was quite carefully drawn between unjust enrichment and estoppel in that each of the judges dealt with estoppel in relation to certain contractual defences and then moved on as quite a separate issue to discuss the restitution of the plaintiffs deposit money.[292] It can be expected that the courts will continue to search for clear lines to draw between estoppel, contract and unjust enrichment, between reliance, expectation and restitution.[293]

(n) **Defences**

Against a claim in equitable estoppel, a party may either argue that any one of the elements of the doctrine has not been made out or raise any of the general defences to an equitable suit.[294] The availability of the equitable defences seems to be assumed in the recent authorities because of the supposed origins of the doctrine in equity.[295]

While a general discussion of the equitable defences is not proposed here, one particular defence has received considerable attention in the cases and merits some consideration. This is the defence that the court ought not to exercise its discretion in granting relief on an equitable estoppel where to do so would undermine the effect of a particular statute. Two issues arise in relation to such a defence: (i) the issue of when a court should refuse to exercise its discretion to grant relief because of the danger of undermining a statutory provision, (ii) the issue of whether the complex law of part performance has been rendered otiose in Australia by developments in estoppel, given that a court might sometimes

---

[292] *Foran* v *Wight* (1989) 168 CLR 385 at 413 *per* Mason CJ, at 432 *per* Brennan J, at 438–439 *per* Deane J at 455 *per* Dawson J and at 459 *per* Gaudron J.

[293] These distinctions have also found favour in the state courts, see *Update Constructions Pty Ltd* v *Rozelle Child Care Centre Ltd* (1990) 20 NSWLR 251. See also generally, J Carter, "Contract, Restitution and Promissory Estoppel", (1989) 12 *UNSWLJ* 30.

[294] For example, set off, release, delay, the application of a statute of limitations either directly or by analogy, illegality and unclean hands. For a discussion of the general equitable defences with particular reference to Australia see M Spence, "Equitable Defences" in P Parkinson (ed.), *The Principles of Equity* (Sydney, LBC, 1996).

[295] For example, it seems assumed in *Budmore Pty Ltd* v *Johnson* (1993) 6 BPR 13,574 at 13,580 that a party seeking to rely upon an equitable estoppel must have "clean hands".

offer relief where a statute might otherwise disallow it and might do so in the expectation measure.

(i) Estoppel and statute

The problem of when a court should refuse to exercise its discretion to grant relief on an equitable estoppel because to do so would undermine the effect of a particular statute arose in the case of *Waltons* itself. It was argued on behalf of Waltons that section 54A of the *Conveyancing Act* 1919 (NSW) precluded the application of equitable estoppel. Section 54A(1) provides:

> "No action or proceedings may be brought upon any contract for the sale of or other disposition of land or any interest in land, unless the agreement upon which such action or proceedings is brought, or some memorandum or notice thereof, is in writing, and signed by the party to be charged or by some other person thereunto by him lawfully authorised."

In considering the effect of the section, Brennan J held that if the true assumption founding the equitable estoppel was that a binding agreement was in existence (either generally or because exchange had taken place), then that estoppel prevented the denial that the contract was enforceable.[296] A similar approach was adopted by Deane[297] and Gaudron JJ[298] Alternatively, Brennan J argued that if the true assumption was that a contract would be concluded in the future, the equitable estoppel gave rise to an equity and did not create a contract to which the section might apply.[299] Neither of these approaches offered a satisfactory solution to the conflict between estoppel and the requirement of writing because neither paid more than lip-service to the statutory provision.

The problem of estoppel potentially underming the effect of a statutory provision was again directly relevant to *Verwayen*. The plaintiff in *Verwayen* sought to estop the defendant from raising a statute of limitation in defence.[300] If the assumption upon which the plaintiff had relied in that case was that the defendant would waive the limitation defence, a question logically prior to the application of estoppel was whether the limitation defence was one ever capable of being waived, however its waiver may have been effected, or whether it established a condition precedent to the exercise of jurisdiction by a court. In answering that question, Brennan J claimed that:

---

[296] *Waltons* at 432.

[297] Ibid. at 446.

[298] Ibid. at 464.

[299] Ibid. at 433. This passage was relied upon in *Dahlenburg v Dahlenburg* (1996) 7 BPR 14,885

[300] The relevant provision, section 5(6) of the *Limitations of Actions Act* 1958 (Vic) read: "No action for damages for negligence . . . where damages claimed by the plaintiff consist of or include damages in respect of personal injuries to any person, shall be brought after the expiration of three years after the cause of action accrued."

"... it is a characteristic of a right susceptible of waiver that it is introduced solely for the benefit of one party, a condition precedent to the jurisdiction of a court to grant relief cannot be waived: *Park Gate Iron Co.* v *Coates* (1870) LR 5 CP 634."[301]

A similar test was adopted – albeit under sometimes quite differing reasoning and for different purposes – by Mason CJ,[302] and Dawson,[303] Toohey,[304] Gaudron,[305] and McHugh JJ[306] None of the judges held that the limitation defence was inherently incapable of being waived.

What is frustrating, however, is that it is not clear what the effect on the plaintiff's argument in equitable estoppel would have been had they done so. Imagine that the plaintiff had been able to establish that he relied upon the assumption, not simply that the limitation defence would be waived, but that the defendant admitted liability and would provide compensation.[307] Could he then have argued that his claim was brought in equitable estoppel and not in negligence and thus not covered by the relevant statutory provision? Could he still have recovered by means of equitable estoppel an amount that he could not have recovered in tort?

To have allowed recovery in such a situation would certainly have been in line with the treatment in Waltons of the writing requirement. Yet to have done so would also arguably have been anomalous. In *Verwayen*, Gaudron J claimed that:

"The general principal is that 'an individual cannot waive a matter in which the public have an interest': *Graham* v *Ingleby*, *per* Alderson B."[308]

If the justification for holding a statutory provision inherently incapable of being waived is that it has been enacted for public rather than private benefit, it must be equally against the public interest that the provision be circumvented by means of equitable estoppel. If Parliament has decided that it is not merely inconvenient for, or even unfair to, defendants but positively against the public interest that a tort be remedied after a particular time period, and has taken jurisdiction to provide such a remedy away from the courts, surely it would be against public policy to entertain a plea that liability has been admitted.[309]

The answer to this dilemma might actually be found in *Verwayen* itself. It might be found by combining the *Verwayen* distinction between provisions enacted essentially for private benefit and those in which the public have an

[301] *Verwayen* at 425.
[302] Ibid. at 404–405.
[303] Ibid. at 456.
[304] Ibid. at 473–474.
[305] Ibid. at 486.
[306] Ibid. at 496.
[307] As, in fact, Brennan, Deane and Dawson JJ seem to have thought that he was in *Verwayen* at 428, 447 and 462–463 respectively.
[308] Ibid. at 486.
[309] This dilemma is not dissimilar to the problem that entertaining a plea of estoppel in administrative law could potentially mean requiring an administrative authority to engage in otherwise *ultra vires* activity.

interest, with the discretionary nature of relief under equitable estoppel. Surely a relevant consideration in determining whether or not to apply equitable estoppel in any particular fact situation is whether the plaintiff would thereby be circumventing a statutory provision enacted to confer a public benefit. For example, under section 45 of the *Builders Licensing Act* 1971 (NSW) a contract to carry out building work by the holder of a licence is not enforceable "against the other party to the contract unless the contract is in writing signed by the parties . . . and sufficiently describes the building work."[310] A court might determine that the purpose of this statutory provision was to protect the public at large (e.g., by improving business practices in the building industry) and not to confer a benefit upon a particular contracting party (e.g., by protecting him from uncertainty as to the precise terms of his contract with the builder). If that were its understanding of the provision, then the court should refuse to apply equitable estoppel wherever to do so would undermine the policy of the statute.

This approach of deciding whether or not to grant relief under a common law doctrine on the basis of whether doing so might undermine the object of a particular statute, is one with which the courts are already familiar even in contexts in which the relevant common law doctrine is not expressly discretionary. It is, for example, the approach to conflicts between restitutionary claims and statutory provisions adopted by a majority of the High Court of Australia in *Pavey & Matthews Pty Ltd v Paul*,[311] a case dealing with section 45 of the *Builders Licensing Act* 1971 (NSW). It is also the approach to the enforcement of illegal contracts by an "innocent" party that Devlin LJ took in the leading case of *Archbolds (Freightage) Ltd v S Spanglett Ltd.*[312]

Further, this approach has been the one that has so far been adopted by the Australian courts in dealing with potential conflicts between equitable estoppel and various statutory provisions. In *Day Ford Pty Ltd v Sciacca*[313] Macrossan CJ relied upon the decisions in *Kok Hoong v Leong Cheong Kweng Mines Ltd*[314] and *Maritime Electric Co v General Dairies Ltd*[315] to support such an approach. His Honour said that the test to apply was:

> ". . . 'whether the law that confronts the estoppel can be seen to represent a social policy to which the court must give effect in the interests of the public generally or some section of the public' . . . [and that] in deciding whether an estoppel might be set up against the operations of a statute 'the Court should first of all determine the nature of the obligation imposed by the statute, and then consider whether the admission of an estoppel would nullify the statutory provision.' "[316]

---

[310] Discussion of the policy underpinning this section can be found in *Pavey & Matthews Pty Ltd v Paul* (1986) 162 CLR 221 at 228–230 *per* Mason CJ and Wilson J.

[311] (1986) 162 CLR 221. See also J Beatson, "Unjust Enrichment in the High Court of Australia", (1988) 104 *LQR* 13 at 15–16 and J Beatson, *The Use and Abuse of Unjust Enrichment* (Oxford, Clarendon Press, 1991) at 8–11.

[312] [1961] 1 QB 374.

[313] [1990] 2 Qd R 209.

[314] [1964] AC 993 at 1016.

[315] [1937] AC 610 at 620.

[316] *Day Ford Pty Ltd v Sciacca* [1990] 2 Qd R 209 at 216.

A similar approach was taken in *Road Construction Authority* v *McBeth*.[317] In this case, applying equitable estoppel would have meant that a right given to one party by statute was effectively deprived of meaningful operation. This was an important ground for the refusal of relief under the doctrine. In *Public Trustee* v *Kukula*,[318] the abolition of the action for breach of promise to marry by section 111A of the *Marriage Act* 1961 (Cth) was taken to mean that "Courts of Equity cannot treat the repudiation of an executory contract of marriage as unconscionable conduct".[319] In *Silovi* v *Barbaro* the court was careful to enquire whether "the law, in the light of the *Local Government Act*, s 327AA, prevent[ed] an equity of the kind asserted by the plaintiffs from coming into existence." This was treated as a threshold question involving a consideration of the purpose and operation of the group of provisions of which section 327AA formed a part.[320] In *Krygger* v *Commonwealth of Australia* estoppel could not be used to circumvent the statutory abolition of a right of action.[321] In *Webb Distributors (Aust) Pty Ltd* v *Victoria* estoppel was not allowed to override a system of priority between creditors in the winding up of a building society provided for by statute.[322] Finally, in *Haraszti* v *Derunovsky* it was held to "be against public policy to allow a party to avoid obligations created by a Contract Determination made by an Industrial Tribunal according to law . . . by seeking to assert circumstances giving rise to an estoppel."[323]

It is suggested that this approach to the question of whether the application of equitable estoppel would undermine a statutory provision is appropriate and ought to be continued. It would clearly be against public policy for the courts to provide relief directly in the face of a legislative enactment intended to confer a public benefit.

(ii) Estoppel and part performance

Equitable estoppel might therefore sometimes be used to give relief where a statute is held otherwise to disallow it, provided that granting relief in such circumstances does not undermine the purpose of the statute. Moreover, equitable estoppel might offer relief in the expectation measure in such circumstances. These two possibilities give rise to the question whether equitable estoppel will render otiose the complex law of part performance in Australia.[324]

---

[317] (1988) 68 LGRA 216.

[318] (1990) 14 Fam LR 97. This case was applied in *Stowe and Devereaux Holdings Pty Ltd* v *Stowe* (1995) 19 Fam LR 409.

[319] Ibid. at 101. It is interesting that Handley JA should have mentioned the statute when it was unlikely that mere failure to perform an executory promise would amount to unconscionable conduct in any case.

[320] *Silovi* v *Barbaro* (1988) 13 NSWLR 466 at 473 *per* Priestley JA.

[321] (1992) 8 SR(WA) 338.

[322] (1993) 67 ALJR 961 at 970.

[323] (1995) 60 IR 135 at 144 *per* Marks J.

[324] A failure which, notwithstanding the reassurances of Mason CJ and Wilson J in *Waltons* at 405, left some commentators concluding that equitable estoppel would be an easier was of

The equitable doctrine of part performance, which was abolished in England by sub-section 2(8) of the Law of Property (Miscellaneous Provisions) Act 1989 (UK) but which survives in Australia, allows a court to order specific performance, an injunction, or damages in lieu thereof, to enforce a contract which has been rendered unenforceable by a statutory requirement of writing in circumstances in which the contract has been partly performed. This doctrine is, however, of limited application. As Brennan J described in *Waltons*:

> "In order that acts may be relied on as part performance of an unwritten contract, they must be done under the terms and by the force of that contract and they must be unequivocally and in their nature referable to some contract of the general nature of that alleged: *Regent* v *Miller* (1976) 133 CLR at 683"[325]

Part performance seems to have had its origins in some form of estoppel,[326] although at least by the time of the leading case of *Maddison* v *Alderson*[327] these doctrines had been distinguished and the shape of the doctrine of part performance outlined by Brennan J in *Waltons* was beginning to emerge.

The possibility raised by recent developments in equitable estoppel is obviously that part performance might be absorbed back into a broader doctrine of estoppel. A plaintiff who had partly performed a particular contract which is ineffective for lack of writing might be able to argue that the terms of the apparent contract constituted an assumption induced by the defendant, that he had relied upon that assumption by his acts of part performance, that it would be unconscionable for defendant to resile from that assumption, and that the appropriate way for the court to protect his reliance upon that assumption would be to award him the expectation measure of relief. This argument might be said to have an enhanced chance of success because the courts are used, under the doctrine of part performance, to presuming that insisting upon the statute and resiling from the assumptions induced under the contract is unconscionable in situations in which there has been reliance, albeit reliance of a more narrowly defined type than that anticipated under equitable estoppel.[328] The plaintiff

circumventing writing requirements than the doctrine of part performance (see J Phillips and L Proksch, "Waltons Stores (Interstate) Ltd v Maher: Implications for the Law of Contract" (1989) 19 *UWALR* 171 at 184). On the interrelation of estoppel and part performance see *ANZ Banking Group Ltd* v *Widin* (1991) 102 ALR 289 and R P Meagher, W M C Gummow and J R F Lehane, *Equity: Doctrines and Remedies* 3rd edn (Sydney, Butterworths, 1992) at 417.

[325] *Waltons* at 432 *per* Brennan J.

[326] For an account of the process whereby estoppel and part performance came to be distinguished see R D Mulholland, "The Equitable Doctrines of Estoppel and Part Performance" (1989) 7 *Otago LR* 69.

[327] *Maddison* v *Alderson* (1883) 8 App Cas 467.

[328] Although it is sometimes expressed as an independent requirement for the application of the doctrine of part performance (*Francis* v *Francis* [1952] VLR 321 at 340 *per* Smith J), the unconscionability inherent in an insistence on the fulfilment of the statutory requirement of writing in face of acts of part performance is usually assumed. As Meagher, Gummow and Lehane claim: "It may be possible to conceive of a case where the doing of acts of part performance, otherwise sufficient, does not, in particular circumstances, make it inequitable for the defendant to plead the statute . . . ; but there does not seem to be any reported instance" (R P Meagher, W M C Gummow, J R F Lehane, *Equity: Doctrines and Remedies* 3rd edn (Sydney, Butterworths, 1992) at 520).

would then be able to achieve by way of estoppel what he might not be able to achieve under part performance because of that latter doctrine's strict requirements that the alleged acts of part performance be "done under the terms and by the force of that contract and . . . unequivocally and in their nature referable to some contract of the general nature of that alleged."[329]

This possibility might be exemplified by reference to *Collin v Holden*[330] in which a contract which would clearly not have been enforceable under the doctrine of part performance became the assumption founding an equitable estoppel upon which an award in the expectation measure was made. Similarly, Brennan J did not believe that the purported contract in *Waltons* was specifically enforceable under the doctrine of part performance, and yet that purported contract induced the assumption founding an equitable estoppel upon which an award in the expectation measure was made.[331]

It is submitted, however, that there is no reason why the doctrine of equitable estoppel, properly understood and applied by the courts, should usurp the function of the doctrine of part performance. As outlined above, awards in the expectation measure ought not normally to be the measure of relief in equitable estoppel. A plaintiff who seeks specific performance of a partly performed contract invalid for want of writing, will therefore be able to place his claim on a firmer footing if he can satisfy the requirements of the doctrine of part performance. Indeed, respect for those requirements may well be a reason for the courts to exercise more than usual caution in making awards in the expectation measure under equitable estoppel. This point was made in the judgment of Mason CJ and Wilson J in *Waltons* in which they said:

"Because equitable estoppel has its basis in unconscionable conduct, rather than the making good of representations, the objection, grounded in *Maddison v Alderson*, that promissory estoppel outflanks the doctrine of part performance loses much of its sting . . . Equitable estoppel, though it may lead to the plaintiff acquiring an estate or interest in land, depends on considerations of a different kind from those on which part performance depends. Holding the representor to his representation is merely one way of doing justice between the parties."[332]

The doctrines of part performance and estoppel therefore have arguably distinguishable rôles to play in Australian law.

---

[329] *Waltons* at 432 *per* Brennan J.
[330] *Collin v Holden* [1989] VR 510.
[331] *Waltons* at 432 *per* Brennan J.
[332] *Waltons* at 405 *per* Mason CJ and Wilson J. This point was also made in *Carr v McDonalds Australia Pty Ltd* (1994) 63 FCR 358.

III

The Utility of Equitable Estoppel

1. INTRODUCTION

In Chapter One a moral principle at work in the equitable estoppel cases – the duty to ensure the reliability of induced assumptions – was described and justified. A sketch map was drawn of the law relating to induced assumptions. In Chapter Two it was shown that equitable estoppel could be developed to give appropriate expression to that principle. The task of this chapter is to demonstrate that equitable estoppel could be a useful addition to the law.

To do this, I will take a group of cases that the common law of obligations has found difficult to resolve – all cases arising at the edge of contract – and show how the new doctrine might have been useful in resolving those cases. I will show either that existing doctrines were unable to account for the results achieved in the cases and that equitable estoppel could have done so, or that the application of the doctrine of equitable estoppel could have led to more satisfactory results. In this introductory section the possible co-existence of equitable estoppel and the existing law of contract is considered and the four problem areas discussed in this chapter are briefly introduced.

(a) Equitable Estoppel and Contract

There are two questions regarding the interrelation of contract and equitable estoppel that must be considered. First, will equitable estoppel prove too great a rival to contract, providing relief too often in situations in which no contract can be established? This question is particularly important because an assumption founding an equitable estoppel may be induced by a representation of intention and because remedies in the expectation measure can be awarded. A party may therefore be prevented from changing his mind and resiling from an assumption that he has induced regarding his intentions by the award of relief in the expectation measure, a form of liability that seems very close to contract but without its limitations. Second, will equitable estoppel too often provide a mechanism for undoing contractual arrangements by preventing a party from insisting upon his contractual rights?

(i) Equitable estoppel as a rival to contract

In relation to the first of these issues it is submitted that equitable estoppel will not provide a rival to contract on four grounds.

First, contract and equitable estoppel are not coterminous doctrines because contract is built upon the duty to keep promises and equitable estoppel is built upon the duty to ensure the reliability of induced assumptions.[1] A promise is just one of the ways in which an assumption may be induced for equitable estoppel. Conversely, there will be many situations in which a promise (which may or may not be enforceable as a contract) has been broken and yet equitable estoppel is not available.

For example, if I promise to supply widgets at £2 each but fail to do so causing you to purchase them elsewhere at £2.50, you may well have an action in contract. It is not clear in this situation, however, that you have suffered any detriment in the sense of being worse off than had the assumption that I would supply the widgets for £2 never been induced. Moreover, it is not clear that my resiling from the promise will represent unconscionable conduct. Mere "failure to fulfil a promise does not of itself amount to unconscionable conduct".[2] Even if the promise has been relied upon "something more would be required".[3]

Second, the remedial consequences of applying contract and equitable estoppel are different. Contract remedies paradigmatically fulfil expectations, while remedies in equitable estoppel compensate for reliance loss.[4] Contract damages are not awarded conditionally in the way in which remedies for equitable estoppel may be. Plaintiffs will generally want to sue in contract where they can because the value of their expectations will generally exceed the value of their reliance. Only very rarely will it be appropriate to protect reliance by an award in the expectation measure. Incidentally, where a plaintiff's reliance loss exceeds his expectation loss, the difficult question arises whether the contract price ought to set a ceiling for reliance based recovery. This parallels a similar debate in the field of restitution for unjust enrichment.[5] Although it is early in the

---

[1] It is submitted that comments in the literature such as the following are patently erroneous: "Advisors should now be aware the *liability for breach of promise* may be based on contract or promissory estoppel" (D Khoury, "Promissory Estoppel – A Sword Unsheathed", (1990) 64 *Law Inst J* 1054 at 1056 (emphasis added)).

[2] *Waltons* at 404 *per* Mason CJ and Wilson J.

[3] Ibid. at 406 *per* Mason CJ and Wilson J.

[4] See, for example, the comments of Brennan J in *Waltons* at 423–424: "The object of the equity is not to compel the party bound to fulfil the assumption or expectation; it is to avoid the detriment which, if the assumption or expectation goes unfulfilled, will be suffered by the party who has been induced to act or to abstain from acting thereon. If this object is kept steadily in mind, the concern that a general application of the principle of equitable estoppel would make non-contractual promises enforceable as contractual promises can be allayed."

[5] See, for example, Lord Goff of Chieveley and G Jones, *The Law of Restitution* 4th edn (London, Sweet & Maxwell, 1993) at 426–428, G J Palmer, "The Contract Price as a Limit on Restitution for Defendant's Breach", (1959) 20 *Ohio St LJ* 264, R Childres and J Garamella, "The Law of Restitution and the Reliance Interest in Contract", (1969) 64 *Nw U L Rev* 433.

development of the doctrine to consider such issues, if it is accepted that there exists a valid distinction between the duty to keep promises and the duty to ensure the reliability of induced assumptions, there would seem to be no reason why reliance based recovery should be so limited.

Third, whereas some relief in contract will be available as of right upon proof of breach, relief in equitable estoppel will only be available on a discretionary basis. It is therefore unlikely that many parties will choose to argue their case in equitable estoppel when a cause of action in contract would be available. The editor of the *Australian and New Zealand Conveyancing Report* made the following comments about relying upon estoppel to ensure the renewal of a lease:

> "While estoppel enables the Court in many situations to achieve justice, or to prevent unconscionable behaviour, it is not an acceptable conveyancing solution in actual transactions . . . It is suggested that the correct legal advice remains strict adherence to proper conveyancing procedures . . ."[6]

Fourth, where a party wishes to ensure that his dealings with another party do not attract legal consequences except under the law of contract, he is always free to warn the other party that the assumptions he induces ought not to be relied upon. While such a warning to the other party will not automatically preclude liability in equitable estoppel, it will often constitute an attempt to prevent reliance upon an induced assumption causing harm and therefore count against a finding of unconscionability.

Thus, I would argue that equitable estoppel will not prove a rival to contract because (i) the doctrines are built upon different principles and are not coterminous, (ii) the remedial consequences of applying the doctrines will differ, (iii) contract remedies are available as of right while equitable estoppel operates as a discretionary doctrine, and (iv) parties are free to warn those with whom they deal that the assumptions they induce, other than as a part of a contract, ought not to be relied upon.

Indeed, it might be that equitable estoppel is contract's appropriate complement rather than its rival. There seem to be two opposing demands that parties involved in transactions make of the law. On the one hand, those parties are said to require control over the content of their agreements, control over *when* their agreements give rise to legal obligations,[7] and a court system that enforces those agreements with certainty.[8] On the other hand, parties to transactions are said to expect a court to treat their dealings with some flexibility and to fashion just

---

[6] (1991) ANZ Convey Rep 181.

[7] These first two ideas are often discussed together under the rubric of "freedom of contract", see P S Atiyah, *An Introduction to the Law of Contract* 5th edn (Oxford, Clarendon Press, 1995) Ch 1, H Collins, *The Law of Contract* 3rd edn (London, Butterworths, 1997) Ch 2, W H Holmes, "The Freedom Not to Contract", (1986) 69 *Tul L Rev* 751.

[8] For an English, an Australian, a Canadian and a United States example see G H Treitel, *Doctrine and Discretion in the Law of Contract* (Oxford, Clarendon Press, 1980) at 20, J W Carter and D J Harland, *Contract Law in Australia* 3rd edn (Sydney, Butterworths, 1996) at 13, J E Côté, *An Introduction to the Law of Contract* (Edmonton, Juriliber, 1974) at 3, R Pound, *An Introduction to the Philosophy of Law* (New Haven, Yale U P, 1922) at 133.

solutions to transactional disputes. Thus Atiyah notes "a desire to escape from the rigidity . . . thought inseparable from contract doctrine proper"[9] and a growing body of empirical work questions the model of parties insistent on the letter of their "deal".[10] Over-rigorous notions of certainty are said to have "highly undesirable consequences" in the commercial world.[11] It might be that the recognition of both a strict contract doctrine and a more flexible doctrine of equitable estoppel could equip the law to meet these opposing demands in a balanced way. The enforcement of promises could be effected by a strictly applied contract doctrine. The enforcement of the duty to ensure the reliability of induced assumptions could be effected by the more flexible doctrine of equitable estoppel. In this way the two doctrines might together achieve the balance of party control, certainty, and flexibility seen as a desirable in the legal treatment of transactional relationships, a balance that neither doctrine could of itself achieve. Whether the two doctrines can achieve this balance will be tested in the latter part of this chapter when their operation in four problem cases at the edge of contract is considered.

(ii) Equitable estoppel as undoing contractual obligations

The other way in which equitable estoppel might be a threat to contract is as a mechanism for undoing existing contractual obligations. I would argue that this would be less the case, however, than it might be under the estoppel theory outlined in *Spencer Bower and Turner*.

Under the theory outlined in *Spencer Bower and Turner* an existing contractual obligation could be modified by the application of the doctrine of "promissory" estoppel. In relation to existing contractual rights, this doctrine would apply in almost the same situations as equitable estoppel. The only relevant additional situations in which equitable estoppel might apply are arguably (i) where an assumption has been induced in pre-contractual negotiations and reliance takes the form of entry into a binding contract,[12] and (ii) in contexts in which assumptions relating to contractual rights are induced by silence. In the majority of cases in which contractual obligations might be affected by an estoppel, however, both promissory and equitable estoppel could equally be applicable.

In such cases, I would argue that traditional promissory estoppel is likely to produce a result more threatening to the security of contractual rights than would equitable estoppel. First, some writers argued that promissory estoppel

---

[9] P S Atiyah, "When is an Enforceable Agreement not a Contract?", (1967) 92 *LQR* 174 at 179

[10] For example, S Macauley, "Non-Contractual Relations in Business: A Preliminary Study", (1963) 28 *Am Soc Rev* 55, H Beale and T Dugdale, "Contracts Between Businessmen: Planning and Use of Contractual Remedies", (1975) 2 *Br J Law Soc* 45.

[11] L M Freidman and S Macauley, "Contract Law and Teaching", [1967] *Wis L Rev* 805 at 816

[12] Although it had been suggested in Australia even before *Waltons* that promissory estoppel could apply in this situation see *State Rail Authority (NSW) v Heath Outdoor Pty Ltd* (1986) 7 NSWLR 170.

always modified rights *per se* and thereby automatically protected expectations.[13] Second, even if promissory estoppel did not always modify rights, it was always up to the party against whom the estoppel was sought to show that he was able to revoke his promise and to restore the other party to his original position. It was up to the party against whom the estoppel was sought to show why simply reliance, and not expectations, should have been protected. With equitable estoppel the burden of proof is reversed. The emphasis is on protecting reliance and it is up to the party seeking to establish the estoppel to show why his expectations should be enforced. It is therefore less likely that an award in equitable estoppel would lead to the permanent modification of existing contractual rights. On this basis, I would argue that equitable estoppel is far less a threat to security of contract than is the existing doctrine of promissory estoppel. Fears that equitable estoppel would lead to the undoing of large numbers of contracts would seem simply misplaced.

(b) Introducing the four problem areas

I turn, then, from considering the possible co-existence of equitable estoppel and contract to examine how the doctrine might operate in four cases that the existing law of contract has found problematic.

In two of these situations one party has relied upon an anticipated or apparent agreement, but no agreement has actually been finalised, either in substance or in form. The first of these situations is that of work requested and undertaken during pre-contractual negotiations towards performance of a contract that is never concluded. The party who has undertaken such work might seek compensation for it, even though the work is not covered by any contractual arrangement. The second of these situations is the "battle of forms" in which two parties exchange their standard terms of business intending to contract, but those standard terms of business are so different that no *consensus ad idem* is achieved and a contract is not formed. In this situation parties might rely upon an agreement that they believe to be in place, and seek compensation for the performance that they have rendered, even though no contract exists between them.

In the other two of these situations one party has relied upon an actual agreement between the parties, but that agreement is unenforceable as lacking consideration. The first of these situations is that of firm offers to contract in the construction industry. In this situation a general contractor who is tendering a bid for a construction contract relies upon quotations for work from subcontractors in calculating his bid. These quotations are not normally contractually binding for want of consideration, though they are often expressed to be "good" for a particular period of time. The general contractor can have his tender

---

[13] See above at p. 22.

accepted and be bound to complete the construction project for a price based upon the quotation from the subcontractor, while the subcontractor remains free to revise his quotation upwards. The general contractor might seek compensation for his reliance upon the subcontractor's bid even though the subcontractor is not contractually bound. The second of these situations is that in which parties to a contract informally vary its terms. Contracts can only be modified by contract. Contractual modifications must be supported by consideration. An undertaking to perform a pre-existing contractual duty cannot constitute valid consideration,[14] although the courts in England have shown some flexibility in relation to what might constitute consideration for these purposes.[15] A contractual modification must be in writing if it was required for the original contract.[16] Under pre-*Waltons* law, unenforceable contractual modifications could sometimes be given effect in the limited, defensive, way made possible by the doctrine of promissory estoppel, but parties often relied upon contractual modifications which they were unable to enforce for want of consideration.

Although *prima facie* no contractual liability will arise, there has been a remarkably resilient intuition that parties who render performance in these four situations ought at least sometimes to be compensated. Take the situation of pre-contractual negotiations. Most modern commercial negotiations involve at least three stages. These are (i) a stage involving preliminary negotiations in which each party feels perfectly free to withdraw, (ii) a stage in which agreement "in principle" has been reached, that agreement often being expressed in a "letter of intent" or similar document, and (iii) a stage in which the contract is complete.[17] Writers such as Ball and Farnsworth have shown that the parties to negotiations often expect that activity directed towards performance of the contract should commence at the second of these stages, and that the risks involved in reliance upon the anticipated contract should fall, not upon the relying party, but upon the party who has induced the assumption.[18] This may be so whether

---

[14] *Stilk* v *Myrick* (1809) 2 Camp 317.

[15] *Williams* v *Roffey Brothers & Nicholls (Contractors) Ltd* [1991] 1 QB 1. The principle in this case was reformulated and applied in the Australian decision of Santow J in *Musumeci* v *Winadell Pty Ltd* (1994) 34 NSWLR 723.

[16] *Gross* v *Lord Nugent* (1833) B & Acr 58.

[17] This process is described in S N Ball, "Work Carried out in Pursuance of Letters of Intent – Contract or Restitution?", (1983) 99 *LQR* 572, E A Farnsworth, "Precontractual Liability and Preliminary Agreements:Fair Dealing and Failed Negotiations", (1987) 87 *Colum L Rev* 217 and H L Temkin, "When Does the "Fat Lady" Sing?: An Analysis of "Agreements in Principle" in Corporate Acquisitions", (1986) 55 *Fordham L Rev* 125.

[18] Ball claims that "the use made of letters of intent by businessmen differs markedly from the assumptions made by the law about their use" (S N Ball, "Work Carried out in Pursuance of Letters of Intent – Contract or Restitution?", (1983) 99 *LQR* 572 at 580). In support of this contention Ball (at 580) cites *Turiff Construction Ltd* v *Regalia Knitting Mills Ltd* [1972] EGD 257 and *Peter Lind & Co Ltd* v *Mersey Docks & Harbour Board* [1972] 2 Lloyd's Rep 234. He might also have pointed to cases such as *William Lacey (Hounslow) Ltd* v *Davis* [1957] 1 WLR 932. Farnsworth makes a similar claim, pointing out that by the second stage of negotiations, one party's investment in the particular deal may already have become substantial and may not be of a type which can be spread out

the agreement "in principle" already reached is almost complete, though not contractual, or much more open textured.[19] Similarly, in the context of the battle of forms, it is clear that parties expect activity directed towards performance of the apparent agreement should commence on the exchange of forms and in this one situation it can be assumed that they believe themsleves to bound by contract. Perhaps for this reason, the battle of forms is rarely litigated. Indeed, the corporate counsel for IBM Canada has claimed that, although his company entered into 18,000 arrangements a year between 1963 and 1980 that were potentially subject to a battle of forms, there was in that period "no single instance where a customer . . . tried to repudiate a deal or . . . resisted a claim for payment on the grounds that there was no valid contract or the contract contained contradictory terms".[20] In the context of firm offers, Lewis and Schultz have shown that construction industry subcontractors who make firm offers generally feel themselves in some way obliged – if not necessarily contractually obliged – to protect general contractors from the loss involved in a price change.[21] This expectation is presumably the basis of §2-205 of the United States UNIFORM COMMERCIAL CODE (1978) which provides that firm offers to buy or sell goods made in signed writing by a merchant are irrevocable for up to three months[22] and of the Law Commission recommendation that firm offers made in the course of a business should be binding for a period not exceeding six years.[23] Finally, in the context of informal variations to contract, academic commentators have long assumed that parties expect their agreements to vary a contract

over other similar deals (E A Farnsworth, "Precontractual Liability and Preliminary Agreements: Fair Dealing and Failed Negotiations", (1987) 87 *Colum L Rev* 217 at 250). He cites (at 262) *Gundersen & Son* v *Cohn* 596 F Supp 379 (1984), *Borg-Worner Corp* v *Anchor Coupling Co* 156 N E 2d 513 (1958) and *APCO Amusement Co* v *Wilkins Family Restaurants of America Inc* 673 S W 2d 523 (1984). He might also have cited cases such as *Hoffman* v *Red Owl Stores* 133 N W 2d 267 (1965). In the context of the mining industry, Trower points out that parties use letters of intent – even though non-contractual – because they want "an accord which secures their property position, allows drilling to commence, commits the remainder of the year's exploration budget, or otherwise accomplishes their business objective" (E A Trower, "Enforceability of Letters of Intent and Other Preliminary Agreements" (1978) 24 *Rocky MMLI* 347 at 350). In *Holiday Inns Inc* v *Broadhead* (1974) 232 E G 961 and 1087 at 1089 the managing director of Holiday Inns argued that ample justification for reliance in business was the "agreement [of] a man I thought was a gentleman". Examples of reliance at this second stage of negotiations which is clearly perceived to be commercially justified, and deserving of compensation, could be multiplied from the cases.

[19] See E A Farnsworth, "Precontractual Liability and Preliminary Agreements:Fair Dealing and Failed Negotiations", (1987) 87 *Colum L Rev* 217 at 249–264 and the categories of case discussed in *Austotel Pty Ltd* v *Franklins Selfserve Pty Ltd* (1989) 16 NSWLR 582 at 588–616 *per* Priestley JA.

[20] G Murray, "A Corporate Counsel's Perspective of the "Battle of Forms", (1980) 4 *Can Bus LJ* 290 at 293.

[21] See R Lewis, "Contracts Between Businessmen; Reform of the Law of Firm Offers and an Empirical Study pf Tendering Practices in the Building Industry", (1982) 9 *J Law Soc* 153 at 163 and F M Schultz, "The Firm Offer Puzzle: A Study of Business Practice in the Construction Industry", (1952) 19 *U Chi L Rev* 237 at 283. For evidence of similar expectations in a different field of activity see Sir Robert Goff, "Commercial Contracts and the Commercial Court", [1984] *LMCLQ* 382 at 384.

[22] See also the N.Y. GENERAL OBLIGATIONS LAW §5-1109 (McKinney 1989).

[23] Law Commission, *Working Paper No. 60: Firm Offers* (1975) at 26.

to have some type of legal effect. They point out that variations of contract arise "over and over again in the ordinary transactions of mankind"[24] and, indeed are necessary if business dealings are to respond to changing market conditions. They point out that it is wrong to imagine that a party requesting variation is necessarily unconscientious or inept[25] and urge the courts to "sustain . . . reasonable commercial practice"[26], "reasonable arrangements between businessmen".[27] The intuition that parties who rely upon anticipated or apparent contracts ought sometimes to be compensated is very resilient indeed.

For this reason, the courts, commentators and legislators have been tempted to distort contract doctrine so as to provide contractual remedies to parties who have relied upon anticipated or apparent contracts. These distortions will be considered in the following sections of this chapter when each of the four fact situations is considered in greater detail. At this stage it is sufficient to point out that there are real dangers in forcing contractual solutions to the problem of reliance upon anticipated or apparent contracts. In the situations of work undertaken in anticipation of contract and the battle of forms, the imposition of contractual liability could have the disadvantage of threatening party-control over the terms of the agreement. It could lead the courts unfairly to prioritise the interests of one party over those of the other, simply awarding one party a result for which he was unable, or did not, bargain and to which the other party has never consented. If one party to unsuccessful pre-contractual negotiations has not promised to compensate the other for work undertaken in anticipation of contract, the courts must be careful not to treat him as if he had. If one party to a battle of forms has failed to secure consent to his standard terms, the courts must be careful to see that those terms are not given unfair priority over those of the other party to the putative contract. In the situations of firm offers to contract and informal variations of contract, the imposition of contractual liability could have the disadvantage of threatening party-control over which agreements ought to have binding legal effect. As suggested in Chapter One, it seems probable that parties do not expect their agreements to be legally binding unless they are in some way reciprocal or the parties have completed a legal formality such as the provision of a peppercorn consideration or the execution of a deed. A subcontractor may be surprised to find himself under a contractual obligation to provide services to a general contractor whom he knows to be under no obligation to accept those services. A party who accedes to an informal variation of contract as a concession to another party's poor planning may be surprised to find he has made a promise having legal effect, a promise potentially binding even if the reasons for granting the assumption turn out to be unfounded. Each

---

[24] *Tyers v Rosedale & Ferryhill Iron Co* (1873) LR 8 Exch 308 at 318 *per* Martin B.

[25] S J Stoljar, "The Modification of Contracts", (1957) 35 *Can Bar Rev* 485 at 485.

[26] G C Cheshire and C H S Fifoot , "*Central London Property Trust v High Trees*", (1947) 63 *LQR* 283 at 290.

[27] M P Furmston, *Cheshire, Fifoot and Furmston's Law of Contracts* 13th edn (London, Butterworths, 1996) at 577.

of these disadvantages to imposing contractual solutions in the four situations of reliance upon anticipated or apparent contracts is considered in greater detail in the following sections.

Alternatives to contract as a basis for the protection of reliance upon anticipated or apparent contracts have also proved problematic.

Remedies in tort will not normally be available. In each situation, reliance will normally be upon an assumption regarding the intentions of the other party, an intention that may be truthfully expressed at the time of the reliance. In the first situation, the relevant assumption will be that the party inducing it will complete a binding contract. In the other situation, the relevant assumption will be that the party inducing it will honour the commitments undertaken as part of the apparent, or unenforceable, agreement. Neither relief in deceit nor in negligent misstatement will be available where the relevant assumption is induced by a truthful representation of intention.

A remedy in restitution for unjust enrichment might sometimes be available in situations of reliance upon anticipated or apparent contract, but may be unsatisfactory for four reasons. First, in many cases it will be difficult to identify a benefit that has been rendered by the party seeking relief. This difficulty, which is considered below in relation to situations of pre-contractual negotiations, is particularly acute when the alleged benefit that one party has received under an anticipated, apparent or unenforceable agreement is the provision of a requested service. Second, restitutionary remedies may be inadequate to compensate reliance, designed as they are to reverse an unjust enrichment. Third, restitutionary solutions to these situations may unfairly prioritise the interests of the party who has received the alleged benefit over those of the party who has rendered it. Often a party who has received a benefit, particularly if the benefit has consisted in the provision of services, has experienced losses flowing from reliance upon assumptions about the timing or quality of the alleged benefit. If a restitutionary solution to the problem of reliance upon anticipated, apparent or unenforceable agreements forces him to pay for the benefit received without compensating his losses, he may feel justly aggrieved that the law is unfairly prioritising the interests of the other party. This problem will briefly be considered in relation to the problem of reliance upon pre-contractual negotiations and then considered more fully in discussion of the "battle of forms". Third, there may be situations in which no benefit at all has been conferred and yet relief may still be appropriate. In particular, there may be situations in which the duty to ensure the reliability of induced assumptions has been broken and no restitutionary remedy is available.

It is the argument of this chapter that equitable estoppel could provide relief on a principled basis in each of these four situations. My argument is not that there is no place for contract, tort or restitution in each of these situations. It is that existing cases show these three heads of liability to be inadequate to provide relief, or appropriate relief, in all situations in which it is arguable that relief ought to be available. The following sections of this chapter examine a limited number of reported cases from each situation to consider how equitable estoppel might have been used to resolve the problems they raise. In relation to each group of cases, existing attempts to find solutions in contract, tort or restitution will be considered. The facts of each case will then be analysed as they might be by a judge applying equitable estoppel. In relation to reliance upon anticipated contracts, it will be shown that equitable estoppel could have provided a justification for the relief actually awarded in the cases, but awarded on an unexplained and apparently unjustified basis. In relation to the battle of forms and informal variations of contract, it will be shown that equitable estoppel could have enabled the courts to analyse the facts of the cases considered more clearly than they did, and thereby to have achieved more satisfactory results. In relation to the problem of firm offers, it will be shown that equitable estoppel could provide relief in cases in which no relief is currently available, but in which relief would be available in the United States. I am aware that, in selecting a limited range of reported cases in each field, I am open to the charge of only examining those cases most suited to my argument. However, the cases chosen include those that dominate the discussion of each area in both the reported judgments and the literature. The limited range of cases treated has a certain self-selecting character.

2. WORK UNDERTAKEN IN ANTICIPATION OF A CONTRACT THAT DOES NOT MATERIALISE

The problem of work requested and undertaken in anticipation of a contract that does not materialise is, of course, the problem that confronted the High Court in *Waltons* itself. But the problem was not new to the law. In this section, six earlier cases struggling with the same problem shall be examined. In four of those cases the party who had undertaken work during pre-contractual negotiations was awarded relief. Of the six cases, four are English decisions, one is from New South Wales and one is from New Brunswick. Arranged chronologically they are *Jennings and Chapman Ltd* v *Woodman, Matthews & Co*,[28] *Brewer Street Investments Ltd* v *Barclay's Woollen Co Ltd*,[29] *William Lacey (Hounslow) Ltd* v *Davis*,[30] *Construction Design & Management Ltd* v *New Brunswick Housing Corporation*,[31] *Sabemo Pty Ltd* v *North Sydney Municipal Council*,[32] and *British Steel Corp* v *Cleveland Bridge & Engineering Co. Ltd.*[33]

---

[28] [1952] 2 TLR 409 (hereafter "*Jennings*").

[29] [1954] 1 QB 428 (herafter "*Brewer Street*").

[30] *William Lacey (Hounslow) Ltd* v *Davis* [1957] 1 WLR 932 (hereafter "*William Lacey*").

[31] (1973) 36 DLR (3d) 458 (hereafter "*Construction Design & Management*").

[32] *Sabemo Pty Ltd* v *North Sydney Municipal Council* [1977] 2 NSWLR 880 (hereafter "*Sabemo*").

[33] *British Steel Corp* v *Cleveland Bridge & Engineering Co Ltd* [1984] 1 All ER 504 (hereafter "*British Steel*").

In none of the cases in which the plaintiff was successful did the judge provide a clear exposition of the basis on which the remedy was being awarded. In one of the cases[34] the judge did not address the question at all, and such explanations as did emerge from the other three cases, and their commentators, do not account for the decisions made. These explanations will be considered and then the cases analysed in terms of equitable estoppel to determine whether that doctrine might provide the "missing" justification for the results achieved. It will also be considered whether equitable estoppel, while still explaining why liability might have arisen in each of these cases, would actually have led to a more satisfactory result in at least one of them.

Jennings and *Brewer Street* each involved alterations to property by prospective lessors in anticipation of a lease which the parties were negotiating but into which they never entered. In *Jennings* the failure to arrive at an agreed lease was because a head lessor, whose consent was required, failed to approve the proposed alterations. The prospective sublessee, a solicitor, had known, because it had been drawn to his attention, that the head lessor's consent was required for the grant of the sublease, but had also known that such consent could not be withheld if he was "responsible or respectable". The prospective sublessee had not known, because it was not brought to his attention, that the head-lessor's consent was also required for the alterations that were proposed. In *Brewer Street* the failure to arrive at an agreed lease was because of an inability to agree a term in the lease regarding the future sale of the property. The prospective lessees were seeking to include a term giving them an option to purchase the property within sixty days of signing the lease. The prospective lessors were only prepared to grant a lease coupled with a right of first refusal should they have decided to sell the property within two years of the date of the lease. In *Brewer Street* the Court of Appeal held that the prospective lessors were entitled to recover the cost of the alterations from the prospective lessees and in *Jennings* it held that the prospective sublessors were not.

William Lacey, *Construction Design & Management* and *Sabemo* also provide contrasting outcomes on similar sets of facts. Each case involved negotiations for a building project. In each case the party who was to carry out the building undertook considerably more work in preparing plans and other documents for the party proposing the development than might normally be expected. In *William Lacey* the owner of premises which had been damaged during the second world war asked a firm of builders, who were led to believe that they would receive the contract for rebuilding the premises, to prepare at least two different sets of estimates of the cost of rebuilding for submission to the War Damage Commission. The owner of the premises subsequently sold them instead of proceeding with the reconstruction and the builders claimed for the reasonable value of their services in preparing the estimates. In *Construction Design & Management* a public housing corporation called for proposals for

---

[34]   *British Steel.*

the construction of a senior citizen's housing project. An architectural, engineering and building firm submitted a proposal for the project which was accepted, but it was understood that the project would only proceed to contract if the project was approved by another public corporation which was to finance it. Obtaining the approval of the finance corporation took much more time than was expected and involved the builders in considerable work amending their plans. Eventually the delay became such that the builders claimed that they could no longer undertake the project at the price originally quoted and, a substantial increase in that price having been rejected by the housing corporation, withdrew from the project. The building firm brought an action for the cost of preparing the plans for the project. In *Sabemo* a local Council called for proposals for an extremely large project, the construction of a civic centre. A development company submitted a proposal for the project which was accepted. The company and the Council began working closely together on putting the development into place. This close relationship continued for three years, although at no time were the company and the Council contractually bound. After an enormous amount of work by both parties obtaining planning approval for, and reworking the design of, the civic centre, the Council suffered a political change of heart and the plan was dropped. The company brought an action for the reasonable value of the work that they had done in preparation for the project. In *William Lacey* and *Sabemo* the claim of the party who had undertaken the preparatory work was successful and in *Construction Design & Management* it was not.

In *British Steel* an engineering company were building a bank at Dammam in Saudi Arabia. As a part of their unusual design for the building, the engineering company required steel nodes which they asked an iron and steel manufacturing company to design and produce. The steel company were required to supply the nodes quickly and so work began on their design and production while contract matters such as price, progress payments and liability for late delivery were still under negotiation. All but one of the nodes were then manufactured and delivered. However, the nodes were not delivered according to an agreed sequence, some were delivered late and some were of an unsatisfactory quality. Negotiations then broke down, the steel company brought a *quantum meruit* action against the engineering company, and the engineering company counterclaimed for damages for breach of contract for late delivery. The value of the counterclaim far exceeded the value of the *quantum meruit*. Goff J rejected the engineering company's counterclaim and awarded the steel company the reasonable value of the nodes supplied.

(a) Contract and work undertaken in anticipation of contract

Attempts have been made to explain the cases of work undertaken during precontractual negotiations on the basis of contract, and contract-like, doctrine.

First, it has been argued that in each of the four cases in which a claim for pre-contractual performance was successful, recovery was provided for by an implied contract collateral to that which was the subject of the negotiations. Stoljar examines the basis upon which liability arose in *Brewer Street, William Lacey, Sabemo,* and *British Steel* and concludes:

"Where two parties proceed upon a joint assumption that a contract will be entered into between them, and one does work beneficial for the project, but work which normally is not expected to be done gratuitously, the one party is entitled to compensation if the other decides, unilaterally, to abandon the project not because of any bona fide disagreement but for his own reasons alone.

It should be clear that this final principle, despite its choice of non-contractual language, is . . . decidedly contractual in nature, admitting as it does the parties' agreement that certain preparatory or interim work is to be done for recompense."[35]

In another place Stoljar comments that the claim in these cases was:

". . . an essentially contractual claim, for the simple reason that the claim is both for solicited and renumerative work, being work done in pursuance of an initial agreement."[36]

Stoljar argues that liability in these cases is liability on a collateral contract evinced by the circumstances of the cases.

Second, it has been argued that liability in these cases was not established on the basis of contract *stricto sensu,* but on the basis of a contract-like doctrine concerned with fulfilling the parties' reasonable expectations. Under this approach, a judge presented with a case of pre-contractual reliance must ask whether it would be reasonable to expect the party who has undertaken the pre-contractual performance to do so gratuitously. If it would not be reasonable to expect work of the type undertaken to be provided gratuitously, then the judge should imply a promise to pay. Thus in *William Lacey* an obligation was imposed because:

"The plaintiffs are carrying on a business and, in normal circumstances, if asked to render services of this kind, the obvious inference would be that they ought to be paid for so doing. No one could expect a business firm to do this sort of work for nothing, and again, in normal circumstances, the law would imply a promise to pay on the part of the person who requested the services to be performed."[37]

The argument from reasonable expectations differs from the argument in implied contract in that, whereas the argument in implied contract focuses on the actual intentions of the parties even where it uses reasonable expectations as a means of ascertaining those intentions, the argument from reasonable expectations acknowledges that it is the *law* which is implying the relevant promise to

---

[35] S J Stoljar, *The Law of Quasi-Contract* 2nd edn (Sydney, LBC, 1989) at 244.
[36] Ibid. at 193.
[37] *William Lacey* at 935.

pay and that such a promise cannot be inferred from the behaviour of the parties' themselves. In the words of Barry J in *William Lacey*:

> ". . . the court will look at the true facts and ascertain from them whether or not a promise to pay should be implied, irrespective of the actual views of the parties at the time when the work was done or the services rendered."[38]

The argument from reasonable expectations imposes liability irrespective of the parties' proved intentions.

Before considering the argument from implied contract more fully, the argument from fulfilling the parties' reasonable expectations should briefly be rejected. It is a concept novel to English law that a plaintiff should have the right to be paid whenever it is reasonable that he should be. It is also a concept leading to liability of a very uncertain kind. It is unclear when will it be "reasonable" for a plaintiff to expect payment. It is also telling that the two passages cited from *William Lacey* speak of the law implying a *promise* and not an *obligation* to pay. It may be, despite the avowed independence of this obligation from contractual reasoning, that the courts are actually using reasonable expectations as a means of determining the parties' intentions at the time that the preparatory work was undertaken. If they are, then Stoljar is right, and those intentions ought to be given effect, if at all, by means of the law of contract.

Turning to the argument from implied contract, it is submitted that contract doctrine is unable to explain the facts of the four cases in which there was recovery for pre-contractual performance. While it would always be open to negotiating parties to make a collateral agreement relating to pre-contractual performance, the argument that these decisions were based on contract is flawed for at least three reasons.

First, in each of the decisions contractual reasoning was considered and specifically rejected. It is true that the liability imposed in these cases might, as Stoljar claims, be essentially contractual in nature however the judges expressly classify it. But the express disavowal by so many judges that they are imposing contractual liability ought not lightly to be ignored. Only Somervell and Romer LJJ in *Brewer Street* seem to have based their argument in contract and their contractual reasoning is difficult to justify. As Denning LJ pointed out, any collateral agreement that could have covered the work undertaken in *Brewer Street* was an entire one and the work was never completed.

Second, in *Brewer Street*, as in each of these decisions, it is an odd approach to say that work which was purportedly undertaken in pursuance of an agreement at which the parties never arrived but which they were confident was forthcoming, was in fact undertaken in pursuance of a collateral agreement of which the parties would not even have been aware.[39] In that the parties held

---

[38] Ibid. at 936.
[39] Not only is this an odd approach, but it is difficult to reconcile with the courts' reluctance to imply contracts in contexts in which the parties "might have acted exactly as they did in the absence of a contract" (*The Aramis* [1989] 1 Lloyd's Rep 213 at 224 *per* Bingham LJ).

liable in these cases promised to assume responsibility for the preparatory work, it is submitted that they promised to do so as a part of the responsibilities they were assuming under the anticipated contract and not as a separate obligation. As Barry J put it in *William Lacey* they did not:

> ". . . actually intend to pay for the work otherwise than under the supposed contract, or as a part of the total price which would become payable when the expected contract was made."[40]

Third, a contractual explanation of these decisions is very difficult to reconcile with the apparent flexibility of the principle that was apparently being applied. For example, Somervell LJ in *Brewer Street* claimed that the issue of whether the party at whose request the work was done must pay for it, is in some way (but not always) linked to the issue of whose "fault" it was that negotiations for the principal agreement broke down. In this, he said, "[e]ach case must be judged on its own circumstances."[41] The value of this approach based on "fault" will be considered below. At this point it is important to highlight the impact of such "fault" considerations upon a contractual explanation of the cases. The contractual argument becomes even more tenuous if the courts must imply into the parties' purported collateral agreement an undertaking to pay for preparatory work only if negotiations for the principal contract break down on particular grounds. And it cannot help to claim, as Stoljar does,[42] that this is essentially contractual liability mitigated by a general duty of good faith in contractual bargaining. There is no hint in the cases that the judges intended to introduce such a general duty;[43] nor is it clear why the breach of such a duty in relation to negotiations for one contract, should *prima facie* render void a collateral contract providing for payment for interim performance.

The majority of the judges in *Brewer Street*, *William Lacey*, *Sabemo* and *British Steel* would seem justified in their claim that the liability imposed in those cases was essentially non-contractual in nature. Moreover, it is submitted that, in absence of a clear collateral agreement, it is undesirable to force the facts of cases concerning work undertaken during pre-contractual negotiations into a contractual framework.

---

[40] *William Lacey* at 939.
[41] *Brewer Street* at 434.
[42] S J Stoljar, *The Law of Quasi-Contract* 2nd edn (Sydney, LBC, 1989) at 244.
[43] Moreover, *Walford v Miles* [1992] 2 AC 128 at 138 implicitly rejects the concept. In *Walford v Miles* a negotiating party sought damages for breach of an alleged contract collateral to the contract for which he was negotiating, an agreement for the purchase of a business. It was argued that under the alleged collateral contract the party selling the business had agreed not to enter into negotiations for its sale with anyone other than the party alleging the contract and had also agreed to conduct negotiations with that party in good faith. The alleged contract was said to be operative for a reasonable time period. The House of Lords found that, if any such a contract could be proved, it was void for uncertainty.

(b) Tort and work undertaken in anticipation of contract

It is clear that in none of the pre-contractual reliance cases did the courts rely upon arguments in deceit or negligent misstatement. As might be expected, none of these cases involved a misrepresentation of fact to which those doctrines could attach. Nevertheless, two tort-like arguments were made in the cases and have attracted academic comment. These arguments focus on the concepts of "risk-allocation" and "fault", concepts very familiar to tort lawyers.

First, an argument of "risk-allocation" was enunciated in *Brewer Street*[44] and taken up in cases such as *Sabemo*.[45] This approach centres on the question of who should bear the risk of loss. It is unclear, however, what these cases mean when they speak of "risk" and in particular whether they could possibly mean the risk of loss through accidental damage with which tort lawyers are familiar. Stoljar explains:

> "What this [approach] overlooks is that the 'risk' now spoken of is not the sort of risk we know in the law of torts, nor indeed a special risk peculiar to restitution; in fact, when everything is said, the so-called risk as it arises in present circumstances is simply the risk we run where an agreement in which nothing is said about remuneration might yet be construed as remunerative, particularly where the work done during that agreement cannot be considered to be gratuitous."[46]

If this is the "risk" to which cases such as *Brewer Street* and *Sabemo* are referring, then the question as to who should bear that risk is simply a reformulated version of the question of who should be liable to pay for pre-contractual preparations, the very question at issue in these cases. The concept of "risk" does not then provide any telling reason why one party should bear the cost of those preparations rather than another and begs the question that is central to these decisions.

Second, an argument concerned with "fault" has also been important to these cases.[47] This approach does not seek to establish a generalised duty of good faith in bargaining. Nevertheless, it does involve the judge asking whose "fault" it might be that pre-contractual negotiations have broken down and allocates liability for the cost of pre-contractual preparations to that party. It is submitted that this approach is far from ideal because "fault" in the breakdown of pre-contractual negotiations is very difficult to identify. Jones writes:

> "It may be . . . unhelpful to conclude that the plaintiff or defendant was or was not 'at fault.' Fault is a slippery and pejorative concept; for example, is a defendant at fault if he withdraws because of an unexpected financial reversal?"[48]

---

[44] *Brewer Street* at 437.

[45] *Sabemo* at 893 and 901.

[46] S J Stoljar, *The Law of Quasi-Contract* 2nd edn (Sydney, LBC, 1989) at 243–244.

[47] See, for example, *Brewer Street* at 434 *per* Somervell LJ, at 437 *per* Denning LJ, at 438–439 *per* Romer LJ and *Sabemo* at 900 *per* Sheppard J.

[48] G Jones, "Services Arising out of Anticipated Contracts which do not Materialize" (1980) 18 *U Western Ontario L Rev* 447 at 454.

Brewer Street provides a good example of the uncertainty of the concept of fault. In this case Denning LJ found that neither the plaintiffs nor the defendants were at fault while Somervell and Romer LJJ claimed that only the plaintiffs were "innocent". It will be recalled that the defendants had wanted to lease certain property with an option to purchase it within sixty days of signing the lease. The plaintiffs were only prepared to grant a lease coupled with a right of first refusal. While negotiations were underway, the plaintiffs undertook certain alterations to the property at the request of the defendants. Somervell LJ claimed:

> "It is plain that the matter went off because of the defendant's own course of conduct in adhering to the condition that they should get an option when it had been made clear to them that the plaintiffs were not willing to grant an option."[49]

Yet surely to adopt such a position is to expose negotiating parties to the constant risk of being found "at fault" for the failure of particular negotiations. There are almost no negotiations in which at least one of the parties involved does not wish to persuade the other to move from a position which he adopts at the beginning of the process. If "fault" lies in failing to realise early enough that the other party is not going to change position, then it is very difficult to know when "fault" will arise. Moreover, each of the parties is usually trying to persuade the other to his point of view. Why was the "fault" in *Brewer Street* with the defendants for failing to realise that they would only be granted a right of first refusal and not with the plaintiffs for failing to realise that the defendants would not take the lease without the option? It is little wonder that the judges in this case were not able to determine whether any fault arose at all, or that Somervell LJ conceded that "the area is somewhat difficult".[50] "Fault" is simply too unstable a concept to provide a solution to the pre-contractual performance problem.

(c) Restitution and work undertaken in anticipation of contract

A third approach to the problem of work undertaken in anticipation of contracts that do not materialise is based on the principle of restitution for unjust enrichment. This approach has enjoyed some academic popularity. However, although resitution may provide a satisfactory solution in many cases involving pre-contractual performance, it is unable to account for all such cases, and indeed, for many of the major reported decisions. In this sense it is like the contractual explanation of these cases considered above. In order to justify such a proposition, it will be necessary to consider at some length the rather complex restitutionary accounts of these cases which have emerged in recent years.

[49] *Brewer Street* at 434.
[50] Ibid. at 434.

The unjust enrichment theorists begin by rebutting the implied contract explanation of cases such as *Brewer Street*, *William Lacey*, *Sabemo* and *British Steel*. Those cases deal, they claim, with obligations imposed at law, rather than with contracts to pay a reasonable sum implied in fact: ". . . the concept of implied contract is, in this context, a meaningless, irrelevant and misleading anachronism."[51] They then claim that the obligation imposed in these cases does not begin with the intention of the parties but with the fact of an unjust enrichment of the defendant at the expense of the plaintiff. Wherever the defendant has been unjustly enriched at the plaintiff's expense, he must make restitution of that enrichment or its value in money. The receipt of a benefit by the defendant thus both partly justifies and measures the *quantum meruit* obligation on a rationale similar to that underpinning the action for money had and received.

The central difficulty with this approach to the pre-contractual performance cases is that the relevant pre-contractual performance will often not benefit the party requesting its provision in any immediately apparent way. For example, in *Brewer Street* it is hard to see how the prospective lessees were benefitted by alterations made to a property in which they had never had any interest. Indeed, the defendants' counsel stressed that the cost of the alterations ought to have fallen on the prospective lessors and not the prospective lessees precisely because it was the prospective lessors who benefitted by improvements carried out to their own property. In *Jennings*, a case with facts very similar to those in *Brewer Street*, it was said that because the prospective sublessee was never able to take possession of the property and the improvements that he had requested, he had "never, of course, had the slightest benefit or interest in these works."[52]

This difficulty in identifying a "benefit" of which restitution can be made is particularly acute in situations in which the pre-contractual performance has consisted in, and compensation is sought for, the provision of some service. Services do not automatically fit into the concepts of "benefit" or "enrichment". They cannot be restored *in specie*, they may not have any worth independent of that at which the recipient values them, and they need not even result in an end product that has a clear or easily realisable exchange value. Goff and Jones admit that "[t]he receipt of money always benefits the defendant. But *services* may not do so."[53]

In order to overcome this problem in the analysis of *Jennings*, *Brewer Street*, *William Lacey*, *Sabemo* and *British Steel*, Birks relies upon the concept of "free acceptance".[54] Birks argues that "free acceptance" can be used by a plaintiff to

---

[51] Lord Goff of Chieveley and G Jones, *The Law of Restitution* 4th edn (London, Sweet & Maxwell, 1993) at 10.

[52] *Jennings* at 413 *per* Somervell LJ.

[53] Lord Goff of Chieveley and G Jones, *The Law of Restitution* 4th edn (London, Sweet & Maxwell, 1993) at 18.

[54] P Birks, *An Introduction to the Law of Restitution* revised edn (Oxford, Clarendon Press, 1989) at Ch VIII. Note that in *Brewer Street* and *Jennings* even the application of "free acceptance" reasoning requires some degree of ingenuity on Birks's part. He deals with each case by turning it

establish that services rendered were a benefit to the defendant, to overcome what he calls the problem of "subjective devaluation". He argues that if the defendant freely accepted the services, he must have considered them a benefit at the time of their provision and so cannot now deny that they were. Birks also argues that "free acceptance" can sometimes be used to show that the retention of a benefit would be unjust. On the basis of the concept he then develops a three stage pattern of "weak" unjust enrichment. For that pattern to apply:

> (a) the recipient must have requested or acquiesced in the doing of the work; (b) he must have known that the work was not intended to be gratuitous; and (c) the events which have happened must not be events whose risk was borne by the intervener.[55]

It will be clear that each of these criteria will often be satisfied in a context of performance rendered during pre-contractual negotiations. Thus, if the weak unjust enrichment pattern can be accepted, a restitutionary analysis of the existing pre-contractual performance cases may well be possible. Conversely, if unjust enrichment is inadequate to provide an explanation of the pre-contractual performance cases, it must be because of some inherent difficulty with the concept of "free acceptance" itself.[56]

I would argue that there is indeed an inherent difficulty with the concept of free acceptance and that the pattern of "weak" unjust enrichment is an inadequate way of describing many of the pre-contractual performance cases, in particular those involving the provision of services. This difficulty is that "free acceptance" masks in restitutionary language a justification for the imposition of obligation on a basis other than benefit or enrichment. Under the "free acceptance" analysis, whether that concept is being used at the "unjust" or the "benefit" stage of restitutionary reasoning, "acceptance" or "consent" is doing the work of distinguishing between situations in which liability will arise and

---

on its head and dealing with it, not as raising issues about why the plaintiff prospective landlord is or is not entitled to a remedy for work done to his own property, but rather as a case dealing with why the landlord is or is not himself liable for the benefit which he has received. The assumption seems to be that in a case where the would-be landlord would not have been liable if the prospective tenant had himself provided the benefit to the landlord's property, the tenant ought to be liable if the landlord renders that benefit and *vice versa*. This is all very well in that reciprocity of rights between situations in which the landlord and the tenant render the relevant benefit is generally desirable. Yet it almost openly abandons the claim that the landlord's rights are somehow based in an unjust enrichment of the plaintiff. It does not solve the problem that *Brewer Street* involves recovery by a party providing services in a context in which only he, if anyone, can be said to receive a benefit.

[55] P Birks, "Restitution for Services", [1974] *Current Leg Prob* 13 at 30.

[56] Slightly different, but essentially similar to this concept of "free acceptance", at least in relation to the "benefit" stage of unjust enrichment reasoning, is Burrows' notion of the "bargained for" benefit. Burrows claims that at the level of establishing a benefit, "free acceptance" is inadequate to overcome the problem of subjective devaluation because it may be that a person who accepts a service does not regard it as a benefit but is merely indifferent to whether or not it is performed. For this reason he intensifies the concept and requires that the defendant actually has "bargained for" the service or other benefit he receives. See A Burrows, "Free Acceptance and the Law of Restitution", (1988) 104 *LQR* 576.

those in which it will not. It is surely therefore fictional to say that "benefit" is the source of the relevant obligation.

Indeed, that such a claim is fictional has often been acknowledged. Beatson claims that cases such as *Brewer Street* and *British Steel* are concerned with "consent", "acquiescence", "reliance", "fault" and "risk" rather than "enrichment" or "benefit", and that grouping cases dependent upon "consent" or "acquiescence" with cases dependent upon "benefit" does not "succeed in grouping together most "like" cases and separating most "unlike" cases."[57] He points out that "[n]ot even a relatively broad use of "enrichment"/"receipt" justifies the treatment of the remedy in cases such as . . . *Sabemo* v *North Sydney MC* as based on the defendant's "receipt" or "enrichment"."[58] Similarly, Hedley writes of the "free acceptance" cases:

> "[The defendant] is liable because he created an expectation of payment and encouraged detrimental reliance on that expectation. We can describe this as Contract, or as Restitution, or as both together, but to describe it as 'benefit' is simply a random departure from the meaning of that word."[59]

One way in which unjust enrichment theorists have tried to avoid the obvious artificiality of the "free acceptance" approach to restitution has been simply to ignore the most obvious practical issue arising from their analysis. Jones admits that "free acceptance" is just an extended notion of "request".[60] Therefore the question obviously arising when "free acceptance" is used either at the unjust or benefit stage of restitutionary reasoning is just how much "request", "acquiescence", "bargain" or "consent" is necessary to render something a benefit and thus the source of an obligation. Yet Mead points out that Birks fails to explain what steps a recipient must go to in order that he will not come under an obligation to pay and that Birks' notion of a "reasonable opportunity to reject" does not satisfactorily answer this dilemma because of its inherent uncertainty.[61] By failing to give this crucial question its real weight, writers such as Birks deflect attention from the process of acceptance itself and thus from the artificiality of claiming that cases focused upon "acceptance" or "consent" are really about "benefit" and "enrichment".

In view of this inherent problem with the concept of "free acceptance", I would argue that restitutionary reasoning may satisfactorily provide an answer to some situations of pre-contractual performance (for example, where money has been paid from one party to another during the course of pre-contractual negotiations) but that it is unable to do so in all such situations (for example, where the pre-contractual performance has primarily consisted in the provision

---

[57] J Beatson, "Benefit, Reliance and the Structure of Unjust Enrichment", [1987] *Current Leg Prob* 71 at 79 and *The Use and Abuse of Unjust Enrichment* (Oxford, Clarendon Press, 1991) Ch.2.

[58] Ibid. at 81.

[59] S Hedley, "Unjust Enrichment as the Basis of Restitution – An Overworked Concept", (1985) 5 *LS* 56 at 63.

[60] G Jones, "Restitutionary Claims for Services Rendered", (1977) 93 *LQR* 273 at 295.

[61] G Mead, "Free Acceptance: Some Further Considerations", (1989) 105 *LQR* 460 at 464.

of services). In particular, I would argue that it is unable to provide a convincing explanation of the most important existing cases in this area.

In addition, some of the pre-contractual negotiations exemplify a further difficulty with a restitutionary solution to reliance upon anticipated, apparent or unenforceable agreements. This is the difficulty, suggested above, that a restitutionary solution may unfairly prioritise the interests of the party who has rendered the alleged benefit over those of the party who has received it. Take, for example, the situation in *British Steel*. In that case there was a disparity between the way in which the plaintiffs and defendants were treated that is at best difficult to justify. The reasonable value of the services supplied by the plaintiffs was assessed as a price for the nodes including a reasonable profit element. Accordingly, the plaintiffs received "approximately what [they] always expected".[62] The defendants, however, were left without a remedy because they were unable to establish any contractual or restitutionary claim. The defendants had suffered substantial losses because of the plaintiffs' defective performance which was left to go unremedied, while the plaintiffs were allowed to profit from the project. The only alternative open to the defendants would have been to reject the nodes altogether but, as Ball notes, that would hardly have helped them to build a bank in Saudi Arabia.[63] A restitutionary treatment of a case such as *British Steel* may lack the subtlety needed to treat both plaintiff and defendant justly. Possible solutions to this problem drawn from the law of restitution itself are considered below in the section of this chapter dealing with the "battle of forms". In this section, *British Steel* is used simply to illustrate that the problem would not even arise if the situation of reliance upon anticipated, apparent or unenforceable agreements were resolved by the application of equitable estoppel.

(d) Equitable estoppel and work undertaken in anticipation of contract

I turn, therefore, from considering the three current explanations of the pre-contractual negotiation cases to consider whether the doctrine of equitable estoppel might on the same facts more easily justify the results given in those cases, or perhaps dictate a more suitable result.

(i) *Jennings, Brewer Street, William Lacey, Construction Design & Management and Sabemo*

First I will consider cases in which the doctrine of equitable estoppel could justify the results actually given in the cases more satisfactorily than the reasoning there employed. *Jennings* and *Brewer Street* will be examined and then *William*

---

[62] S N Ball, "Work Carried out in Pursuance of Letters of Intent – Contract or Restitution?", (1983) 99 *LQR* 572 at 577.
[63] Ibid. at 577.

Lacey, Construction Design & Management, and *Sabemo*. These two provide useful groups of cases because each group consists of cases of contrasting results on almost identical facts. It is therefore interesting to see whether the application of equitable estoppel would also lead to contrasting results in these cases and, if so, whether it is able to provide a coherent justification for those differing outcomes.

It will be recalled that *Jennings* and *Brewer Street* each involved alterations to property by prospective lessors in anticipation of a lease into which the parties did not eventually enter. In *Jennings* this was because a head lessor, whose consent was required, failed to approve the proposed alterations. In *Brewer Street* this was because of an inability to agree terms.

Applying equitable estoppel to the facts of these cases, a judge would first have to identify the actual assumptions induced in the cases. In each case, the prospective lessees induced the prospective lessors to start work on alterations to a property in reliance upon an assumption that the prospective lessees would bear their cost. In *Brewer Street* it is relatively clear that the assumption induced was that the lessors would be paid whether or not the lease went ahead.[64] For example, as Romer LJ pointed out, some of the work was paid for directly by the prospective lessees without any suggestion that such payment was to be conditional.[65] In *Jennings* the assumption induced seems to have been simply that the lessor would pay, without any contemplation that the lease might not go ahead.

Having identified the relevant assumption, a judge applying equitable estoppel would then have to consider the reliance and detriment issues. Reliance may be presumed in the manner described in Chapter Two. In any case, in both fact situations the alterations made to the property were to the specific requirements of the potential lessees, a fact which is emphasised in *Brewer Street*, and so it is likely that the alterations were undertaken in reliance upon the assumption of payment. Further, in each case the detriment suffered by the prospective lessors was easily quantifiable.

A judge applying the doctrine of equitable estoppel on these facts would finally have to determine whether it would be unconscionable in each case for the prospective lessees not to remedy the detriment suffered by the prospective lessors.

In doing so the judge would have to balance the factors determining the question of unconscionability. He would have to weigh those factors which, on the facts of the case, would lead to a finding of unconscionability, against those which, on the facts of the case, would militate against such a finding.

---

[64] *Brewer Street* at 432–433 *per* Somervell LJ, at 438 *per* Romer LJ. The idea that the defendant might not have been liable if the negotiations had been broken off by the plaintiff is only dealt with as a defence. If the case were to be treated as one raising an equitable estoppel, it could be said that the assumption was clearly that the plaintiff would be paid for the pre-contractual performance even if nothing came of the negotiations, and that the subsequent behaviour of the parties was going to unconscionability.

[65] *Brewer Street* at 438.

I shall first consider, therefore, those factors which in these cases might support a finding of unconscionability. In relation to the mode of inducement, in each case this was by express representation and thus more likely to give rise to liability in equitable estoppel than it would have been had it been by a less direct mode of inducement. In relation to the parties' relative interest in the activities in reliance, in each case it was the potential lessees who were most interested in the relevant activities in reliance. In *Brewer Street*, just as in *Waltons*, the party inducing the assumption was insistent that the work on the premises be completed by a specific time, which time-frame put great pressure on the negotiations. As Romer LJ emphasised:

> "The truth of the matter is that [the prospective lessees] were in a very great hurry to get into these premises because the lease of their own premises was running out, and because of that hurry they did things which in the normal course they would not have done."[66]

In relation to the context of the inducement, although these were commercial negotiations, neither party anticipated any problem with the lease going ahead and the context was one of trust and close co-operation. Finally, it is significant that in neither case did the party inducing the assumption take any steps at all to ensure that it did not cause preventible harm. For example, in neither case did the party inducing the assumption warn the party relying upon it that it was not their intention to pay for the works if the lease were not negotiated.

In summary of this first group of criteria I would suggest that, at least in *Brewer Street*, the strong interest of the prospective lessees in the relevant activities in reliance, together with their express inducement of an assumption that the alterations would be paid for (probably even if the negotiations never came to fruition) could lead to a *prima facie* conclusion that it would be unconscionable for them not to remedy the detriment that the lessors had suffered by reliance. The remedy *prima facie* available would be the cost of the alterations, the remedy in fact awarded in *Brewer Street*.

Considering those factors which might militate against a such finding of unconscionability, a judge using equitable estoppel to decide these cases might turn first to the issue of the content of the induced assumption. In each case the induced assumption was one of intention, which type of assumption we have seen ought less often to give rise to liability in estoppel. Against this, however, must be weighed the fact that, at least in *Brewer Street*, the prospective lessees did not give any indication that they might possibly change their mind, that the induced assumption related to a mere reversible intention. On the contrary, they stressed the urgency of the completion of the work. This was not a situation in which the induced asssumption related to some general plan for the future.

However, there is also a second factor which might militate against a finding of unconscionability in these cases. Indeed, I would argue that this second fac-

---

[66] *Brewer Street* at 438.

tor actually accounts for their differing results. This factor is the relative knowledge of the parties. In *Brewer Street* both the parties had equal knowledge of
the likelihood of the reliance leading to the prospective lessors' detriment. In
Jennings, however, the parties were not in so equal a position as regards knowledge. Only the prospective sublessors knew that the alterations to the property
were subject to approval by a head lessor, and thus only the prospective sublessors knew that there was a very real possibility that the lease would not be
finally negotiated. This knowledge would have seriously undermined the
prospective sublessee's interest in the relevant activities in reliance, the most
important of those factors counting towards a finding of unconscionability in a
case such as *Brewer Street*. Somervell LJ said:

> "[The prospective sublessee] had not the slightest interest in agreeing with what
> should be done in these premises unless he was going to be the sublessee of them, and
> that must have been obvious to the plaintiff."[67]

Indeed, not only did the knowledge of the risk undermine the prospective
sublessee's interest in the activities in reliance, it may well have suggested that
the relevant activities were primarily in the prospective sublessors' interest.
Denning LJ said:

> "The plaintiffs were doing work on their own property which might perhaps be of
> some use to them if the underlease was not granted, but could be of no possible use to
> the solicitor unless it was granted."[68]

The relative knowledge of these parties might thus be seen to outweigh their relative interest in the relevant activities in reliance.

I would argue, therefore, that in the balancing of criteria involved in the application of equitable estoppel, a judge deciding *Brewer Street* might award a remedy laying particular emphasis on the parties' relative interest in the activities in
reliance. But equally, a judge deciding *Jennings* could argue that the issue of the
parties' relative interest in the activities in reliance took second place to the issue
of their relative knowledge, and thus, all else being equal, that liability ought not
to arise. Equitable estoppel might therefore more neatly account for these decisions and the difference between them than any of the alternative explanations
set out above.

Having seen how equitable estoppel might be deployed on the facts of
Jennings and *Brewer Street*, we turn to consider whether it might similarly be
deployed on those of *William Lacey*, *Construction Design & Management* and
Sabemo.

It will be recalled that each of these cases involved negotiations for building
projects. In each case the party who was to carry out the building undertook
considerably more work in preparing plans and other documents for the party
proposing the development than might normally be expected. In *William Lacey*,

---

[67] *Jennings* at 413.
[68] Ibid. at 414.

where the relevant pre-contractual reliance involved preparing estimates of the cost of rebuilding for submission to a grant making body, the War Damages Commission, the negotiations did not give rise to a contract because the party proposing the development sold the premises instead of proceeding with the reconstruction. In *Construction Design & Management* the party which was to carry out the building decided not to proceed with its bid for the project. In *Sabemo* the party proposing the development, a local council, changed its plans for political reasons. As to remedies, in *William Lacey* the party which was to carry out the building was awarded the reasonable value of its services, in *Sabemo* no award was made but the judge suggested that an appropriate award would have been Sabemo's costs in preparing the various building schemes, and in *Construction Design & Management* the plaintiffs were unable to establish any liability on the part of the defendants.

In applying equitable estoppel to these cases a judge would again have to identify an assumption induced by the defendants upon which the plaintiffs may be said to have relied. This is an important enquiry and it divides these cases from the outset.[69]

In *William Lacey* the assumption induced was that the plaintiffs would be remunerated for their pre-contractual performance only under the terms of the anticipated contract, but that the anticipated contract would certainly eventuate. In *Sabemo* the assumption induced was that the anticipated contract would go ahead unless there was a "bona fide failure to reach agreement on some point of substance in such a complex transaction."[70] Sheppard J found that the parties understood that an agreement might not eventuate but that the assumption induced by the council was that it would not simply change its mind. Moreover, he found that the detriment for which the plaintiffs were claiming relief arose because this particular assumption, that the Council would not simply change its mind, proved unjustified and that agreement would otherwise have been reached.[71] In *Construction Design & Management* there was neither the assumption induced that the plaintiffs would be paid for their pre-contractual performance, nor the assumption induced that a contract would necessarily eventuate.

This distinction between the assumptions induced in the various decisions is important because it shows why liability would not arise in *Construction Design & Management* even were a judge to apply the doctrine of equitable estoppel. The plaintiffs in that case could not rely upon an assumption that they would be remunerated for the work they did, even that they would be remunerated under an eventual contract for construction, because such an assumption was never induced. As Hughes CJNB put it:

---

[69] It also, I would suggest, distinguishes them from *Brewer Street*, in which the assumption induced was that the defendants would bear the cost of the alterations no matter what happened in relation to the central contract.

[70] *Sabemo* at 901.

[71] Ibid. at 901.

"The distinction between the *Lacey* case and the one which we are considering is that in the former the unqualified understanding of both parties was that the building was to be constructed and the plaintiff was to be given the contract . . . In the instant case the understanding was qualified."[72]

Leaving this case to one side, therefore, we turn to *William Lacey* and *Sabemo*. In these decisions, reliance and detriment would be relatively easy to establish, even without the aid of the presumption regarding reliance. In *William Lacey* the plaintiffs would not have undertaken the preparation of the estimates if they had not been led to believe that they would be given a contract. In *Sabemo*, while the plaintiffs may have undertaken the relevant work even in light of the chance that a contract would not have eventuated, it was "unthinkable that the plaintiff[s] would have been prepared to do what [they] did, if [they] had thought that the defendant might change its mind about proceeding with the proposal."[73] In each case the plaintiffs had incurred costs in, and lost alternative income by, working on building plans for the defendants. In *Sabemo* the work had gone on for three years.

Reliance and detriment thus established, a judge applying the doctrine of equitable estoppel on the facts of these cases would then have to consider the question of unconscionability. Would it be unconscionable in either case for the defendant not to remedy the detriment suffered by the plaintiffs by reason of their reliance upon the assumption induced?

Starting with *William Lacey* and those aspects of the facts that could count towards a finding of unconscionability, it might be highlighted that the relevant assumption was induced by express representation. It might then be emphasised that the relevant activities in reliance were clearly in the interests of the inducing party. Not only was the work performed at the request of the inducing party but he was able to use the estimates prepared by the plaintiffs to increase the value of the property on sale. It is also clear that the defendant knew that the plaintiffs were relying upon the assumption that the contract would be granted, and for at least some of the relevant period perhaps also knew that he would not be proceeding with the work.[74] However he took no steps to avoid the possible detriment that the plaintiffs would suffer by assuming that the project was going ahead.

Against these factors pointing towards a finding of unconscionability, a judge deciding this case on the basis of equitable estoppel would have to weigh the fact that the parties were of apparently equal bargaining power and the fact that the assumption upon which reliance was placed was an assumption relating to the

---

[72] *Construction Design & Management* at 646.

[73] *Sabemo* at 901.

[74] This is the factual issue which I would suggest actually swayed the court in *William Lacey* but which is nowhere directly addressed in the decision. The implication that the defendant never intended to proceed with the re-building work may be drawn from the fact that it told the plaintiff that another firm of builders was being given the work when, in fact, it sold the premises. Presumably, had it been possible to prove that the defendant did not actually ever intend to undertake the rebuilding, an action would have been available in deceit.

future. Balancing this latter consideration, however, was the fact that the assumption was not one as to general future plans but one upon which the defendant could already be seen to be taking action, that is, submitting estimates to the War Damage Commission.

Weighing these two sets of factors against each other, I would argue that a judge deciding *William Lacey* on the basis of equitable estoppel may well arrive at a finding of unconscionability. If he did, he would then have to determine what remedy he might apply in the decision.

In examining remedy I would argue that a judge applying equitable estoppel could enunciate far more clearly the reason for his award than did Barry J in his judgment. Rather elusively, Barry J said:

> "The plaintiffs are entitled to a fair renumeration for the work which they have done, but they cannot, in my view, quantify their charges by reference to professional scales."[75]

What it seems Barry J was driving it, was that the plaintiffs were not entitled to expectation damages for the work they had done. They were not entitled to charge what they could usually expect to be paid for providing these estimates. Even on the basis of equitable estoppel their *prima facie* remedy would be reliance damages calculated on the "narrower" basis from *Verwayen*,[76] in other words compensation for the actual cost of providing the services. A judge considering the facts on the basis of equitable estoppel could set out more clearly both the reasons for his award and the justification of its amount.

Turning finally to *Sabemo*, a judge would find facts which, on the application of equitable estoppel, would as clearly demand a remedy as did those in *Brewer Street* and *William Lacey*. While equitable estoppel could be used to justify the result given on the facts of *Sabemo*, it would also enable a judge to compare the case more closely with the facts in *Brewer Street*, upon which decision the judge who decided the case actually based his reasoning.

Considering first those factors which might lead to a finding of unconscionability in this case, the most important is the length of the relationship between the plaintiffs and the defendant. The assumption that the defendant was committed to the building project was reinforced by three years of trust and co-operation. Yet throughout these three years the defendant took no steps at all to prevent the plaintiff from suffering harm. There was no suggestion at all that the council might change its mind. It seems to have been this history of trust which particularly impressed the judge in the decision.

Added to this factor might be the fact that the work was in the interests of the council and undertaken at its special request. Sheppard J highlighted the fact that the pre-contractual performance was in the interests of the council in that it was leading to a project:

---

[75] *William Lacey* at 940.
[76] See above at pp. 68–69.

"... which would give it adequate accommodation for its various activities free from any obligation to pay therefor, and with the knowledge that, in due course of time when the lease expired, all would revert to it."[77]

Against this would have to be set the fact that the work was also in the interests of the plaintiffs in that it was leading to a project from which Sabemo hoped to make a substantial profit.

Factors telling against a finding of unconscionability in this case might include the fact that the plaintiffs were at no time expressly assured that the council would not change its mind. At best the assurance was made impliedly, although admittedly over the course of three years. Moreover, these were large commercial negotiations. The parties must be presumed to have had equal knowledge that the defendant was under no legal obligation to continue with the project and that as a local council it was subject to political vicissitudes. Sheppard J acknowledged:

"It is true that the defendant is a council the members of which are elected from time to time, and that, therefore, it might not be expected necessarily to be as consistent in its approach to problems as a different sort of undertaking."[78]

It will be equally evident from the preceding two paragraphs both that equitable estoppel could be used to justify the decision in *Sabemo* and that a finding of unconscionability would not *necessarily* be the result were that doctrine applied and the issues brought to light by that doctrine more carefully considered. What should be clear from this discussion, however, is that analysing the case in terms of the doctrine of equitable estoppel would allow a judge to analyse the facts far more carefully than did a simple application by analogy of the decision in *Brewer Street*.

Were the doctrine of equitable estoppel in fact applied successfully to this case it would probably yield the remedy which was, in fact, suggested by the judge. Sheppard J suggested that the plaintiffs were entitled to the:

"... direct cost to [them] of preparing the various plans and models, and attending the various conferences which were held with the defendant and other authorities in connection with the planning and design of the project."[79]

This is clearly the reliance measure of relief.

(ii) British Steel

At this point we should turn from pre-contractual negotiation cases in which the application of equitable estoppel could justify the result achieved in each case, to a case in which the application of the doctrine could arguably have led to a more satisfactory result. That case is *British Steel*.

---

[77] *Sabemo* at 901.
[78] Ibid. at 901.
[79] Ibid. at 903.

It will be recalled that an important feature of this decision is the disparity with which the plaintiff and defendant were treated. The plaintiff steel company received the reasonable value of the nodes supplied. The defendant engineering company was left without remedy, although the nodes had been supplied late and in a sequence that inconvenienced them, and although some of the nodes were of an unsatisfactory quality. Equitable estoppel could prove a useful doctrine in this situation. It could equip the law to treat parties in the position of the plaintiffs and defendants in *British Steel* with greater parity.

A party in the position of British Steel, who had tendered defective goods or services in the course of pre-contractual negotiations, may well be able to claim payment on the basis of equitable estoppel. That party could well claim that the other party had induced an assumption that he would be paid for the work undertaken and that he had relied on that assumption by commencing work. Provided that all the requirements of the doctrine outlined in Chapter Two were met, there is no reason why that doctrine ought not to provide compensation to the party who has relied upon the assumption that he would be paid. Of course, that compensation would normally be in the reliance, and not in the expectation, measure. But, given that the party undertaking the work has failed to secure the reward for his work that he expects in contractual negotiation, there is good reason for the law to be reluctant to award him more than the reliance measure.

More importantly, however, equitable estoppel could also provide a remedy to the party who had received the defective goods or services in the course of contractual negotiations. Defendants in the position of Cleveland Bridge & Engineering will often suffer damage as a result of reliance upon assumptions induced by the other party to pre-contractual negotiations regarding the timing or quality of pre-contractual performance. Provided that all the requirements of the doctrine described in Chapter Two are met, there is no reason why that doctrine ought not to provide compensation to protect this reliance so that the party who is required to make payment for defective goods or services (on the basis of equitable estoppel or otherwise) will have a counter-claim to make. Of course, this compensation will not *prima facie* be compensation in the expectation measure, but neither will the party who has provided the defective goods or services be likely to receive compensation in that measure.

The facts of *British Steel* are presented in the report in insufficient detail to examine how successful a claim in equitable estoppel might have been for either this plaintiff or defendant. Nevertheless, it is clear that approaching the case on the basis of equitable estoppel would have given rise to a result more just in its treatment of both plaintiff and defendant than was the result actually awarded.

It is submitted therefore, that equitable estoppel would be a useful addition to the treatment of pre-contractual negotiation cases. It both offers a convincing justification of many of the existing cases in which remedies have been awarded on an otherwise inexplicable basis, and could have provided a better guide to a result in at least one of those decisions.

3. THE "BATTLE OF FORMS"

As Atiyah points out, the battle of forms "which must be extremely common in practice, has rarely been litigated in England."[80] Almost all discussion of the battle of forms both in England and Australia has focussed on just one decision, *Butler Machine Tool Co Ltd* v *Ex-Cell-O Corp (England) Ltd*,[81] which is the only appellate decision dealing with the problem.

In *Butler Machine Tool* the sellers of a certain machine offered to deliver it to the buyers ten months from the date of the offer for a provisional price of £75,535. The offer came with a particular set of terms including a price variation clause. Under the price variation clause, the final cost of the machine was to be determined at the time of delivery.

The prospective buyers of the machine wrote accepting the sellers' offer but in terms which "could not be reconciled in any way" with those contained in the sellers' quotation.[82] Most importantly, the purported acceptance contained no price variation clause; but there were also other material differences between the two sets of terms. For example, the purported acceptance:

  (i) provided for installation as an additional item at a cost of £3,100,
 (ii) provided for delivery within ten to eleven months, while the sellers' standard terms provided for delivery in just ten,
(iii) stipulated that the price of the goods included the cost of delivery to the buyers' premises while the sellers' standard terms had allocated this cost to the buyers,
 (iv) provided that the buyers would be entitled to cancel for delay in delivery while the sellers' standard terms had expressly provided that no liability for delay would be accepted and that cancellation of the order could only be effected with the express consent of the sellers, and
  (v) provided that the buyers would be entitled to reject the goods if they were found to be faulty, while this type of liability had been expressly excluded under the sellers' standard terms.

The purported acceptance had a tear-off acknowledgment for signature and return. The sellers returned the slip with a covering letter stating that delivery was to be "in accordance with [their] revised quotation . . . for delivery within 10/11 months."

---

[80] P S Atiyah, *An Introduction to the Law of Contract* 5th edn (Oxford, Clarendon Press, 1995) at 66.

[81] *Butler Machine Tool Co Ltd* v *Ex-Cell-O Corp (England) Ltd* [1979] 1 WLR 401 (hereafter "*Butler Machine Tool*"). Other recent cases in the area include *BRS* v *Arthur Crutchley & Co* [1968] 1 All ER 811, *OTM Ltd* v *Hydranautics* [1981] 2 Lloyd's Rep 211, *Uniroyal Ltd* v *Miller & Co Ltd* [1985] SLT 101, *Sauter Automation Ltd* v *Goodman (Mechanical Services) Ltd* (1986) 34 Build LR 81, *Chichester Joinery Ltd* v *John Mowlem & Co Plc* (1987) 42 Build LR 100, *Buchanan* v *Brook Walker & Co Ltd* [1988] NI 116 and *Rutterford Ltd* v *Allied Breweries* [1990] SCLR 186.

[82] *Butler Machine Tool* at 405 *per* Lawton LJ.

The machine was ready for delivery five months late, and the buyers had to reorganise their production schedule. Accordingly, they were unable to take delivery of the machine until seven months after the anticipated delivery date. The sellers sought to rely on the price variation clause contained in their original offer to charge a price commensurate with the value of the machine as at eighteen months after their original offer. The buyers argued that no price variation clause had been agreed and that the cost of the machine was £75,535. The sellers brought an action for £2,892 allegedly due under the price variation clause of the contract of sale.

Both the trial judge and Court of Appeal sought contractual solutions to this problem. The trial judge found for the sellers and awarded them the £2,892 they claimed. The Court of Appeal reversed this decision, finding that a contract had been concluded on the buyers' terms and that no additional payment was due.

(a) Contract and the "battle of forms"

Although Lord Denning MR and Lawton and Bridge LJJ all agreed that the law of contract was sufficient to solve the dispute in *Butler Machine Tool*, their reasoning differed.

Lawton and Bridge LJJ utilised the traditional "mirror image" approach to contract formation. Because the buyers' purported acceptance was in terms different to those of the sellers' original offer, it took effect as a counter-offer and not an acceptance. This counter-offer was accepted by the sellers' return of the tear-off slip. The phrase "in accordance with our . . . quotation" in the letter accompanying the slip was simply intended to confirm the price and the identity of the machine. It was not intended to propose that the other terms of the original offer be incorporated into the contract. A contract was therefore formed on the buyers' terms which did not include the price variation clause.

Lord Denning MR claimed that:

> "[O]ur traditional analysis of offer, counter-offer, rejection, acceptance and so forth is out of date . . . The better way is to look at all the documents passing between the parties – and glean from them, or from the conduct of the parties, whether they have reached agreement on all material points – even though there may be differences between the forms and conditions printed on the back of them . . . The terms and conditions of both parties are to be construed together. If they can be reconciled so as to give a harmonious result, all well and good. If the differences are irreconcilable – so that they are mutually contradictory – then the conflicting terms may have to be scrapped and replaced by a reasonable implication."[83]

Applying this approach to the facts, Lord Denning MR held that the tear-off slip and accompanying letter were decisive documents making it clear that the contract was being concluded on the buyers' terms.

[83] *Butler Machine Tool* at 404–405.

There have been critics of each of these contractual approaches to the battle of forms.[84] It has been suggested that the traditional approach (i) encourages businessmen to extend the exchange of standard forms in the hope of making the last offer, (ii) puts the party receiving the last offer in a no-win situation in that either there is no contract and he cannot complain of non-performance or there is a contract by reason of his accepting performance and that contract is necessarily on the other party's terms, and (iii) leaves reliance between the time of the last offer and the time of implied acceptance unprotected.[85] The approach of Lord Denning MR has been criticised because it has been said to provide too little guidance as to when agreement has been reached.[86] It would therefore "produce a flood of litigation."[87]

Less often criticised is the focus of all the judges in *Butler Machine Tool* on contract as providing a solution to the battle of forms dilemma. Where a contractual solution to cases such as *Butler Machine Tool* is readily available, it is generally agreed to be preferable.[88] Although I argue below that equitable estoppel is able to handle the claims of both parties to a battle of forms justly, the only way in which adequately to protect the expectations of both parties is if a genuine *consensus ad idem* can be found.

What is unclear, however, is just what constitutes a genuine *consensus ad idem* and just how far the courts should go in attempting to discover it. For example, in *Butler Machine Tool* Bridge LJ seemed to have little doubt that "there was a complete contract in existence and the parties were ad idem"[89] and Atiyah labels the suggestion there was no contract in this case as "absurd".[90] Yet, as even Atiyah admits, "[t]he truth is that the parties were never really

---

[84] As there have been of almost all contractual solutions to the battle of forms dilemma internationally. Thus the legislative answer to the problem contained in the United States UNIFORM COMMERCIAL CODE §2-207 (1978) has been subject to fierce criticism. For a summary of how this section operates and of recent criticisms of it, see E Jacobs, "The Battle of the Forms: Standard Term Contracts in Comparative Perspective", (1985) 34 *ICLQ* 297 at 308–312, J E Murray, "The Chaos of the "Battle of the Forms": Solutions", (1986) 39 *Vand L Rev* 1307, S Corneill, "On Ending the Battle of the Forms: Problems with Solutions", (1991) 80 *KLJ* 815. Similarly, Article 19 of the United Nations Convention on Contracts for the International Sale of Goods, another attempt to deal with the problem contractually, has also had its critics. For a summary of how this article operates and of recent criticisms of it, see F Vergne, "The 'Battle of Forms' under the 1980 United Nations Convention on Contracts for the International Sale of Goods", (1985) 33 *Am J Comp L* 233, C Moccia, "The United Nations Convention on Contracts for the International Sale of Goods and the "Battle of the Forms"" (1989) 13 *Fordham Int'l L J* 649. If Von Mehren is right that all contractual solutions to the battle of forms involve a choice between competing notions of intention, then inevitably all such solutions are open to criticism (A T Von Mehren, "The 'Battle of the Forms': A Comparative View" (1990) 38 *Am J Comp L* 265 at 294–298.

[85] See R Rawlings, "The Battle of Forms" (1979) 42 *MLR* 715 at 717.

[86] G H Treitel, *The Law of Contract* 9th edn (London, Sweet & Maxwell, 1995) at 45.

[87] R Rawlings, "The Battle of Forms", (1979) 42 *MLR* 715 at 720.

[88] See E McKendrick, "The Battle of the Forms and the Law of Restitution", (1988) 8 *OJLS* 197 at 220.

[89] *Butler Machine Tool* at 407.

[90] P S Atiyah, *An Introduction to the Law of Contract* 5th edn (Oxford, Clarendon Press, 1995) at 69.

agreed on the terms which were to govern the sale of the machine".[91] The sellers intended to sell a machine on terms which were "contrary in a number of vital respects" to the terms on which the buyers wished to purchase it.[92] If the truth was that the parties had never reached agreement on the central terms of their arrangement, then it is difficult to see how contract was the appropriate basis of the buyers' liability and how contract could determine whether the price variation clause would apply. It is suggested that the court went too far in *Butler Machine Tool* in the search for a consensus position. It constructed, rather than discovered, *consensus ad idem*. There is the danger that any agreement constructed on such facts will be artificial in nature and arbitrary in its terms. An artificially constructed consensus, however determined, might give unjustifiable priority to the claims of one party over those of the other.

The critics of the different approaches to offer and acceptance in this case would be better to focus their attentions on the insistence on a contractual solution to the battle of forms itself. A contractual solution to the problem doubtless has its advantages, but on many sets of facts it is simply unavailable. Indeed, as the edition of Cheshire and Fifoot current at the time of *Butler Machine Tool* put it:

> "In theory there is much to be said for the [no contract position] since there is neither agreement nor apparent agreement on the terms of the contract."[93]

(b) Tort and the "battle of forms"

As in the case of work undertaken in anticipation of contract, neither the tort of deceit nor of negligent misstatement has been important to the discussion of the battle of forms. This is presumably again because of the difficulty of identifying a representation of fact upon which there has been reliance.

However, just as it did in the cases concerning work undertaken in anticipation of contract, "fault" does seem to have played some rôle in the imposition of liability in *Butler Machine Tool*. It clearly impressed at least Lord Denning MR that the price escalation clause only became an issue because of the seller's default in delivering the machine on time.

> The important thing is that the sellers did not keep the contractual date of delivery which was March/April 1970. . . . [T]he buyer's production schedule had to be re-arranged . . . Meanwhile the sellers had invoked the price increase clause. They sought

---

[91] P S Atiyah, *An Introduction to the Law of Contract* 5th edn (Oxford, Clarendon Press, 1995) at 67.

[92] *Butler Machine Tool* at 407 *per* Bridge LJ.

[93] M P Furmston, *Cheshire and Fifoot's Law of Contract* 9th edn (London, Butterworths, 1976) at 151. See also J Adams, "The Battle of Forms" [1983] *JBL* 297 at 301 where that writer concludes: "Often the fairest result, as in the *Cleveland Bridge* case, will be achieved by holding that neither party's terms apply, and by dealing with the apportionment of compensation under the principles of restitution and reliance."

to charge the buyers an increase due to to the rise in costs between . . . when the order was given . . . and . . . when the machine ought to have been delivered.

There is more than a hint in this passage that Lord Denning was reluctant to allow the sellers to benefit from a situation that they themselves had caused.

Perhaps because the price escalation clause was expressed to apply however the delay was caused, the concept of "fault" was not specifically developed in *Butler Machine Tool*. Moreover, it is submitted that "fault" is too unstable a concept to resolve problems in the battle of forms. *Butler Machine Tool* was an unusual case in that the "fault" could relatively easily be identified. In most situations of the battle of forms, the only relevant "fault" will have been neglect in reading the terms of the other party's offer or acceptance and both parties will have been equally neglectful. Fault seems no more helpful a concept in resolving battles of forms than it did in compensating work undertaken in anticipation of contract.

(c) Restitution and the "battle of forms"

Largely because of the difficulties with a contractual solution to the battle of forms, an approach to cases such as *Butler Machine Tool* based on the principle of restitution for unjust enrichment has been proposed. In his article, "The Battle of the Forms and the Law of Restitution", McKendrick writes:

"Professor Atiyah was wrong to state that it would have been 'absurd' to suggest in a case such as *Butler* that no contract had been concluded between the parties . . . [T]he fact situation in *Butler* can be accommodated within a restitutionary framework . . ."[94]

Applying this approach to the facts of *Butler Machine Tool* and assuming that no contract was agreed, McKendrick argues that the buyers were under an obligation to make restitution of the reasonable value of the machine to the sellers. This was because:

". . . it [was] clear that the buyers were enriched by the receipt of the machine tool because they requested it, that the enrichment was at the expense of the sellers and that it was not unjust that the buyers should recompense the sellers because when they requested the machine tool the buyers knew that the sellers were not doing the work gratuitously."[95]

The reasonable value of the machine would roughly have equated with the value determined under the price variation clause:

"[H]ad no contract been concluded in *Butler* and the case had been decided on restitutionary grounds, the case may have been decided in favour of the sellers because the benefit would have been valued at the date of delivery of the machine tool. At that date

[94] E McKendrick, "The Battle of the Forms and the Law of Restitution", (1988) 8 *OJLS* 197 at 220.
[95] Ibid. at 208.

the market price of the machine tool must have been very close to the amount demanded by the sellers because the price variation clause and the sum demanded by the sellers was based upon 'prices ruling upon date of delivery'."[96]

Thus the sellers might have achieved by way of restitution what they were unable to achieve under the law of contract.

There would no doubt be many situations in which the law of restitution would be able to provide a satisfactory solution to a battle of forms. There are, however, serious difficulties both with this approach to the battle of forms in general and to the facts of *Butler Machine Tool* in particular.

First, McKendrick's approach is necessarily based on the concept of "free acceptance", a concept which is open to all the criticisms outlined in the preceding section.

Second, McKendrick acknowledges that the restitutionary approach does not deal well with the claims of the buyers in *Butler Machine Tool*. This is the problem, illustrated above in relation to *British Steel,* that a restitutionary solution to the problem of reliance upon anticipated, apparent or unenforceable agreements may not treat the provider and recipient of an alleged benefit equitably. The whole point of *Butler Machine Tool* was to decide whether or not there was any ground for payment equivalent to that provided for by the price variation clause. Under a restitutionary analysis this would have become a matter of the time at which the so-called "benefit" was to be assessed. McKendrick argues that this was at the time when the machine was delivered because before that there had been no "benefit" to the buyers.[97] Therefore the suppliers could recover the additional payment. However, such an analysis would entirely ignore any expense which the buyers might have incurred by relying upon the assumption that they would have a machine of a particular type at a particular time in the organisation of their production schedule. It would allow the sellers to benefit from their own failure to comply with the original arrangements by arguing that the machine was of greater value to the buyers than it would have been at the earlier date. Indeed, not even on a contractual analysis did the trial judge in *Butler Machine Tool* award the sellers as much as they could receive under McKendrick's restitutionary reasoning. For the £2,892 that the trial judge awarded represented the increased price due under the variation clause at the time when the machine *ought to have been delivered*, rather than when it actually was. It is clear that under McKendrick's restitutionary reasoning the sellers' claims would be given unfair priority over those of the buyers.

Moreover, suppose that the production schedules of buyers in the position of the defendants in *Butler Machine Tool* gave them no choice but to accept a machine which was of a different type to that which they had ordered and which would thereby cause them loss, but which was of the same realisable market

---

[96] E McKendrick, "The Battle of the Forms and the Law of Restitution", (1988) 8 *OJLS* 197 at 219.

[97] Ibid. at 219.

value as the machine they had ordered. Their reliance upon the induced assumption that they would receive a machine of a particular type (for example, by not ordering the machine elsewhere or by not organising their production schedule differently earlier) would go without compensation if they were required to make restitution of the same value as the value of the machine that they had assumed they were getting.

McKendrick claims that this problem regarding the buyers' claims can be overcome by a sensitive analysis of the issue of "benefit" on the basis of "free acceptance", an analysis that can take into account the buyers' assumptions about the machine that was to be delivered in determining whether they have freely accepted the machine that was delivered.[98]

The difficulty with this approach, however, is that it uses "benefit" to determine a far broader range of issues than the concept can conceivably handle. McKendrick has an extremely long list of things a court should take into account in determining the value of a "benefit":

> "In cases involving the battle of the forms the court must inevitably look to the standard terms issued by both parties. These will no doubt be detailed documents and there may even be agreement reached on certain points. Such documents will provide a useful foundation for the judgment of the court. Where these standard terms conflict then the court must look to other factors. Other factors relevant would be the market value of the goods or services, the terms of the request made by the buyer, the extent of the compliance with the request, the reason for any departure by the seller from the terms of the request and the reasons why no agreement had been reached on a particular point at issue (including an assessment of the 'fault' of both parties and whether the risk of such eventuality had been accepted by either party)."[99]

This is clearly not the allocation of liability on the basis of unjust enrichment. Liability might be imposed because one party has made a particular request; liability might be imposed because one party was at "fault" in the parties' failure to reach agreement; liability might be imposed because one party has accepted the risk of a certain eventuality. But it is unintelligible to say that these potential justifications for imposing liability – each of which would attract a different measure of relief – can simply be collapsed into the questions of whether one party has received a "benefit" of which he ought to make restitution and the value of that benefit.

This overworking of the concept of "benefit" and corresponding inability to provide a convincing way of taking into account the claims of *both* the parties to a battle of forms, is a strong reason for avoiding a restitutionary analysis in many battle of the forms situations. In particular, a restitutionary analysis of *Butler Machine Tool* shows how overworking the concept of "benefit" can collapse an important question which should be faced directly (i.e., "Ought the additional payment to be made and why?") into an enquiry which is not

---

[98] Ibid. at 212.
[99] Ibid. at 219.

obviously related to any of the issues relevant to whether liability ought or ought not to arise (i.e., "At what time should benefit be assessed in restitutionary situations?").

Because of these difficulties, therefore, a restitutionary analysis can be seen as useful in the context of some, but not all, battle of forms situations. McKendrick himself admits that a restitutionary approach to the battle of forms "is not alone in being a fruitful" approach and that "some fruit may be derived from taking an approach based upon reliance".[100] In particular, a restitutionary approach is unsatisfactory to handle the facts of *Butler Machine Tool* and any case where defective performance has been rendered which has caused loss to the party receiving it. We turn, therefore, to consider whether those facts might more adequately be handled by the application of equitable estoppel.

(d) Equitable estoppel and the "battle of forms"

In applying equitable estoppel to this case we will first deal with the sellers' claim for payment for the machine delivered to the buyers. We will then consider whether the buyers' might have counter-claimed for losses consequent upon late delivery.

(i) *The seller's claim for payment*

A judge applying the doctrine of equitable estoppel to the facts of *Butler Machine Tool* would begin by identifying the assumption upon which the sellers might be said to have relied. There would be three possibilities. The buyers might have induced the assumption (i) that the sellers would be paid for the tool, (ii) that the sellers would be paid £75,535 for the tool or (iii) that the sellers would be paid a price for the tool determined by the price variation clause. However, I would argue that the only assumption which was induced was that the sellers would be paid for the machine. It is clear that the sellers never held the assumption that they would be paid £75,535 and so the second of these assumptions is not relevant. As to the third, the sellers might argue that the buyers' silence induced in them the assumption that the buyers would pay a price for the machine determined according to the price variation clause. However, in the confusion of the terms of exchange it would be hard to demonstrate that the sellers' price expectations were caused by the buyers' silence and not, for example, by their confidence that their own standard terms of dealing would prevail. Thus the assumption that the buyers in *Butler Machine Tool* would seem to have induced in the sellers was simply that the sellers would be paid for the machine.

---

[100] E McKendrick, "The Battle of the Forms and the Law of Restitution", (1988) 8 *OJLS* 197 at 220–221. See also J W Carter, "Services Rendered under Ineffective Contracts", [1990] *LMCLQ* 495 at 498 and 508.

Even without the presumption of reliance, detrimental reliance upon this assumption would not be difficult to establish in that the sellers clearly manufactured and delivered the tool in reliance upon the assumption that they would be paid.

Assuming, then, that the sellers relied upon the induced assumption that they would be paid for the machine tool by manufacturing and delivering the tool to the buyers, the question becomes whether it would be unconscionable for the buyers not to compensate any detriment that the sellers might have suffered by their reliance.

Factors pointing towards a finding of unconscionability in this context would be (i) that the assumption was induced by an express representation, (ii) that the relevant activities in reliance were strongly in the buyers' interest (indeed, that they enjoyed the fruits of those activities in whatever use they were able to make of the tool) and (iii) that the buyers took no steps to ensure that the sellers did not suffer the preventible harm by the relevant activities in reliance.

Factors counting against a finding of unconscionability would be (i) that the representation was as to the future, (ii) the commercial context of the dealings and, (iii) that the sellers were in just as strong a position to assess the risk of detriment by reliance as were the buyers. The first of these factors might be somewhat discounted, however, because although the representation was as to intention, reliance on the assumption was intended to follow closely after its inducement. This was not a general statement of intention. It was a statement that was intended to be no less reliable than any statement of present fact. As to the second of these factors, the commercial context of the inducement has to be set against the fact that both parties believed that they were bound by an existing contract. Thus although *legally* this was a context involving unrelated parties, *factually* it was a context involving a not inconsiderable degree of anticipated trust and co-operation.

Balancing these two sets of criteria, therefore, it would seem that a judge applying equitable estoppel to the facts of *Butler Machine Tool* would determine that it would be unconscionable for the buyer in this case not to remedy the sellers' reliance upon the induced assumption that he would be paid for the machine.

A final issue to be determined would be the measure of relief that would be required to compensate such reliance. The goal of equitable estoppel remedies is to put the party relying upon the induced assumption into as near a position as he would have been had the assumption never been induced. For the sellers in *Butler Machine Tool* this would *prima facie* be the cost of making and delivering the machine. Of course, the sellers might always argue that this was a case in which the expectation measure of relief ought to be awarded to protect their reliance loss. If this argument was successful, the question would again arise of whether an award in the expectation measure would consist in an award of the provisional price of the machine or the price of the machine determined according to the price variation clause. However, this choice would not be as unrestrained as it could be on contractual reasoning because the court would be choosing between the two *quanta* on the specific basis of which might be said better to reflect the sellers' reliance loss. This is a question which it would be easier to answer *ex post facto* than the question of which *quantum* better reflected the parties' intentions.

(ii) The buyer's counter-claim

As outlined above, one of the potential weaknesses of forced contractual and restitutionary solutions to the battle of forms cases is that they tend to give undue priority to the claims of one party over those of the other. Remember that, although contract is the only way in which fully to compensate disappointed expectations, there is also a problem of the disparity with the which the claims of the buyers and sellers are treated if a *consensus ad idem* is artificially constructed. Forcing a contractual analysis of *Butler Machine Tool* might arguably have led the court to give undue priority to the buyers' terms. A restitutionary analysis of *Butler Machine Tool* might be seen as giving undue priority to the claims of the sellers.

It is important, therefore, to note that the buyers in *Butler Machine Tool* might have had a claim in equitable estoppel to set off against any which the sellers could establish. Argument for the most obvious of such claims would seem to run as follows: (i) the sellers induced in the buyers the assumption that the machine tool would be delivered on a particular date, (ii) the buyers relied upon that induced assumption by organising their production schedule in a particular way, (iii) this assumption proved unjustified, and (iv) it would be unconscionable for the sellers not to compensate the losses which the buyers suffered by relying upon the induced assumption.

Of course, the reported facts give far too little information to examine such a claim in any detail. The unconscionability question would be particularly difficult to determine on the state of the given facts. Nevertheless, it is important to recognise that such a claim might potentially exist. The existence of such a claim demonstrates how more just an approach to many of the battle of forms cases might be found in the law of equitable estoppel than by artifically constructing a contract or by compensating just one party under the law of restitution. Once again this is an area in which the development of the doctrine of equitable estoppel is to be welcomed.

4. FIRM OFFERS IN THE CONSTRUCTION INDUSTRY

We turn, then, from two cases at the edge of contract in which a remedy will not normally be available in contract because agreement will not be complete, to two cases in which a remedy will not normally be available in contract for want of consideration. The first of these is the situation of firm offers in the construction industry.

It will be recalled that this is the situation in which a subcontractor submits a bid to a general contractor for work as part of a larger project for which the general contractor is tendering. The offer is expressed to be good for a certain period of time. The general contractor relies upon the subcontractor's bid in submitting his own tender, is successful in the award of the head contract and goes on to accept the subcontractor's bid within the stipulated period only to find it withdrawn or revised upwards. The general contractor is then locked into a head contract which he may no longer be able to perform at a profit. As outlined above, there is a resilient intuition both in the construction industry and the academic literature that the general contractor ought, at least sometimes, to be protected by the subcontractor from experiencing such losses.[101]

A slight variation in methodology will be required in this part. This is because there are no reported English cases dealing with the fact situation just outlined. Presumably this is not because English general contractors do not suffer loss in this way, nor because they feel that the law ought not to compensate such loss. Rather, the dearth of reported English cases in this area can probably be attributed to the certainty which English law has attached to the rule that firm offers – at least for bilateral contracts – may be revoked at any time prior to acceptance. The rule has probably been established since the early nineteenth century,[102] and certainly since *Dickinson v Dodds*.[103] Accordingly, the methodology adopted in this section will be first to consider the merits of various contractual solutions to the firm offer problem that have been proposed. Second, we will take the facts of four of the United States firm offer cases and consider how those facts might be handled by a judge applying the doctrine of equitable estoppel.

(a) Contract and the firm offer problem

One solution to the firm offer problem is to impose a contractual obligation upon the subcontractor to keep his offer open for the stipulated period. This is the solution to the problem found in §2-205 of the United States UNIFORM COMMERCIAL CODE (1978) which provides that firm offers to buy or sell goods made in signed writing by a merchant are irrevocable for up to three months.[104] It is also a solution that has been recommended by the Law Commission who have argued that firm offers made in the course of a business should be binding for a period not exceeding six years.[105]

It is suggested, however, that such a solution is simply to transform a potential injustice to the general contractor into a potential injustice to the subcontractor. This is for two reasons.

---

[101] See above at p. 84.
[102] See, for example, *Routledge v Grant* (1828) 4 Bing 653.
[103] (1876) 2 Ch D 463 .
[104] See also the N.Y. GENERAL OBLIGATIONS LAW §5-1109 (McKinney 1989).
[105] Law Commission, *Working Paper No.60: Firm Offers* (1975) at 26.

First, in most of these cases there is nothing to suggest that an option contract could not have been negotiated, had the parties agreed that the subcontractors should have been bound to keep the offer open. Indeed, the general contractors attempted to negotiate such a contract in one of the cases to be considered in this section.[106] Some might argue, therefore, that the law ought not effectively to award the general contractors what they failed to obtain in open commercial negotiation. Subcontractors will rarely want to withdraw their bids for capricious reasons and it might be argued that the risk of loss arising from an unforeseen need to change bids ought to be allocated by contract or left to lie where it falls.

Second, even the development of a legal rule protecting the reliance of the general contractor, let alone a rule enforcing firm offers irrespective of reliance, has been strongly criticised on the basis that such a rule could encourage "bid shopping".[107] "Bid shopping" is a practice whereby a general contractor will try to obtain lower bids for the subcontracts involved in a project even after he has been awarded the head contract. This practice has seriously detrimental effects upon the bidding process.[108] It also gives rise to the reciprocity problem that, although the subcontractor may be bound to protect the general contractor's reliance, the general contractor is free to "shop" for a better deal. It will be considered below whether "bid shopping" would be encouraged by the imposition of liability in equitable estoppel, but it is clear that it would be encouraged by the imposition of liability in contract.

(b) Equitable estoppel and the firm offer cases

In a majority of the United States, the firm offer problem has been solved by the recognition of potential liability under the flexible doctrine of promissory estoppel. This doctrine is described in the RESTATEMENT (SECOND) OF CONTRACTS §90 (1979):

> "A promise which the promisor should reasonably expect to induce action or forbearance is binding if injustice can be avoided only by enforcement of the promise. The remedy granted for breach may be limited as justice requires."

[106] *Northwestern Engineering* v. *Ellerman* (1943) 10 NW 2d 879 (1943).

[107] Not surprisingly, this view has been particularly strongly expressed by subcontractors, see R Lewis, "Contracts Between Businessmen; Reform of the Law of Firm Offers and an Empirical Study of Tendering Practices in the Building Industry" (1982) 9 *J Law Soc* 153. For a more general discussion of this problem see L Lederman, "Once Around the Flag Pole: Construction Bidding and Contracts at Formation", (1964) 39 *NYU L Rev* 816, J B Gaides, "The 'Firm Offer' Problem in Construction Bids and the Need for Promissory Estoppel", (1968) 10 *Wm & Mary L Rev* 212, K L Schriber. "The Problem of Offer and Acceptance in the General Contractor-Subcontractor Relationship", (1968) 37 *U Cin L Rev* 798, T P Lambert, "Bid Shopping and Peddling in the Construction Industry", (1970) 18 *UCLA L Rev* 389, R A Oertli, "Construction Bidding Problem: Is there a Solution Fair to both the General Contractor and Subcontractor?" (1975) 19 *St Louis U L J* 552. See also K Llewellyn, "What Price Contract? An Essay in Perspective", (1931) 40 *Yale L J* 704, M L Closen and D G Weiland, "The Construction Bidding Cases", (1980) 13 *J Marshall L Rev* 565.

[108] See T P Lambert, "Bid Shopping and Peddling in the Subcontract Industry", (1970) 18 *UCLA L Rev* 389.

The application of RESTATEMENT (SECOND) OF CONTRACTS §90 (1979) to reliance on an unaccepted offer was affirmed by the inclusion of §87(2).[109]

The §90 principle of promissory estoppel provides a solution to the firm offers problem which has neither the difficulty of always favouring, nor of always unfairly prejudicing, the general contractor. Instead the courts "have tended to apply [this] doctrine flexibly, considering the facts and equities in each case."[110] Thus:

> "Courts have refused to apply the doctrine of promissory estoppel in cases in which the equities lie with the subcontractor. [For example] some courts have refused to apply promissory estoppel when the subcontractor's bid was so 'glaringly low' as to put the general contractor on notice that a mistake had been made. In such cases courts view the general contractor's reliance on the bid as unreasonable."[111]

Indeed, it has even been argued that promissory estoppel is able to solve the "bid shopping problem". Although without explanation, one of the decisions to be considered in this section provides that:

> "... a general contractor is not free to delay acceptance after he has been awarded the general contract in the hope of getting a better price."[112]

A comparison of the two doctrines is outside the scope of this book,[113] but promissory estoppel seems to provide the type of flexible answer to the firm offer problem that I argue is appropriate and could be provided by the doctrine of equitable estoppel.

Of the four cases examined in this chapter, two are cases in which liability was established on the basis of United States promissory estoppel (*Northwestern Engineering Co v Ellerman*,[114] a decision of the Supreme Court of South Dakota, and *Drennan v Star Paving Co*,[115] a decision of the Supreme Court of California) and two are cases in which liability was not established on application of the same doctrine (*Robert Gordon Inc v Ingersoll-Rand*,[116] a decision of the Circuit Court of Appeals, Seventh Circuit, and *MacIsaac & Menke Co v Freeman*,[117] a decision of the District Court of Appeals, Second District, California).

---

[109] §87(2) reads: "An offer which the offeror should reasonably expect to induce action or forbearance of a substantial character on the part of the offeree before acceptance and which does induce such action or forbearance is binding as an option contract to the extent necessary to avoid injustice."

[110] J McPeters Murphy, "Promissory Estoppel: Subcontractor's Liability in Construction Bidding Cases", (1985) 63 NC L Rev 387 at 395.

[111] Ibid. at 394.

[112] *Drennan v Star Paving Co* 233 P 2d 757 (1958) at 760 *per* Traynor J.

[113] The difference between these two doctrines was considered in *Waltons* at 401–402 by Mason CJ and Wilson J as being that §90 estoppel operates as an alternative to consideration in the founding of contractual liability while equitable estoppel operates as an independent cause of action. For an alternative account of the relationship between the two doctrines see A Robertson, "Situating Equitable Estoppel within the Law of Obligations", (1997) 19 SLR 32.

[114] *Northwestern Engineering Co v Ellerman* (1943) 10 N W 2d 879 (1943) (hereafter "*Northwestern*").

[115] *Drennan v Star Paving Co* 233 P 2d 757 (1958) (hereafter "*Drennan*").

[116] 117 F 2d 654 (1941) (hereafter "*Robert Gordon*").

[117] 15 Cal Rptr 48 (1961) (hereafter "*MacIsaac*").

Taking the cases chronologically, *Robert Gordon* involved bidding for the project of installing heating and ventilating machinery in a university hall. Robert Gordon and their principal competitor, Mehring & Hanson, both made bids based upon an identical sub-bid from Ingersoll Rand regarding the cost of supplying certain refrigeration machinery. Both companies had extensive experience of acquiring and installing machinery of the relevant type. The bidding engineer at Robert Gordon understood the sub-bid to set out a price for the supply of two refrigeration machines. He prepared his company's bid on the basis of that assumption and that bid was accepted by the university. The bidding engineer at Mehring & Hanson thought that the sub-bid was vague but, from his knowledge of the prices of such machines, that it could not refer to two machines. He therefore checked with the suppliers and found that the price in the sub-bid was for one machine only. After his company's bid had been accepted, the bidding engineer from Robert Gordon spoke to the university's consulting engineer who pointed out that the sub-bid could only have been for one machine. The bidding engineer from Robert Gordon then had a similar conversation with the bidding engineer from Mehring & Hanson. The university's consulting engineer agreed to convince the university to allow Robert Gordon to withdraw their bid. However Robert Gordon decided to continue with their bid and brought proceedings against Ingersoll Rand for breach of contract, relying on the doctrine of promissory estoppel, in failing to supply the two machines at the given price. The action for breach of contract was not successful.

In *Northwestern* two construction companies entered into a written agreement that, if the first company, Northwestern Engineering, was successful in their bid to construct water supply, storage facility, sewerage disposal and treatment works for the United States airforce, the second company, Ellerman & McLain, would undertake the laying of a sewer system at a particular price. As evidence of their good faith, Ellerman & McLain provided a bidder's bond from a surety company. Northwestern Engineering was awarded the head contract by the airforce. Ellerman & McLain, however, refused to proceed on the terms agreed and Northwestern Engineering brought an action for breach of contract, relying again on the doctrine of promissory estoppel, claiming the difference between the price agreed for laying the sewer and the cost of alternative performance. The action for breach of contract was successful.

In *Drennan*, Drennan was a building contractor bidding on a school construction project. His bid for the construction project had to include the names of almost all subcontractors and had to be guaranteed by a bond in the amount of ten per cent guaranteeing that he would enter the contract if it was awarded to him. A part of the project involved paving, the cost of which varied around one hundred and sixty per cent in the relevant locality. On the day of the bid, as was customary in the locality, Drennan received sub-bids by telephone from various subcontractors for different parts of the project, including a sub-bid from Star Paving for the paving. This sub-bid was received by a secretary, with Drennan listening in on another telephone, who asked for the sub-bid to be repeated because accuracy was so important. Drennan submitted his bid for the school project on the basis of the Star Paving sub-bid, but was told the following morning that the company would not be able to provide the paving for the given price. Drennan, relying on the doctrine of promissory estoppel, brought an action for breach of contract, claiming the difference between the cost of the paving given in the sub-bid and the price at which he eventually obtained alternative performance. His action was successful.

Finally, *MacIsaac* involved a bid for the construction of a university building in Los Angeles. The specifications for the project included sections "DD", entitled "Plumbing and Steamfitting", and "EE", entitled "Heating, Ventilating and Cooling". MacIsaac & Menke intended to bid for the project and invited selected subcontractors to submit sub-bids for its different parts. The defendant, Freeman, obtained a copy of the section of the specifications "DD" and one of his employees submitted a sub-bid for the work by telephone. When the employee called MacIsaac & Menke to submit his sub-bid, that company's estimator was very busy and so the two had a conversation lasting less than a minute. Freeman's employee said that the sub-bid was for "Plumbing only. No heating." The estimator understood the sub-bid to relate to all the work described in section "DD" of the specifications for the project and submitted his company's bid for the project on that basis, but Freeman's employee only intended it to relate to the plumbing and not the steam fitting work described in that section. Freeman refused to complete the whole of the work described in section "DD" for the given price and MacIsaac & Menke, relying on the doctrine of promissory estoppel, brought an action for breach of contract to recover the difference between the given price and the cost of alternative performance. The action was not successful.

The application of equitable estoppel to these fact situations yields results parallel to those achieved by the application of United States promissory estoppel. Examing those facts in the light of the equitable estoppel, however, reveals how helpful a tool to unlock the firm offer problem the emerging doctrine could be.

(i) Northwestern *and* Drennan

Applying equitable estoppel to the facts of these cases, a judge would first have to consider the issues of inducement, reliance and detriment. In *Drennan* and *Northwestern* general contractors were induced by express representation to assume that subcontractors would perform work at a particular price. In each case the general contractors clearly relied upon that assumption, though the presumption proposed in Chapter Two would operate to relieve the general contractors of the need to prove reliance. In *Drennan* the court pointed out that the general contractor neither sought to reopen bargaining with the subcontractors nor delayed acceptance of the subcontractors' offer once the head contract had been awarded, either of which might negate the presumption of reliance.

Moreover, the general contractors' reliance was in both cases clearly such that they would have suffered detriment had the induced assumption proved unreliable. Once again this was particularly true in *Drennan* in which the general contractor was subject to forfeiture of a "bid bond" if he did not proceed to contract with the school board to which he had submitted his own bid.

Once a court had determined that there had been an assumption induced by the subcontractors and reliance upon that assumption to the detriment of the general contractors, the question would then become whether it was unconscionable for the subcontractors not to remedy that detriment.

Factors leading to a finding of unconscionability in these cases would start with the mode of the relevant inducement. In *Northwestern* the assumption was induced by a detailed document which each of the parties believed to have contractual force. The detail of this document was something which clearly impressed the court.[118] Moreover, the document contained a "bid bond" guaranteeing performance by the subcontractors. The mode of the inducement could hardly have been more conducive to a finding of unconscionability. In *Drennan* the inducement was by repeated oral representation during a telephone call. This mode of inducement might seem less likely to lead to a finding that the defendant had failed to ensure the reliability of induced assumptions because a representation made during a brief telephone call is self-evidently less reliable than a representation made as a part of a formal "legal" document. However, the mode of the inducement in *Drennan* has to be considered in light of a proved local custom for "general contractors to receive the bids of subcontractors by telephone on the day set for bidding and to rely on them in computing their own bid."[119] Indeed, the representation was required to be carefully repeated to ensure accuracy. It is suggested that in these cases the mode of the relevant inducement would be a factor pointing towards a finding of unconscionability.

So, too, would be the relative state of the parties' knowledge in these cases. The defendants in these cases had knowledge of all the relevant circumstances which could lead to the plaintiffs' harm, they possessed all the information required to make reliable bids and were aware that any bid they did make would be used by the plaintiffs as a part of their tenders. Moreover, it seems probable that in *Drennan* the defendant knew that the general contractor had to name the subcontractors in his tender and provide a "bid bond" to secure his entry into the head contract. It is submitted that this knowledge was sufficient to impose upon the defendants a relatively strong duty to ensure the reliability of the assumption induced. The plaintiff, for his part, had no opportunity to know that reliance upon the assumption might lead to his harm. This is because "there was usually a variance of 160 per cent between the highest and lowest bids for paving in the desert around Lancaster."[120]

---

[118] *Northwestern* at 884.
[119] *Drennan* at 758.
[120] Ibid. at 761.

Another factor supporting a finding of unconscionability in these cases is that reliance upon the assumption by the general contractors was not only in the interests of the general contractors but was also strongly in the interests of the subcontractors. This is again a point which is made much of in the *Drennan* judgment:

> "Though the defendant did not bargain for this use of its bid neither did defendant make it idly, indifferent to whether it would be used or not. On the contrary it is reasonable to suppose that defendant submitted its bid to obtain the subcontract . . . Defendant had reason not only to expect plaintiff to rely on its bid but to want him to. Clearly defendant had a stake in plaintiff's reliance on its bid. . . . [I]t was motivated by its own business interest."[121]

Of course, this consideration is not as important as it would have been had reliance upon the assumption been wholly in the interests of the inducing party, but it is clearly relevant.

A final factor pointing towards a finding of unconscionability in these cases is that in neither case did the subcontractors take any steps at all to ensure that the induced assumption did not cause preventible harm. Thus, as was again important in the *Drennan* decision, in neither case did the subcontractors intimate that the induced assumption might be unreliable, that the offer to perform at a particular price might be revoked.

Of course, against these factors lending support for a finding of unconscionability, a judge applying equitable estoppel to the facts of *Northwestern* or *Drennan* would have to weigh those factors telling against such a finding. Chief amongst these must be the commercial context of these dealings. There is nothing in either case to suggest a disparity of bargaining power between the plaintiffs and defendants. I have already suggested that the courts must be wary of effectively granting parties what they failed to achieve in commercial negotiation, and that in *Northwestern* there had been an attempt to negotiate an option contract which had failed. Perhaps for this reason, there is a reluctance in a significant minority of the United States to apply promissory estoppel to the situation of reliance upon unaccepted offers.[122]

However, I would argue that this issue of the commercial context of these dealings might not tell as strongly against a finding of unconscionability in these particular cases as it might in some other situations. Usually in commercial cases the duty to ensure the reliability of induced assumptions places a very low burden on the inducing party because in a competitive environment each party is expected to take a high level of responsibility for the reliability of the assumptions upon which he relies. This is not true in the context of firm offers in the construction industry in which the general contractor will usually be expected to rely upon the subcontractor's bid without securing an option contract. Indeed

---

[121] Ibid. at 760–761.

[122] This minority position focuses on the decision of Learned Hand J in *James Baird Co v Gimbel Bros* 64 F 2d 344 (1933).

it might not be possible for the general contractor to secure an option contract in the short time that the bidding process allows. In *Drennan* evidence was taken to the effect that reliance upon such bids without an option contract was customary amongst prudent business people. Therefore the general contractor following standard construction industry procedure in relation to firm offers is in a position of unusual vulnerability and is not in the position usually occupied by those in commercial dealings. The subcontractor will know of this vulnerable position of the general contractor and therefore owes a higher duty to ensure the reliability of induced assumptions than he would in other commercial negotiations.

A further factor weighing against a finding of unconscionability in these cases would be the content of the assumption induced, that the assumption is one relating to the future. Again, however, I would argue that this factor is less important than it might at first appear. In each case the time for reliance came extremely close on the heels of the inducement of the relevant assumption. This was not a vague assumption of general intention which it was evident was less reliable than a statement of present fact. It was an assumption intended to be acted upon immediately.

Weighing these two sets of factors – those telling for and those against a finding of unconscionability – a judge deciding both *Northwestern* and *Drennan* would probably decide these cases in favour of the general contractors. Considerations relating to the mode of the relevant inducement, the relative knowledge of the parties, the relative interest of the parties in the relevant activities in reliance, the failure to take any steps at all to prevent the harm to the party relying upon the assumption, would here seem to outweigh the commercial context of the inducement and the fact that the assumption induced was one as to the future. In that there is any doubt that this would be the finding of such a judge, it is because the facts appear in the reported decisions only as they have been filtered through a different legal doctrine so that it is difficult to know what might have emerged had the facts been presented within the framework of equitable estoppel. In particular, §90 of the RESTATEMENT (SECOND) OF CONTRACT (1979) differs from equitable estoppel because the considerations that a judge may take into account in determining whether it would be "unjust" for one party to resile from a promise are more indeterminate than the list of criteria to be weighed in finding unconscionability.

(ii) Robert Gordon and MacIsaac

I turn, then, from two fact situations in which the application of equitable estoppel would probably lead to an award in the reliance measure, to two fact situations in which I would submit that such an award would not be made.

Considering these situations in turn, I begin with the facts in *Robert Gordon*. Applying the doctrine of equitable estoppel to those facts, a judge would have to begin with the question of whether the relevant assumption – that the two refrigeration machines would be supplied for $26,450 – was induced by the sub-contractors in the mind of the engineer at Robert Gordon. This is not at all clear from the facts of the case and would depend upon the view that the court took of the subcontractors' bid. It may be, for example, that the court would find that the subcontractors' bid was not sufficiently unequivocal in its inducement because of the ambiguous way in which it was expressed. It would have to tell against the general contractors that the engineer at Mehring & Hanson regarded the sub-bid as confusing and rang the subcontractors to have its terms clarified.

Assuming, however, that inducement was found on these facts, the next issue would be whether there was detrimental reliance by the general contractors upon the assumption induced. Here again there was some question on the facts of the case because, although, even without the help of a presumption of reliance, it is clear that the general contractors relied upon the assumption, it is likely that their reliance was not to their detriment. It was apparent from the evidence that the university would have been prepared to allow them to submit a revised tender. Thus the general contractors' reliance need not have been to their detriment.

Yet, again assuming that the hurdle of showing detrimental reliance could be overcome, a judge applying equitable estoppel to the facts of this case would then have to examine the issue of unconscionability. Several factors would count against a finding of unconscionability in this situation. First, this was an assumption regarding the future which was induced in a commercial context, although these factors could probably be discounted in the way in which they were in the earlier discussion of *Northwestern* and *Drennan*. Second, and less easy to discount, is the issue of the relative knowledge of the parties. It was clear on the evidence of the case that the general contractors were in just as good a position as were the subcontractors to know that reliance upon the induced assumption was potentially harmful. The general contractors were extremely experienced in the installation of ventilating, heating and air-conditioning machinery and a price of $26,450 would have been "absurdly low"[123] for two machines of this type. It is clear from the evidence that the engineer at Robert Gordon must have known that a mistake had been made in the sub-bid or, in the words of the other bidding engineer, that "there was something screwy about [it]".[124] The conclusion of the court was that the engineer at Robert Gordon "could not have reasonably entertained the belief that the Ingersoll-Rand letter intended the price of $26,450 to refer to two full-capacity machines."[125] Even if the general contractors genuinely held the relevant assumption, they were in just as strong a position of knowledge as the subcontractors to know that a mistake had been made. Third, there is the issue of the steps that the inducing party took to ensure that the induced assumption would not cause preventible harm. The

---

[123] *Robert Gordon* at 660.
[124] Ibid. at 656.
[125] Ibid. at 660.

subcontractors had taken the precaution of including the following words in red type on the bid, "Quotations subject to change without notice." The subcontractors had taken the step of warning the general contractors that the bid was not able to be relied upon. Admittedly, this statement was "in small red type, removed somewhat from the body of the letter and not referred to therein, and not as easily readable as the typewritten matter."[126] A court applying equitable estoppel would not necessarily give the inclusion of these words much weight as an attempt to prevent the relying party from suffering harm. Indeed the words were ignored in the *Robert Gordon* decision itself. Nevertheless, express warnings of this type ought not to be regarded too lightly by the courts and might be taken as a factor weighing against a finding of unconscionability. Taken together, these three factors would make a finding of unconscionability very unlikely in such a case.

It is clear, then, that a court applying equitable estoppel to the facts of *Robert Gordon* – a case in which the general contractors would have had difficulty in showing inducement, detriment and unconscionability – would be unlikely to require the defendants to remedy the plaintiffs' detriment.

I turn to consider *MacIsaac*. In seeking relief on the facts of *MacIsaac* on the basis of equitable estoppel, the general contractors would again first encounter a problem with the issue of inducement. It is not at all clear on the facts that the subcontractor was causally responsible for the general contractors' assumption that the quotation included all of the work in section "DD". In fact, the court took extensive evidence of industry usage and found that the estimator at MacIsaac & Menke should have understood the bid in the sense in which the subcontractor's employee intended it. It would have been very difficult in this context to establish unequivocal inducement of the assumption upon which the general contractors relied.

Having established inducement, plaintiffs arguing equitable estoppel on facts identical to those in *MacIsaac* would have no difficulty in establishing detrimental reliance.

Such plaintiffs would encounter more problems, however, when unconscionability came to be considered. Two factors may count in favour of a finding of unconscionability. First, there was the fact that the parties were in relatively equivalent positions of knowledge. The subcontractor's bid was high and there was nothing in the circumstances which ought to have alerted the general contractors to their mistake.[127] Second, the subcontractor took no steps to ensure that reliance upon the induced assumption did not cause harm. However, the mode of the inducement, particularly in the light of its context, would surely count against a finding of unconscionability. This was an oral bid made during a telephone conversation of less than one minute's duration. Even given the practice apparently common in the construction industry of taking telephone bids from subcontractors, an assumption induced by a bid during a hurried con-

---

[126] *Robert Gordon* at 661.
[127] *MacIsaac* at 51.

versation in which the issue of the work the bid was intended to cover was not discussed, must have been self-evidently less reliable than an assumption induced by a bid in other circumstances. The court in *MacIsaac* implicitly made this point when it said that the plaintiffs' estimator "at least should have made further inquiry so that there would be no lack of clarity as to what was intended to be included in the bid."[128] Indeed, if Freeman in any way broke his duty to ensure the reliability of induced assumptions, it seems partly to have been because his engineer was prevented from taking further steps by the speed with which he was hurried off the telephone. When the mode of this inducement is added to its commercial context and thus the reluctance of the courts to find unconscionable behaviour, I would argue that a court applying equitable estoppel would be unlikely to award the plaintiffs their reliance loss. Even were the general contractors arguing this case in equitable estoppel able to overcome the hurdle of proving inducement, they would surely fail to establish unconscionability. Having, then applied the doctrine of equitable estoppel to the facts of these four subcontractor cases, it is clear that in two of the cases the general contractors would be awarded a remedy to protect their reliance and in two they would not be.

(iii) Equitable estoppel and "bid shopping"

Before leaving the firm offer problem, it is worth considering whether equitable estoppel might encourage "bid shopping". The issue is whether equitable estoppel could provide an effective answer to the fear that compensating the general contractor's reliance will simply shift the injustice he potentially suffers to the subcontractor.

I would argue that there are at least four ways in which the application of equitable estoppel in the firm offer situation could discourage "bid shopping". None of these ways could entirely rule out bid shopping, but each could operate as a powerful disincentive to engaging in it.

First, where a general contractor has engaged in bid shopping after the award of the head contract, it might be questioned whether he had relied on the subcontractor's specific bid in the preparation of the estimate for the head contract. Rather, he might be said to have relied upon his own belief that he could negotiate a subcontract at the given price or lower. Bid shopping might be taken as evidence rebutting the presumption of reliance.

Second, given that the equitable defences are available against a claim in equitable estoppel, bid shopping may be taken as evincing the general contractor's present fixed intention to release his claim in equitable estoppel against the subcontractor. There is no reason why such a release ought not to be effective.[129] A general contractor might be less inclined to bid shop if he knew that he was

---

[128] Ibid. at 52.
[129] For a discussion of the defence of release see M Spence, "Equitable Defences" in P Parkinson, *The Principles of Equity* (Sydney, LBC, 1996) at 939–944.

thereby surrendering any claim that he might have against the subcontractor on whose offer he had relied.

Third, it would always be open to the courts to regard bid shopping as a type of "unclean hands" that could bar the general contractor from relief. This would be unlikely, however, given obvious difficulties in determing the sense in which the practice constitutes "legal" impropriety.[130]

The fourth way in which the application of equitable estoppel could discourage bid shopping relates to a countervailing claim that could be brought by the subcontractor. In the usual subcontractor situation, the general contractor will at some point have encouraged the subcontractor whose bid he has used in the belief that, should the head contract be granted, the subcontractor will be given the work. Where this is in fact the case, and where the subcontractor has arranged his affairs on the basis of this assumption but it subsequently proves unjustified, there is no reason why the subcontractor will not himself have a countervailing claim in equitable estoppel. This is how Lambert[131] has argued that the United States doctrine of promissory estoppel should operate to discourage bid shopping. He believes that the opposite responses to the bid shopping problem of "always" or "never" protecting the general contractor's reliance are both too inflexible. Rather, he argues that the bid shopping problem can in many circumstances be resolved by asking whether the subcontractor can show detrimental reliance which also merits protection.

The bid shopping problem is clearly not insurmountable. It ought not to be allowed to undermine the appropriate application of equitable estoppel to reliance by general contractors in the firm offer situation. The law could clearly respond more flexibly and fairly to the puzzle of firm offers if armed with the doctrine of equitable estoppel.

5. VARIATIONS OF CONTRACT UNSUPPORTED BY CONSIDERATION

This section will involve a detailed examination of just two cases, the decision of the English Court of Appeal in *Williams v Roffey Brothers & Nicholls Contractors Ltd*[132] and the equitable estoppel decision of the Supreme Court of New South Wales in *Citra Constructions Ltd v Allied Asphalt Co Pty Ltd.*[133]

In *Williams v Roffey* a general contractor engaged subcontractors to undertake carpentry work on a block of twenty seven flats for £20,000. The agreed price was too low and the subcontractors failed to supervise their workmen

---

[130] *Dering v Earl of Winchelsea* (1787) 1 Cox 318 and see M Spence, "Equitable Defences" in P Parkinson, *The Principles of Equity* (Sydney, LBC, 1996) at 963–970.

[131] T P Lambert, "Bid Shopping and Peddling in the Subcontract Construction Industry", (1970) 18 *UCLA L Rev* 389 at 405–409.

[132] *Williams v Roffey Brothers & Nicholls Contractors Ltd* [1991] 1 QB 1 (hereafter "*Williams v Roffey*").

[133] *Citra Constructions Ltd v Allied Asphalt Co Pty Ltd*, Supreme Court of New South Wales, 28 March 1990, unreported (hereafter "*Citra Constructions*").

adequately. As a result, the subcontractors were in financial difficulties and there was a danger that they might not complete the work. By the time work to the roof of the block of flats had been completed, some work had been done to all twenty seven flats and nine flats had been substantially completed. The general contractor had made part payments totalling £16,200. The general contractor was concerned that the head contract contained a penalty clause for late completion and agreed to pay the subcontractors an extra £10,300 at the rate of £575 for every completed flat. However, by the time eight more flats had been substantially completed, the general contractor had paid only an extra £1,500 and the subcontractors ceased work on the flats and brought an action in contract against the general contractor. The general contractor counter-claimed £18,121.46 for breach of the original agreement.

The trial judge found for the subcontractors and awarded them the sum of £3,500 computed in the following way. First he took a figure of £4,600 (8 × £575) for the completed flats, deducted an amount for defective and incomplete items, added a reasonable proportion of the £2,300 outstanding from the original contract sum and arrived at a subtotal of £5,000. He then deducted the £1,500 which the subcontractors been paid after the agreement in variation and awarded them £3,500.

The Court of Appeal affirmed the trial judge's decision, finding for the subcontractors on the basis that the agreement to pay the extra £10,300 was a contractual variation which the general contractor had broken. The difficulty with this argument was, of course, the issue of consideration. In return for the promised additional payments, the subcontractors had promised to do no more than they were already bound to do and, under the long-standing case of *Stilk* v *Myrick*,[134] a promise to perform an existing contractual duty does not amount to good consideration. The contractual reasoning of *Williams* v *Roffey* is considered below.[135]

In *Citra Constructions* a contract provided *inter alia* for the supply of materials from overseas. No provision was made regarding the impact of currency fluctuations upon the prices to be paid for those goods in Australian dollars. It was claimed that the company supplying the materials would face liquidation unless the other company agreed to absorb any losses due to the devaluation of the Australian dollar and so a variation of the contract in these terms was effected. There was no suggestion that those requesting the variation were guilty of any type of misrepresentation or economic duress. The variation was held to be unenforceable for want of consideration. In this case the application of the doctrine of equitable estoppel was considered but the doctrine was held not to apply.

---

[134] *Stilk* v *Myrick* (1809) 2 Camp 317.
[135] Note that the decision has not, yet, been applied to a promise to accept part payment of a debt *Re Selectmove* [1995] 1 WLR 474.

(a) Contract and variations unsupported by consideration

In *Williams* v *Roffey* the Court of Appeal found consideration for the variation of contract by relying upon the concept of "practical benefit". It was said that although the subcontractors had undertaken to do no more than they were already bound to do, the general contractor had received a benefit greater than a simple promise to perform an existing duty. The general contractor had received the benefit of (i) ensuring that the subcontractors continued work, (ii) avoiding the penalty for delay and, (iii) avoiding the trouble and expense of engaging another subcontractor to complete the carpentry work.

This concept of "practical benefit" picks up on Corbin's frequently cited criticism of the pre-existing duty rule. Corbin asserts that it is either an error of fact or an error of logic to claim that a promise to perform a pre-existing duty does not constitute a benefit to the promisee:

> "It is an error of fact to suppose that one gets no benefit when he gets only that to which he had an existing right. A bird in the hand is worth much more than a bird in the bush; and that is why the promisor bargains to pay more in order to get it. . . . If it be granted that there [is] benefit . . . in fact, but is asserted that there is no 'legal benefit' . . . then the error is one of logic. The addition of the adjective 'legal' simply begs the question. It is merely saying that performance of the duty is not a legally operative consideration because it is not a consideration that is legally operative. The question remains, Why should it not be legally operative, as in the case of other bargained-for equivalents?"[136]

I would argue, however, that Corbin's claim can be rebutted, that the concept of "practical benefit" is vacuous, and that *Williams* v *Roffey* ought not to have been decided on a contractual basis.

First, in a context such as *Williams* v *Roffey* the concept of the "bird in the hand" is misplaced. The party agreeing to the variation in such situations does not receive the "bird in the hand" of actual performance but rather an increased chance that performance to which he is already entitled may eventually be effected. There is no guarantee, of course, that performance will be effected on the varied terms any more than it was on the original terms. If the "practical benefit" the party agreeing to the variation is supposed to be receiving is avoidance of litigation, there is no way of guaranteeing at the time of the modification that he will in fact receive such a benefit. At most he is receiving a calculated improvement in the chance that a promise which he is already entitled to have performed at a lower price will in fact be performed at a higher price and that, perhaps, litigation will be thereby avoided. Seen in these terms it becomes difficult to understand how he is receiving any benefit at all.

This difficulty with the concept of practical benefit also highlights a second problem with the contractual analysis of the *Williams* v *Roffey* situation. That

---

[136] A L Corbin, *Corbin on Contracts (vol 1A)* (St Paul, West, 1963) at 108–109.

situation is not one involving the making of new promises, especially not promises of the type which contract enforces. Rather it is a situation in which one party is granting the other some kind of concession and excusing the other party's inability to perform his contractual obligations on a particular basis.[137] If for some reason the concession were to prove unjustified or unnecessary, it would arguably be more just that the original arrangements should prevail.

However, if a contractual analysis is applied to these cases, the variation takes effect as a binding promise. Accordingly, if the purported variation is given contractual effect it may be binding in contexts in which after variation the party requesting the variation nevertheless completes only part of an arranged project. Imagine that in *Williams* v *Roffey* certain of the flats had been completed and then the subcontractors' company had gone into liquidation. Assuming that the obligation to complete each flat was a severable one, the general contractor might still have been bound to pay the higher price for the completed flats even though there was arguably no longer any "benefit" to him. Similarly, the varied terms might be binding in situations in which the whole basis on which the concession was granted disappears. Imagine that in *Williams* v *Roffey* the flats were completed without any additional payments having been made at all and the subcontractors were found to have prospered from their work and their company not to have gone into liquidation. Imagine further that their suggestion that the company would go into liquidation had involved no type of misrepresentation. The general contractor might still have been bound to pay the higher price even though the whole basis upon which he had granted the concessionary variation would have disappeared.[138] That such results would be unsatisfactory has been recognised by both the English and Ontario Law Reform Commissions.[139]

Indeed, this problem with a contractual approach to the facts of *Williams* v *Roffey* may be tacitly acknowledged in the case itself. Chen-Wishart points out that the £3,500 awarded by the court seems much closer to an estimate of the subcontractors' reliance loss than their expectation loss.[140] There would seem to be a reluctance in the case to grant a full contractual remedy in the expectation measure. Perhaps this is because of the unjust effect of making a concession

---

[137] As Lücke writes: "Arrangements which seek to modify a contractual performance are often arrived at in circumstances which indicate that they are not intended to be promissory and contractual but merely to be concessions by one of the parties in recognition of some difficulty faced by the other. Such "forbearance arrangements" cannot be the equivalent of contractual variations of the terms, but they are not entirely without some effect both at common law and in equity." (H K Lücke, "Non-Contractual Arrangements for the Modification of Performance: Forbearance, Waiver and Equitable Estoppel", (1991) 21 *UWA L Rev* 149 at 181).

[138] This was, in fact, the situation in *Citra Constructions*.

[139] Law Revision Committee, *Sixth Interim Report (Statute of Frauds and the Doctrine of Consideration)* (1937) (Cmd 5449) para. 33–36, 50(3) and 50(4) but particularly 35 and 50(3), Ontario Law Reform Commission, *Report on the Amendment of the Law of Contract* (1987) at 12.

[140] M Chen-Wishart, "Consideration, Practical Benefit and the Emperor's New Clothes" in J Beatson and D Friedmann (eds), *Good Faith and Fault in Contract* (Oxford, Clarendon Press, 1995) at 134.

which is granted on a particular basis binding whether or not that basis proves justified.

Of course, to circumvent this second problem with a contractual approach to the facts in *Williams* v *Roffey*, it would be open to a court to infer that the variation constituted a contract conditional upon the completion of the work and the continued validity of the grounds upon which the variation was granted. It is submitted, however, that this would usually be a matter of implication involving quite a degree of artificiality. The parties will not usually have reached any kind of consensus as to what would happen in either of these circumstances. Thus a better approach would be to say that, where parties do not ensure that the variations to which they agree take effect as binding contracts by providing additional consideration, they ought to be treated as mere concessions not giving rise to contractual liability. If the party who has relied upon the concession is to claim relief, it must be relief of a different kind.

A final difficulty with a contractual analysis of *Williams* v *Roffey* concerns the interrelation of the pre-existing duty rule and the doctrines of frustration and economic duress. Under the doctrine of frustration, the fact that a contractual obligation becomes more onerous does not excuse performance[141] even if the obligation becomes onerous to the point at which the party of whom performance is required is in danger of bankruptcy. This leads Halson to ask why, in a context such a *Williams* v *Roffey*, the "risks" of underpricing or inadequate supervision should not similarly be left with the subcontractor. He answers this question by asserting that in this context the "risks" have been "shifted" by the "freely negotiated modification".[142] The fact that the modification is "freely negotiated" is seen as guaranteed by the modern law of economic duress, which, it is said, guards against the possibility that the party requesting the variation might obtain it by unfairly threatening non-performance.[143] The importance of economic duress is therefore stressed in *Williams* v *Roffey* and the doctrine is often seen as obviating much of the need for the pre-existing duty rule.[144]

It is to be questioned, however, whether the doctrine of economic duress is an appropriate tool for determining which particular variations should attract legal consequences and which should not.

First, the doctrine of economic duress will probably only apply in a limited number of purported variation cases. The law of economic duress is in a state of

---

[141]   *Davis Contractors Ltd* v *Fareham Urban District Council* [1956] AC 696.

[142]   R Halson, "Sailors, Sub-Contractors and Consideration", (1990) 106 *LQR* 183 at 185.

[143]   On the impact of this idea on the orthodox law see B J Reiter, "Courts, Consideration and Common Sense", (1977) 27 *U Toronto L J* 439 at 458–465 and E W Patterson, "An Apology for Consideration" (1958) 58 *Colum L Rev* 929 at 936–938.

[144]   For example, *Williams* v *Roffey* at 1163 and 1170 and M Chen-Wishart, "The Enforceability of Additional Contractual Promises: A Question of Consideration?" (1991) *NZULR* 271 at 279–280. Fleming suggests that a modification which was not obtained by duress might nevertheless be unenforceable under *Williams* v *Roffey* as being involuntary. However, he does not explain the doctrinal basis of this argument and it seems difficult to support, see D Fleming, "Contract – Consideration – Promise to Perform Existing Duty Owed to Promisee", (1990) 49 *CLJ* 204.

development. In England and a majority of the Australian jurisdictions, the doctrine will only apply where there has been:

> ". . . some factor 'which could in law be regarded as a coercion of his will so as to vitiate consent' . . . In determining whether there was a coercion of will such that there was no true consent, it is material to inquire whether the person alleged to have been coerced did or did not protest; whether, at the time he was allegedly coerced into making the contract, he did or did not have any alternative course open to him such as an adequate legal remedy; whether he was independently advised; and whether after entering the contract he took steps to avoid it. . . . It must be shown that the payment made or the contract entered into was not a voluntary act."[145]

This position has been much criticised[146] and in New South Wales the doctrine is of slightly broader application. It will apply wherever "any applied pressure induced the victim to enter into into the contract and . . . that pressure went beyond what the law is prepared to countenance as legitimate."[147] However even in New South Wales "overwhelming pressure . . . will not necessarily constitute economic duress".[148] At least under the first of these approaches to economic duress, and perhaps also under the second, duress will often be very difficult to prove in the *Williams* v *Roffey* situation.[149] The party agreeing to the variation will almost always have had the alternative course of pursuing remedies on the original contract rather than agreeing to the modification. Parties to contractual variations will often have been independently advised. In *Williams* v *Roffey* itself there was evidence that the general contractor's own surveyor was the first to suggest the extra payment.[150] In circumstances such as these it will be hard to demonstrate that the party agreeing to the modification was the subject of duress, that he was not merely "acting under great . . . commercial pressure, and not anything which in law could be regarded as a coercion of his will so as to vitiate consent"[151] or, perhaps, as "pressure . . . beyond what the law is prepared to countenance." [152]

Indeed, take the following example given by Corbin.[153] A contractor purposely bids low in order to get a contract and then refuses to perform after it is

---

[145] *Pao On v Lau Yiu Long* [1980] AC 614 at 635–636.

[146] For debate regarding the concept of the "overborne will", see P S Atiyah, "Economic Duress and the Overborne Will", (1982) 98 *LQR* 197, D Tiplady, "Concepts of Duress", (1983) 99 *LQR* 188 and D Tiplady, "Duress and the Overborne Will Again", (1983) 99 *LQR* 353.

[147] *Crescendo Management Pty Ltd v Westpac Banking Corporation* (1989) 19 NSWLR 40 at 46 *per* McHugh JA.

[148] Ibid. at 46.

[149] See I Brown and T Chandler, "Consideration and Contract Modification" (1990) 54 *Conv* 209 at 213 and J N Adams and R Brownsword, "Contract, Consideration and the Critical Path", (1990) 53 *MLR* 536 at 541.

[150] *Williams* v *Roffey* at 1170 *per* Purchas LJ.

[151] *The Siboen and The Sibotre* [1976] 1 Lloyd's Rep 293 at 336. See, however, *B & S Contracts & Design Ltd v Victor Green Publications Ltd* [1984] ICR 419 and *Atlas Express Ltd v Kafco (Importers & Distributors) Ltd* [1989] QB 467.

[152] *Crescendo Management Pty Ltd v Westpac Banking Corporation* (1988) 19 NSWLR 40.

[153] A L Corbin, *Corbin on Contracts (vol 1A)* (St Paul, West, 1963) at 105–106.

too late to obtain another contract without loss and inconvenience, so the party to whom he has submitted his bid agrees to a price variation. It is unlikely that a court applying the now most common understanding of economic duress would find that the will of the party who has agreed to the variation would be sufficiently overborne as to amount to economic duress. The prospect of "loss and inconvenience" is not generally such as to overbear the will.

Second, and more important than the fact that economic duress will often be difficult to prove in this context, is the fact that it is by nature an inappropriate doctrine to apply here. Economic duress will only be found in a limited range of circumstances because the courts are rightly wary of undoing contractual arrangements. As long as a distinction is made between informal promises and promises which either constitute a "bargain" or are formally made, the latter ought less readily to be denied effect than the former. There will be many situations in which the duress appropriately required to undo a contract cannot be identified, but it would be wrong to suggest that the concession granted by one party to the other was, in Halson's terms, sufficiently "freely negotiated" to justify the transfer of risks assumed under the original contract.[154]

Indeed, the United States law in this area seems to accept this point. While under both the RESTATEMENT (SECOND) OF CONTRACTS[155] and the UNIFORM COMMERCIAL CODE[156] an agreement modifying a contract is valid without consideration, it is only valid if it is "fair and equitable"; which requirement, the commentators point out, goes beyond requiring absence of coercion to requiring an "objectively demonstrable reason for seeking a modification."[157] The United States law appreciates that enforcing a gratuitous concession will only be just where the concession is made even more freely than bargain promises must be made under the law of economic duress.

Accordingly, it is inappropriate to enforce as contracts variations supported only by a promise to perform a pre-existing contractual duty, and leave the work of undoing unfair variations to the doctrine of economic duress. That doctrine is, and ought to remain, far too blunt a tool to determine which of such variations ought, and which ought not, to give rise to legal liability.

On the basis of this and the preceding two objections it is submitted that a contractual approach to the facts of cases such as *Williams* v *Roffey* ought not to be adopted. This conclusion might further be underscored by the seeming injustice of the final outcome of that case. This was a situation in which whatever loss had occurred was attributable to the subcontractors' underpricing and poor management. Yet they alone were protected by the decision of the court. The general contractor's quite substantial losses were left unremedied.

---

[154] R Halson, "Sailors, Sub-contractors and Consideration", (1990) 106 *LQR* 183 at 184–185.
[155] RESTATEMENT (SECOND) OF CONTRACTS §89 (1979).
[156] UNIFORM COMMERCIAL CODE §2-209 (1978).
[157] See RESTATEMENT (SECOND) OF CONTRACTS §89 (1979) Comments at 238 and UNIFORM COMMERCIAL CODE §2-209 (1978) Comments at 58.

A more appropriate approach to this case would arguably have recognised the general contractor's original contractual claim first and then examined the facts to determine whether there was some other basis on which the general contractor was liable to the subcontractors. If so, then those two competing claims could be off-set. We turn now to examine whether an approach to the facts of *Williams* v *Roffey* on the basis of equitable estoppel might not have allowed a court to deal with these facts in this way and thereby to have achieved a more satisfactory result.[158]

(b) Equitable estoppel and variations unsupported by consideration

In a fact situation such as that in *Williams* v *Roffey* the party requesting the variation is often faced with a very difficult choice: should he break the contract or should he continue with performance? It will often be difficult to tell which of these two options will be the most beneficial, and the party making the decision is in a very vulnerable position as he seeks to weigh the probabilities.

Because of this vulnerability, the party of whom the variation is requested must owe the party requesting the variation some type of duty to ensure the reliability of the assumptions he induces regarding the future of their relationship. The party of whom the variation is requested has considerable opportunity to cause the requesting party preventible harm. It is therefore appropriate to determine whether, and how, the doctrine of equitable estoppel might apply to protect the party requesting the variation in fact situations such as those in *Williams* v *Roffey* and the very similar *Citra Constructions*. This is an issue that is, of course, distinct from the issue of whether the party requesting the variation owes contractual liabilities to the party acceding to the variation.

The facts of *Williams* v *Roffey* and *Citra Constructions* have already been outlined. Considering these two cases on the basis of equitable estoppel, a judge would first have to identify the relevant induced assumption and to determine whether the party requesting the variation had acted in reliance upon it. In each case the relevant assumption was that the party acceding to the variation would pay more for goods and services than had been agreed. In each case the party requesting the variation had acted in reliance upon that induced assumption by continuing performance of the original contractual obligation.

At this point, the difficult issue of detriment would arise. "Detriment" in these circumstances would have to be that the party relying upon the assumption that a higher price would be paid would be worse off if that assumption proved unjustified than that party would have been had it never been induced.

---

[158] To turn from consideration based on practical benefit to equitable estoppel is to take a path that the Australian courts are very likely to pursue. Already one court has suggested that *Ward* v *Byham* [1956] 1 WLR 496, upon which the English Court of Appeal relied heavily in *Williams* v *Roffey* to establish the concept of practical benefit, ought to be re-interpreted as an estoppel case (*Sheahan* v *Workers' Rehabilitation and Compensation Corp* (1991) 56 SASR 193 at 203–204).

In *Citra Constructions* it was this issue of detriment which prevented the application of equitable estoppel. The suppliers had not suffered detriment by relying upon the induced assumption; they had prospered by that reliance. All the relevant overseas materials had been purchased and the contract completed. Not a cent of the devaluation claim had been paid and the suppliers had greatly profited from continued performance. There was therefore nothing which the inducing party could be called upon to compensate.

It is important to underscore how much more satisfactory this result in *Citra Constructions* was than a result giving contractual force to the purported variation would have been. The purchasers acceded to the variation only because they believed that the suppliers were about to "go broke". The suppliers did not "go broke" but sought to rely upon a concession made in circumstances in which it had seemed as if they may "go broke" to gain extra profit from the performance of the original contract. A contractual approach would have allowed the suppliers to recover this windfall profit; a denial of a contractual remedy and an examination of the suppliers' position on the basis of equitable estoppel provided a more flexible solution to the facts.

For a judge deciding *Williams v Roffey* on the basis of equitable estoppel, detriment would prove a more difficult issue. Had the general contractor in that case not induced the assumption that he would pay more for the carpentry work than he was bound to, the subcontractors might have decided to breach the contract. Had they done so, they would presumably have been liable for breach at the measure of the difference between the contract price and the cost of hiring someone else to do the work. Moreover, had the general contractor not been able to find anyone else to do the work within a sufficiently short time period, the subcontractors may well have been liable for extensive damages because of the general contractor's liability to pay a penalty under the head contract. On this set of possibilities the subcontractors might not be able to show that they would have been better off had the assumption never been induced than they would be were it to prove unreliable. There would simply have been a delay in their accepting the consequences of their underpricing and poor staff management.

Alternatively, the subcontractors might be able to show that they could not have borne the expense of continuing with the contract at the original contract price but that, had they abandoned the contract, they would have been able to acquire sufficiently remunerative work elsewhere to satisfy the general contractor's claim and thereby have been better off. Or perhaps they could show that they could not have borne the expense of continuing with the contract at the original contract price but that, because of some peculiarity of his situation, the general contractor's damages would not have been as great as their costs in providing the service. On either of these sets of possibilities the subcontractors could establish detriment.

The detriment issue was not discussed in *Williams v Roffey* because, to the regret of at least two of the judges,[159] arguments in estoppel were neither heard

---

[159] *Williams v Roffey* at 1163 *per* Glidewell LJ and at 1167 *per* Russell LJ.

in the first instance court nor developed in the Court of Appeal. However, had the detriment issue been fully canvassed, the court might well have been less eager to compensate a promisee who had neither rendered any real additional benefit to the promisor by way of bargain, nor suffered any real loss because of his reliance. Interestingly, Purchas LJ is the only judge to mention the issue of detriment[160] and he seems the most reluctant to enforce the variation. What is clear is that, had the court not chosen to mask their reasoning in contractual language, but rather acknowledged that no additional bargain was achieved and then examined alternative bases for compensation such as those provided by estoppel, the reasoning of the court would have been more lucid.

I shall assume, however, that a court deciding *Williams* v *Roffey* on the basis of equitable estoppel would be able to find detriment if they took evidence concerning the issue. The question then remains whether equitable estoppel would justify the award made in the decision. Would it be unconscionable for the general contractor not to remedy the detriment suffered by the subcontractors by reason of their reliance upon the induced assumption?

Again this is an issue which it is not at all easy to determine on the facts contained in the report. Factors seeming to lead towards a finding of unconscionability are that the assumption was induced by express representation and that it was induced in a context of co-operation. The parties were, after all, in a contractual relationship. Also pointing towards a finding of unconscionability is the issue of the relative knowledge of the parties. It is clear that the general contractor was aware that the price for which the subcontractors had agreed to do the work was far too low. Accordingly, he might also be taken to have known that, if the subcontractors relied on the induced assumption that a higher price would be paid, they would thereby suffer damage. Finally, the general contractor took no steps to ensure that the subcontractors did not suffer harm by their reliance.

Factors seeming to lead against a finding of unconscionability are that the representation was one concerning intention and that the parties must be taken to have had relatively equivalent interest in the relevant activities in reliance. After all, the subcontractors must be taken to have had an interest in fulfilling their contractual obligations. Also counting against a finding of unconscionability would be the commercial context of the relevant inducement.

If on balancing these sets of factors the court were to determine that it would be unconscionable for the general contractor not to remedy the detriment which the subcontractors might have suffered by their reliance, it would make an award to compensate that reliance. Any damages awarded would then have to be set off against the general contractor's claim for breach of contract. This is a far more satisfactory way of dealing with the ineffective variation of contract problem than is the contractual approach adopted in *Williams* v *Roffey* because it isolates the two separate complaints that the parties in this case might

---

[160] Ibid. at 1172.

justifiably have had against each other. It also provides a mechanism for resolving and comparing each of those complaints.

While there is insufficient evidence in the report to determine how the issues of detriment and unconscionability would be determined by a court applying equitable estoppel to the facts of *Williams* v *Roffey*, it ought to be clear from the preceding discussion that the application of this doctrine would lead to a more lucid analysis of the facts of the case.[161] For this reason it would also presumably lead to a more satisfactory decision than contractual reasoning was able to do.

In this sense equitable estoppel may be seen as a useful addition to the law concerning variations of contract ineffective for want of consideration. In cases in which contractual modification has been made of the type which the law enforces, there is no reason to impose liability in contract. There may well, however, still be a justification for imposing liability upon the party who has agreed to the variation; in particular because he has broken his duty to ensure the reliability of induced assumptions. Equitable estoppel can enable a court to determine when this might be the case and to award a remedy accordingly. It thereby provides a more flexible and just solution to the problem of variations of contract ineffective for want of consideration than the simple choice between imposing, or refusing to impose, liability in contract.

From the four problem areas discussed in this chapter, then, it would seem that equitable estoppel constitutes a useful addition to the armoury of the law. It provides an explanation, and better resolution, of these four problematic cases at the edge of contract. It facilitates the treatment of transactional relationships in a way that seems predictable, flexible and just.

---

[161] As Halyk puts it: "If the courts were to approach future cases similar to *Roffey* through the doctrine of promissory estoppel, judges would be free to articulate the real reasons underlying their decision . . . rather than grasping onto unpredictable and unprincipled notions of practical benefits accruing to the promisor. The judgments of the courts would send a clear signal saying that unconscionable conduct in commercial relations is not to be tolerated." (D Halyk, "Consideration, Practical Benefits and Promissory Estoppel", (1991) 53 *Saskatchewan L Rev* 393 at 414).

IV

Epilogue

We are at a new stage in the mapping of the private law of obligations. Those areas of the map that deal with promissory and restitutionary obligation have been well worked over. A large part of the excitement of the recent Australian developments in estoppel is that, like recent developments in the law of negligent misstatement, they draw attention to the need for obligations dealing with reliance, a much neglected part of the map.

Two tasks regarding the protection of reliance currently face the Australian courts. The first of these tasks is to find a satisfactory and principled structure for the doctrine of estoppel described in cases such as *Waltons* and *Verwayen*. This book has proposed a principled structure for the emergent doctrine of equitable estoppel. It has shown that, if that structure is adopted, the doctrine could equip the law better to handle many fact situations that have proved unyielding to legal analysis. The second of these tasks facing the Australian courts is to identify how equitable estoppel is to fit with other doctrines that purport to protect reliance. This is a task which has been outside the scope of this book. It would be foolhardy to attempt it while the law of negligent misstatement is in such a state of flux. But it is a task that is essential if the law of obligations is to develop in a coherent way. Only if the courts recognise and take up these two tasks will the law of civil obligations come more completely to be charted.

It is appropriate to conclude this book with a brief warning about an important and very real danger in the development of the doctrine of equitable estoppel. This danger is that the courts might begin to see equitable estoppel as a panacea for hard cases and be prepared to find detrimental reliance upon an induced assumption or unconscionability wherever doing so would allow them to remedy what is perceived as an "unjust" situation. This danger is acute because, as Stoljar points out, the courts have been accustomed to think of estoppel as a "stand-by"[1] doctrine, usefully invoked in deserving cases when the courts are baffled as to how to provide a remedy.

If equitable estoppel is to take on a major rôle in the protection of reliance in the way envisaged by this book, this danger will have to be recognised and this attitude to the doctrine will have to be abandoned. As Young J emphasised in *GWH Pty Ltd* v *Commonwealth Bank of Australia*,[2] ". . . estoppel is not to be used as a panacea for people in the commercial community who fail to protect themselves by the ordinary routes in which ordinary people in the situation do

---

[1] S J Stoljar, "Estoppel and Contract Theory", (1990) 3 *JCL* 1 at 2.
[2] (1994) 6 BPR 14,073.

protect themselves."[3] The elements of the doctrine expounded in the book are carefully proscribed. If the courts do not respect the need for proof of those elements, then the doctrine could become a recipe for chaos. For example, there is always the danger that the courts could "uncover" induced assumptions retrospectively where to do so would allow them to offer relief. Similarly, there is always the danger that estoppel could become the worthy plaintiff's contract, that the courts could ignore the criteria for unconscionability set out in this book and use equitable estoppel and remedies in the expectation measure to enforce gratuitous promises whenever they want to find for a particular plaintiff. The doctrine is constrained from being the type of palm-tree justice that many fear only as long as the courts take seriously the proof of its various elements.

As long as the courts remember this, however, there is much to suggest that Anglo-Australian law would be greatly enriched by the development of the doctrine of equitable estoppel; there is much to suggest that the developments of *Waltons* and *Verwayen* are developments to be welcomed.

[3] (1994) 6 BPR 14,073 at 14,087.

Index

duty not to lie, 1, 7–8, 10
duty to ensure reliability of induced assumptions (*see also* equitable estoppel), 1–14, 29, 32, 34, 40–1, 45, 49–50, 59, 66, 69, 71, 78–80, 86, 123–4, 127, 135, 138
  and categories of relationship, 13–14
  constraints on, 12–14
  core factual basis, 11, 13
  distinguished from other duties, 6–8, 11
  factors indicating presence of, 3, 14
  justification of, 4–6
  limitations on, 5–6
  primary obligation arising from, 2, 7
  related to duty not to lie, 10
  related to duty to keep promises, 9–10
  secondary obligation arising from, 2, 7
duty to keep promises, 1, 4–5, 6–10, 71, 79–80
Dworkin, 56

election, 20, 25, 28
Ellinghaus, 15
equitable defences, 71, 127–8
equitable estoppel, 23, 88, 129, 139
  and belief in truth of representation, 36–8
  and contract, 78–87
  and detriment – *see* detriment
  and firm offer cases, 118–28
  and holding of assumption, 34–8
  and inducement of assumption, 50–4, 60–1, 102–3, 106, 114, 121, 124–6, 135
  and nature of assumption, 38–41, 61–2
  and relationship between parties, 14, 31–2, 62–4
  and reliance – *see* reliance
  and the battle of forms, 114–16
  and unconscionability – *see* unconscionability requirement
  and variations unsupported by consideration, 135
  and work undertaken in anticipation of contract, 86–106
  as term for Australian doctrine, 2
  benefit of by privies, 33–4
  burden of by privies, 47–50
  context of, 9–14
  counter-claim in, 106, 116, 128
  danger in development of, 139–40
  defences to, 71–7, 127–8
  description of doctrine, 17
  effect on market place, 16
  elements of, 25–71
  factors promoting development, 15–16
  flexibility of, 57
  history of term, 2
  in state of flux, 17–18
  relation to consideration, 9–10
  relation with common law, 2, 26–30, 48
  remedies – *see* remedies

requirement of acting or refraining, 41–2
role as cause of action or defence, 30–1
utility of, 78–87
value of, 14
estoppel, 1, 136–7, 139
  and part performance, 75–7
  and statute, 72–5
  Australian doctrine of (*see also* equitable estoppel), 1, 15–19, 24–31, 34, 38–40, 45, 64, 68–9, 77
  categories of, 2, 13–14, 19–22, 45
  meaning of term, 13
  single overarching doctrine, 28
estoppel by aquiescence (*see also* proprietary estoppel) , 26–7
  explained, 21
estoppel by convention, 15, 20, 27, 36–8, 50, 64
  explained, 20–1
estoppel by representation, 15, 20, 22–3, 27, 37, 44
  defined, 20
estoppel *per rem judicatam*, 20
Ewart, 25

fact/law distinction, 38–41
Farnsworth, 83–4
fault, 92–4, 97, 110–11, 113
  unstable concept of, 94, 111
Ferguson, 34
fiction, 31
fiduciary
  duty of, 1, 12–13
Fifoot, 85, 110
Finn, 11, 15, 37
Fleming, 132
Fowler (F), 40
Fowler (H), 40
Fried, 9
Friedman, 81
Friedmann, 131
Fry J, 36–7
Fullagar J, 17, 32
Fuller, 7, 9–10
Furmston, 85, 110
fused legal system, 29

Gaides, 118
Galligan, 56, 58
Garamella, 79
Gaudron J, 23–4, 28, 54, 68–9, 72–3
gentleman, 84
Gibbs CJ, 15
Giles J, 60
Gilmore, 9
Lord Goff, 12, 37, 50, 79, 84, 95
Goldring, 59
Gordon, 10
Grice, 7–8, 54